Lights from

THE SHAAR PRESS

Jerusalem

Stories and perspectives from the Holy City

SARA YOHEVED RIGLER

© *Copyright 2007 by* Shaar Press

First edition – First impression / August 2007

ALL RIGHTS RESERVED
No part of this book may be reproduced **in any form,** *photocopy, electronic media, or otherwise without* **written** *permission from the copyright holder, except by a reviewer who wishes to quote brief passages in connection with a review written for inclusion in magazines or newspapers.*
THE RIGHTS OF THE COPYRIGHT HOLDER WILL BE STRICTLY ENFORCED.

Published by **SHAAR PRESS**
Distributed by MESORAH PUBLICATIONS, LTD.
4401 Second Avenue / Brooklyn, N.Y 11232 / (718) 921-9000 / www.artscroll.com

Distributed in Israel by SIFRIATI / A. GITLER
6 Hayarkon Street / Bnei Brak 51127

Distributed in Europe by LEHMANNS
Unit E, Viking Business Park, Rolling Mill Road / Jarrow, Tyne and Wear, NE32 3DP/ England

Distributed in Australia and New Zealand by GOLDS WORLD OF JUDAICA
3-13 William Street / Balaclava, Melbourne 3183 / Victoria Australia

Distributed in South Africa by KOLLEL BOOKSHOP
Ivy Common, 105 William Road / Norwood 2192, Johannesburg, South Africa

ISBN 10: 1-4226-0567-1 / ISBN 13: 978-1-4226-0567-7 h/c
ISBN 10: 1-4226-0568-X / ISBN 13: 978-1-4226-0568-4 p/b

Printed in the United States of America by Noble Book Press
Custom bound by Sefercraft, Inc. / 4401 Second Avenue / Brooklyn N.Y. 11232

For my husband

Leib Yaacov Rigler

ליב יעקב בן דוד הלוי נ"י

A genius in music, an adept in Mussar, a truly humble servant of HaKadosh Baruch Hu, and one of my greatest teachers.

Contents

Acknowledgments 11
Introduction 13

Spiritual Growth

The Party 19
My Rat's Tale 28
Friend or F.O.E. 39
Gabbing About Goodness 47
True Riches 51
Testing ... 1,2,3, Testing 58
Challah: Kneading Our Spiritual Needs 66
Not So Small Miracles 74
Suffering: Interloper or Invited Guest? 85
The Right Tool 92
Choosing Up 96
The Builder and the Terrorist 101
Blake Nordstrom Speaking ... 104
Alice's Cake 110
Growing and Not Just Older 119
Breaking the Comfort Barrier 126
Other People's Shoes 132
Bigger Than You Think 140

The Promised Land

My Home, My History, My Heart 151
At Home, At Last 159

Loving the Land of Israel	163
The Jigsaw Puzzle	172
Laughter in a Time of War	177
Gush Katif: The Night After	186

Contemporary Issues

The Spiritual Roots of Anti-Semitism	193
Who's Minding the Bus?	203
Universalism: Can Loving More Mean Loving Less?	206
The Every-Breath Solution	211
Israel's Vital First Strike	217

Holy Days

Pesach: Born Free?	227
Pesach: Chomping the Big Apple	233
Pesach: My Dayenu Ring	241
Shavuos: Hashem's Greatest Gift	244
Tishah B'Av: Waking Up to a World Without Hashem's Presence	251
Days of Awe: Submitting Your Annual Report	258
Days of Awe: Stalking True Atonement	265
Days of Awe: The Gates of Forgiveness	275
Yom Kippur: Other People's Tears	283
Yom Kippur: Becoming the Person You Could Have Been	289
Yom Kippur: Whom We Hurt	295
Yom Kippur: Through the Gate of Tears	302
Chanukah: The Capture of Saddam	310
Purim: Unmasking the Divine	315
Purim: Hidden Miracles	322

Great People

More Holy Woman	333
A Taste of Heaven	340
Jewish Nobelity	357
Who Will Save the Baby?	368
Holy Woman: The Story Behind the Story	377
Adi's Angel	384
Heroes: A True Story	390
An Ordinary Woman	397
Seeing Clearly: A Blind Woman's Vision	409
Unbelievable Belief: Dr. Melamed-Cohen	417

> My deepest gratitude and appreciation
> to the kiruv website Aish.com,
> where almost all of these story-lessons
> first appeared in a more kiruv-oriented
> version. Without Aish.com and
> its editor-in-chief
> Rabbi Nechemia Coopersmith,
> this book simply would not exist.

The chapter "Holy Woman: the Story behind the Story" first appeared in *Mishpacha Magazine*.

The chapter "Dr. Melamed-Cohen" first appeared in *HaModia*.

With thanks to Feldheim Publishers for permission to reprint an excerpt from *Forever My Jerusalem* by Puah Shteiner and from *Strive for Truth* by Rav Dessler.

Special thanks to Chaya Hertzberg for allowing me to use part of her amazing story about Yehudis Weinberg, which appeared in *Mishpacha Magazine*.

Acknowledgments

To quote the great *tzaddik*, R' Yaakov Moshe Kramer: "How can I thank Hashem Yisbarach for all the good that He has bestowed on me until now, and how can I give praise and thanks to the Master of all the worlds, Who has had such compassion on me?"

My deepest gratitude goes to:

The Rebbe of Amshinov, *shlita*, whose prayers and guidance have filled my life with revealed good.

Rebbetzin Chaya Milakovsky of Amshinov. Where would I be without you, Rebbetzin? (And may you someday permit me to write your story!)

Rebbetzin Tziporah Heller. Most of the wisdom in this book is merely my prosaic translation of her profound Torah teachings.

Rabbi Leib Kelemen. All of the mussar teachings in this book, including the quotations from the Gra and from Rav Shlomo Wolbe, z"l, were transmitted by Rav Kelemen, whose zeal to spread the transforming light of the Mussar Movement is having a major impact on Jews around the world.

Rabbi Noach Weinberg, Rosh Yeshivah of Aish HaTorah, who is one of the greatest of the great people I have been priveleged to meet, for generously giving me his time to clarify important concepts. Without his pioneering outreach, Aish.com would not exist, and therefore few of these chapters would ever have been written. Would that I would ever have half the *ahavas Yisrael* that he has!

Rabbi Nechemia Coopersmith, the editor-in-chief of Aish.com, where all of the chapters in this book (with just three exceptions) were first published. Rabbi Coopersmith was the first person to edit these essays, pruning away the "too-much" and "too-heavy." All of these chapters are better for having passed through his wise and sensitive scrutiny.

The entire staff of Aish.com, for making it the world's leading Judaism website, and thus providing me a top-notch forum for my writing.

Evelyn Rigler, my beloved mother-in-law, for the love and support she lavishes on our family.

Uriela Sagiv, my dear friend and expert adviser on all literary matters. She helped me decide which essays to include, and lent her editing expertise to many of the chapters.

Pamela and Aba Claman, who allowed me to write in the holy atmosphere of their mitzvah-house, overlooking *Har HaBayit,* which certainly inspired the best of these writings.

Judi Dick, my editor at ArtScroll, whose expert hand and discerning eye made many improvements in the manuscript. She is a pleasure to work with.

Shmuel Blitz, Avrohom Biderman, Mendy Herzberg, Eli Kroen, Mrs. Mindy Stern, Nechama Breningstall, Mrs. Tzini Fruchthandler, Sury Reinhold. If it takes a village to raise a child, it takes a competent, expert publishing team to produce a book.

My late parents, **Irving Levinsky (Yisrael ben Yosef Yehuda, z"l) and Leah Lintz Levinsky (Leah bas Yisrael, z"l),** whose living example of *chesed,* devotion, taking responsibility for the welfare of others, self-sacrifice, *shalom bayis,* and true inner greatness remains with me every single day.

My precious children, **Pliyah Esther and Yisrael Rohn,** who filled in for their absentee mother during the final weeks of this book's preparation. They induce me to grow every day, both by the beautiful *middos* they model and the challenges they pose.

To all the people whose stories appear in this book. May they get much merit for sharing their stories and thus inspiring Klal Yisrael.

Introduction

The anatomy class of third-year medical students was standing in the morgue of the University Hospital. The professor removed a piece of blackened lung from the cadaver. "This patient died of lung cancer. Here you can clearly see the damage to the lung caused by nicotine," he said, as he lifted his right hand to display the blackened tissue. In his left hand he held his lit cigarette.

The gap between what we know and what we do is rarely glimpsed as dramatically as in this macabre (but true) episode. For most of us the gap is as subtle as reading a book of Torah ideas, thinking how inspiring it is, closing the book, and going on with our lives while leaving the ideas trapped on the page.

Judaism is a dynamic spiritual path. I was unaware of this for the first thirty-seven years of my life. Raised in the Conservative movement, I did not know a single Jew who regarded Judaism as a spiritual path that led anywhere. The Judaism I witnessed was static. It was like a picture hanging on the wall of my grandmother's apartment, quaint, nostalgic, and framed in a cumbersome, ornate, gold frame.

I intuitively understood that life is about growth and change. Therefore, in my junior year of college, I went off to India in search of a genuine spiritual path.

Seventeen years later, I heard Rabbi Dovid Din, z"l, say, "The word for Jewish law, *halachah*, comes from the root word meaning, 'to walk.' Judaism is a path. It takes you somewhere." With those words, the static picture became animated. It turned into a film, full of action and movement. I hopped onto the path, and two months later it led me to Jerusalem, where I found myself surrounded by fellow travelers who were striving to learn and grow and transform themselves through Torah.

The concept of spiritual growth in Judaism is termed *"teshuvah."* It means, "to return or change direction." No matter how faithfully one is following the precepts of the Torah, there is always room for improvement. *Teshuvah* is always warranted. The contemporary sage Rav Shlomo Wolbe, z"l, was speaking with a student who referred to another student as a *baal teshuvah*. Rav Wolbe's eyes grew big. "What!" he exclaimed. "And you are not a *baal teshuvah?*"

A month after my first book, *Holy Woman*, was published, I received a phone call from a Chassid living in Boro Park. "It's *mamash* a *mussar sefer*," he enthused. This was the highest compliment I could receive. Many readers of *Holy Woman* have told me, "The book changed my life." Indeed, that was its purpose.

Lights from Jerusalem, like *Holy Woman*, was written not to entertain nor to inform, but to inspire — to inspire change and growth. This is the true purpose of all Jewish literature, from *sifrei kodesh* to collections of Chassidic tales. The Ramban, in his famous letter to his son, *Iggeres HaRamban*, wrote: "Take care to always study Torah diligently *so that you will be able to fulfill it*. When you get up from the book, ponder carefully what you have learned; *see what there is in it that you can put into practice.*"

Rabbi Leib Kelemen, at the beginning of our mussar classes, instructs us students to draw a vertical line down the right side of the page in our notebooks. In the area to the left of the line, we are to take notes of the concepts that the Rav is teaching. In the area to the right of the line, we are to write down how we can apply these concepts in our lives.

Lights from Jerusalem is a collection of stories and Torah ideas. I would behoove my readers to use it employing the above method. Keep a blank sheet of paper in the book, and at the end of every chapter, jot down one or two ways in which you can implement the ideas of that chapter in your life. The benefits of not beginning the next chapter until you have, in some way, performed the action you've jotted down are manifold.

Among the wisest words I ever heard were those spoken by a Canadian rabbi on my Old City roof twenty years ago: "There are two kinds of Jews in the world: those who are moving forward and those who aren't." It is my sincere hope that all my readers are (or will become) the first kind of Jew.

Note: The chapters in this book were written over a span of seven years, between 2000 and 2007. This accounts for the discrepancies in how many years I've been in Israel, how many years I've been married, and the ages of my children. All the articles were written in "real time," i.e., during or just after the events they describe. They are dispatches from the field of life.

All the stories, with the exception of the parable "The Party," are true. Some of the names have been changed where appropriate.

SPIRITUAL GROWTH

The Party

Randolph found the invitation slipped under his door. In gilded, embossed letters it read:

> You are cordially invited to a party.
> You will be picked up at your
> residence at noon tomorrow.
> Come as you are.
> All your needs will be provided.
>
> T.M. Goddard

Randolph did not recognize the name "T.M. Goddard." Still, it was an intriguing invitation, and since he was unemployed and alone at the time, he decided to attend.

Promptly at noon the next day, a black limousine pulled up to Randolph's door. He got in. After many hours of driving, they passed through the gates of a grand estate. Verdant lawns, orchards laden with fruit, and splendid gardens bordered the long, winding driveway. Finally, they arrived at the mansion, a huge and magnificent building.

A butler showed Randolph to his room. "I didn't realize I was invited to stay overnight," Randolph commented, perplexed. The room was comfortable, although not lavish. In the closet was a wardrobe of clothes, all perfectly tailored to Randolph's size.

At dinner, Randolph was shown to his place at a table for ten. The other guests greeted him amiably. Much to Randolph's astonishment, they had not arrived that day. Gregory, a loquacious chap who was more than happy to answer all of Randolph's questions, had, in fact, been at the party for more than six years.

"Six years?!" Randolph exclaimed, thoroughly baffled. "What kind of party lasts for six years? And where is our host? I'd like to meet him."

"Oh," Gregory chuckled, "none of us has ever seen Mr. Goddard. They say he lives in the penthouse, but who knows? As far as the party goes, it's grand. Meals are served three times a day. A variety of amusements and entertainments are offered every night. The grounds are extensive, and the gardens are always in bloom."

"Only one thing is required of us," added a pretty brunette named Cecelia. "It seems that Mr. Goddard is a bit of an exercise enthusiast. Every guest is expected to exercise five hours a day. You can choose between swimming, tennis, polo (the horses are thoroughbreds), cricket, ice-skating, skiing (I don't know where they bring the snow in from), golf, soccer, sailing on the lake, jogging, or twenty other sports. Other than that, you're free to do whatever you want."

Randolph was awed. "Such hospitality!" he exclaimed. "Such generosity! Mr. Goddard must be an amazing chap!"

After dinner, a couple from his table, Brendon and Emily, showed Randolph around. The rooms of the mansion were decorated with works of art, the view from the upper balcony was breathtaking, and the "specialty chambers," including several scientific laboratories, music rooms, art studios, and a hothouse filled with tropical plants, seemed to cater to everyone's interests.

Weeks and months passed. Randolph was having a splendid time. Then the cuisine started to bore him. Although some two dozen dishes were offered at every meal, they were the same two dozen dishes every day. And his room started to feel a little cramped. And once he had seen the view from the upper balcony a myriad of times, he became jaded.

Two years passed. One night at dinner, Randolph complained to Gregory, "I've tried every sport here. But what used to be my favorite sport — fencing — isn't available. I think it's an unfortunate omission."

"Quite so," Gregory agreed. "And my favorite sport — snorkeling — is missing as well. They failed to provide a seashore."

"The truth is," Brendon piped up, "I'm not athletic and I don't like sports at all. I don't think it's fair that we be required to spend five hours a day exercising. I would rather paint — or sculpt."

After that, the dinner table conversation every night focused on the party's deficiencies. The entertainment, while first-class, was repetitive. "After all," Emily remarked. "How many times can one see 'Swan Lake,' even when performed by virtuosos?"

"And the clothes," remarked Cecelia. "I admit it was enchanting, the first time I opened my closet, to find an entire wardrobe my size and in my taste, but as the years have passed, the clothes have gone out of style."

As for the host, no one mentioned him anymore.

One evening before dinner, when Randolph had been at the party for four years, seven months, and nineteen days, he found what looked like an invitation slipped under his door. He opened it. In gilded, embossed letters it read:

> *You are cordially invited to leave the party.*
> *You will be picked up in front of*
> *the main entrance at noon tomorrow.*
> *Leave as you are, without taking anything.*
>
> *T.M. Goddard*

Randolph was abashed. He ran to dinner and, with quivering hands, showed his friends the invitation. "It's not fair!" he exclaimed. "I haven't done anything wrong. I've obeyed the rules. I've exercised five hours a day, even when I didn't want to. How dare he do this to me!"

Everyone agreed that it was appalling to ask — really, coerce — someone to leave. "Goddard's not such a great host, after all," Brendon sneered.

"He never was," Emily agreed. "What kind of a host never appears to greet his guests?"

"It's deplorable," Cecelia lamented. "But there's nothing we can do. We're nothing but pawns here."

The next day, Randolph's friends escorted him to the main entrance, where the black limousine was waiting. It was a tearful good-bye, punctuated by exclamations of anger at the host who had treated Randolph so shabbily.

As the limousine pulled away from the curb, Randolph leaned out the window and shouted up toward the penthouse, "It's not fair!" Everyone somberly nodded in agreement.

Time and Entitlement

The two enemies of gratitude are time and a sense of entitlement. One feeds into the other; the more time elapses, the more we feel entitled to what originally we may have perceived as a gift.

For example, the birth of a healthy baby is greeted by the new parents as an incredible, miraculous gift: ten fingers and ten toes and they all move! But how many parents thank Hashem for ten fingers and ten toes on a 2-year-old? A 10-year-old? A child's first smile fills the parents with jubilation. But the hundredth smile?

Actually, human beings are programmed to be ungrateful. Stick your hand in a bowl of hot water, and after a couple of minutes you'll cease to feel the heat. The same is true for all your senses. Live next to the train tracks long enough, and you'll stop hearing the train. Your first intoxicating whiff of jasmine in full bloom is automatically your last; no matter how long you keep your nose stuck in the flowers, your olfactory sense will cease to register the scent. Desensitization is built into the human being. It deadens our awareness over time, and without awareness, there can be no gratitude or joy.

Rav Shlomo Wolbe, *z"l*,[1] has pointed out that the prerequisite of joy is *daas*, or awareness. We may have erroneously believed that the prerequisite of joy is a felicitous life — to have ample quantities of everything we want. Rabbi Wolbe teaches that joy is the result not of having more things, but of having more awareness of what we already have. The same is true for gratitude.

Gratitude begins where a sense of entitlement leaves off. We learn this from our Matriarch Leah. The Patriarch Yaakov

---

1. Rav Wolbe requested that after his passing only *z"l* (*zichrono livrachah*) be used when referring to him, not *zt"l* (*zecher tzaddik livrachah*).

knew prophetically that he would have twelve sons who would become the forebears of the nation of Israel. Since he had four wives, his wife Leah expected that three sons would be born to each wife. When, therefore, she gave birth to her fourth son, the first son she did not feel entitled to, "she said, 'This time I will thank Hashem,' therefore she named him 'Yehudah.'"[*Genesis* 29:35] "Yehudah" is derived from the Hebrew word meaning "thanks." (The word *"Yehudi"* — Jew — is a derivative of "Yehudah," and therefore also connotes "thanks.")

In the battle between entitlement and gratitude, we humans have an inner agenda to favor a sense of entitlement. Either we get what we deserve or we get a free gift undeserved. To assert the former is to empower ourselves with "rights," a boon to the ego. To admit the latter is like receiving charity; it's humbling. Therefore, we've made a fine art of convincing ourselves that whatever we have, we deserve.

For example, the Jerusalem Talmud asserts that one of the most stringent mitzvos in the Torah is the commandment to honor one's parents. This honor is obligatory even if one's parents are inexorably flawed. *Sefer HaChinuch* declares that the "root" of this mitzvah is gratitude. Not only did parents bring the child into the world, but also they fed and cared for him during his initial years of complete helplessness. Most parents continue to feed and take care of their children for at least eighteen years.

Yet most children, instead of feeling overwhelmed by gratitude, feel entitled to everything their parents give them. How many children — teenagers and older — walk into the parental home, toss off a perfunctory greeting, "Hi, Mom! Hi, Dad!" make a beeline for the refrigerator, and then complain that there's nothing good to eat?

Again, in this scenario, time teams up with a sense of entitlement to banish gratitude. If, on the other hand, a child, for whatever reason, had been separated from her parents for most of her life and then reunited with them, she would no doubt feel gratitude for every meal served — at least for the first month!

Humans have a sense of "squatter's rights" that extends to the normal functioning of our bodies, our faculties, our relationships, etc. This means that we feel that we have a right to everything we have simply because we have it. When a circumstance — illness, accident, or loss — divests us of something, we not only feel pain at the loss, but also we feel umbrage at our rights being violated.

The father of a friend of mine died at the age of 91. For two months prior to his death, he was hospitalized with various conditions. He was often unconscious and incontinent, and he suffered all the indignity and pain that are the concomitants of old age, illness, and death. After he died, in addition to mourning the loss of her beloved father, my friend was bitter at Hashem that someone as good as her father should have ended his life like that. Often her bitterness exceeded her sadness.

Instead of feeling grateful for our years at the party, we feel resentful when the party ends.

Up the Down Escalator

Our sense of entitlement makes us take for granted whatever we have. This mind-set dooms us to search for happiness in ever new experiences and relationships. Our trips abroad must be to ever more exotic destinations; each new house must be bigger and better decorated than the one before. New, more, and better becomes the motto of our ever-receding goal.

Alas, such a pursuit of happiness is fated to fail. Every new acquisition eventually becomes old. "More" is never "enough." And today's "better" will always be bested by tomorrow's "better yet." We are, by nature, riding a down escalator. If we stand still, the momentum of our desensitized senses will always carry us downward toward less happiness.

Judaism, the religion that means "thankfulness," offers an antidote: to understand and accept that **everything, at every moment, is a free gift from Hashem.**

The sages have taught us that Hashem recreates the world anew at every moment. So if you can see to read these words, it's because Hashem is giving you the gift of sight, right now. You have sight not because you've always had sight. You have sight, gift-wrapped in a half million precision cones and rods, as a present from Hashem to you in this very moment, because Hashem deigns to give you the gift of sight.

The particular means that Judaism offers to re-sensitize us is blessings. Every blessing is a step up the down escalator. A Jew recites a blessing before and after eating or drinking anything, even a glass of water. The first words upon awakening are, *"Modeh ani,"* expressing gratitude for the gift of another day of life. The morning prayers start with a series of blessings thanking Hashem for everything from sight to the ability to stand erect, from the clothes we wear to the energy that enables us to tackle our day despite tiredness.

We are, every one of us, invited guests at Hashem's party. This means that whether we're served Chivas Regal or soda pop, steak or soybeans, we have no right to lodge complaints against the host. Even if we are very good guests, behaving completely in accordance with the laws of etiquette, we have no right to insist on anything, nor to walk away with the silver forks just because we used them properly. Even the young guests at a 6-year-old's birthday party know not to complain if they're served cake, but no ice cream.

And these junior guests also know, even if they didn't get the exact party favor they wanted, to thank the host as they leave.

My Rat's Tale

It all started with the compost. Several years ago, I ordered, from an American back-to-nature catalog, a large plastic composter to recycle my copious vegetable parings into lush compost for the potted plants in my courtyard garden. I set the composter, which resembled an oversized garbage bin with side vents and a bottom door, in an unobtrusive corner of the courtyard that we share with five other apartments.

One of the upstairs neighbors, Mr. X, an older, divorced man who was on speaking terms with no one in the courtyard, complained. He alleged that the compost smelled and attracted flies. I sniffed. No stench. I looked. No flies. I summoned two of the other neighbors, a veritable sniffing committee, and together we sniffed and looked. No stench. No flies. Although I considered myself an exemplary neighbor, I was not about to get rid of my precious compost heap because of the imaginary grievances of an impossible-to-please neighbor.

Two months ago, Chein, another neighbor's daughter-in-law who lives on a rural moshav, knocked on my door and said, "I know this may sound aggressive, but if you ever want to get rid of your composter, we would love to have it." I thought of Mr. X, who hadn't been well in recent months, and felt guilty. But not guilty enough to part with my composter.

Three days later, my husband, watching me labor in my garden, decided he would make his contribution by turning over the compost. He removed the lid, and with a stick began churning the vegetable parings and dead leaves.

Out jumped a rat. It fled under the courtyard gate into the Old City's labyrinthine lanes, leaving me trembling with horror. My husband remarked that its coat was sleek and shiny. All my carrot peels and parsnip tops had gone to feed a rat!

I sat down in my kitchen, waves of revulsion washing over me, and asked myself: Given that Hashem runs the universe, what am I supposed to learn from this? What is "the rat" in my compost? Could it be my heedlessness of my neighbor's feelings? Apparently Hashem was not a member of my sniffing committee, and He did not concur with its findings. I picked up the phone and called Chein. "You can have the composter," I told her.

The following week, Chein's husband came and carted off the composter. I felt chastened. And relieved to be rid of the rat.

Early one morning a few days later, I entered my kitchen and found a persimmon and an apple partly gnawed. Bits of persimmon skin were splattered on my kitchen counter. Appalled, I called my husband. He called the exterminator.

The exterminator verified that it was a rat, not a mouse, and it had most likely entered through the bottom of the kitchen window, where the chicken wire we had put up against cats was bent up in the corner. He set three rat traps with chocolate, commenting that rats love chocolate. (A chocoholic myself, I pretended not to hear that I have any affinity with disgusting rodents.) The exterminator put one trap under the refrigerator, a second on the windowsill, and a third near the living room couch, where a few weeks before, when my husband had opened the sofa bed for guests, he had found mysterious droppings.

Although I'm always the first one up, and the first one to walk through the kitchen on my way to *daven* in the living room, that night I took my *siddur* to our bedroom, resolving to pray my morning prayers in the bedroom until my husband got up and disposed of the dead rat. Call me a sexist, but it's manifest to me that removing dead rats is a man's job, and all the women I know, even staunch feminists, agree.

The next morning, my half-asleep husband dutifully made the rounds of the three traps and reported to me: No rat.

However, another persimmon had been gnawed. And under the *milchig* sink, I found droppings. The rat had entered the under-sink cabinet from below, through the open space around the drainpipe, and had been feasting on our garbage. I shivered and called the exterminator again.

He moved two of the traps into the cabinet, right next to the drainpipe. The third he left under the refrigerator.

The next morning, as I tried to pray in my room, with my mind on the squished rat under my kitchen sink, my husband again checked and reported: No rat.

Instead, two rags that usually sit on the lateral segment of the drainpipe had fallen onto the traps below. Clearly, the rat had climbed the drainpipe to avoid the traps and had made its way to the garbage pail unscathed.

"Let's give it another night," my husband suggested. "No rat is that smart."

The next morning, the kitchen was flooded with an inch of water. The rat, apparently thirsty, had gnawed a hole in the plastic tubing to our water filter. The hole was barely two feet away from the shunned trap under the refrigerator.

I called the exterminator again. He was baffled. He had been catching rats for twenty-seven years with those very same chocolate-baited traps. No rat had ever before eluded him.

This time he came with a pump sprayer filled with rat repellent. We knew the rat was living under the cabinet, in the 3-inch space between the cabinet and the floor. First the exterminator put a trap right in front of the hole, near the wall, which the rat had been using to enter that space. Then he started spraying under the sink, right into the circle around the drainpipe. He sprayed so much rat repellent that pools of liquid started to ooze out from under the cabinet. We waited for the rat to escape out of his hole right into the waiting trap.

We waited. And waited. No rat.

Finally, the exterminator said he had other work to do, and excused himself. My husband went to his Gemara class. I greased the lateral segment of the drainpipe, so that if the rat tried to climb over it, he would fall onto the two traps waiting below. Then, I went to my computer, two rooms away, and tried to work. Two hours later, I heard a trap spring.

"Finally," I thought. I waited, cowering by my computer, for my husband to come home and remove the dead rat. When he entered the kitchen he reported: The trap beside the hole had indeed sprung, but there was no trace of a rat. Somehow the rat had managed to move the trap, thus setting it off, and had scampered to freedom — somewhere else in the house.

That night, for the first time in a week, we left the kitchen window hospitably open, hoping the rat would get tired of outwitting three human beings and leave for more tranquil territory.

For the next two days, there was no sign of the rat. While our nighttime ritual now included hiding our fruit bowl in the oven and the ripening tomatoes in the microwave, I decided to leave one persimmon on the kitchen floor, to determine whether the rat was still with us.

The next morning, I found the persimmon, gnawed, on the floor on the far side of the *fleishig* counter. Beside myself, I called the exterminator for the fourth time — a record in his long career of eliminating vermin. While we were loathe to cause suffering to any of Hashem's creatures — even a rat

— and had preferred the traps because they killed quickly, now in desperation I told the exterminator to bring poison.

He came armed with two glue traps and three kinds of poison. He found a large hole a few inches away from the gnawed, schlepped persimmon. Clearly, the rat had found a new home beneath the *fleishig* counter. It had only one exit. The exterminator put two packets of poison which take three days to work inside the hole. Then he set the two glue traps outside the hole, so that it would be impossible to exit the hole without getting caught. Then he put fast-acting poison powder on the gnawed persimmon, and placed it on the first glue trap, so that the rat, instead of dying a slow and gruesome death from the glue trap, would eat the poisoned persimmon and die quickly. Just for good measure, in case the rat was hiding elsewhere, he put another poisoned persimmon on the other side of the glue traps. It was a comprehensive, foolproof system.

It didn't work. The next morning my husband reported: No rat, and the persimmons had not been touched.

Incredulous, we stood there staring at our infallible, failed system, and suddenly it occurred to me: This was no ordinary rat. It must be a *gilgul* [reincarnation] of some soul, and it refuses to die until it gets its *tikkun* [spiritual rectification]. Jewish lore is full of tales of *gilgulim*, and although it is a rare punishment for a human soul to have to come back in the body of an animal, it can happen occasionally. How else to explain a rat more intelligent than three human beings?

"That's it," I announced to my stymied husband. "Let's go to Rav Sheinberger [a Kabbalist who lives in our neighborhood], and ask him what *tikkun* this rat needs so it can finally die."

My husband scoffed at my notion, but reluctantly took me to Rav Sheinberger. I told him the whole story, and asked, "Could this rat be a *gilgul,* and what *tikkun* does it need?"

With a dismissive gesture of his hand, Rav Sheinberger replied, "The rat is not a *gilgul.* And the rat doesn't need a *tikkun.*" Then, looking straight at me, he declared: "*You* need a *tikkun.*"

"*Me?*" I asked, aghast. "What *tikkun* do I need?"

"What does the rat say in *Perek Shirah*?" Rav Sheinberger queried. *Perek Shirah* is an ancient poem, attributed to King David, in which every creature and natural phenomenon, from the sky to the desert, from rivers to lightning, from snails to whales, praises Hashem with a particular Biblical verse.

My friend Sarah Yehudit, closely following my rat saga, had called me that morning with the startling news: In *Perek Shirah*, the rat proclaims, "*Kol haneshamah tehallel Kah, Hallelukah!* — Let all souls praise Hashem. Hallelukah!" This is the final, and perhaps most exalted, verse in the Book of Psalms. And it is ascribed to the rat!

I dutifully answered Rav Sheinberger: "*Kol haneshamah tehallel Kah, Hallelukah!*"

"The *tikkun*," he said with authority, "is to stop complaining."

I stared at him as if he had uncovered a secret vice hidden even from me. *Complain? Me?* I'm no kvetch.

Rav Sheinberger continued. "The sages read the verse as: '*al kol neshimah u'neshimah,*' meaning that for every breath you take, you should praise Hashem. Every one of us has received such a wealth of blessings that we should be making a feast of gratitude to Hashem every day. If we don't do that, at the very least we should be praising Hashem for every breath."

I went home, my mind spinning. If I want to get rid of the rat, I need to stop complaining. But do I kvetch that much?

That night I removed both glue traps. The rat was not my enemy, and I refused to inflict such a gruesome death on him. I left one persimmon laced with the fast-acting poison. In the morning, there was no sign of the rat, and the persimmon was untouched.

As usual, I walked my 9-year-old son partway to his Talmud Torah in Geulah. My son hates this 40-minute walk, which his physical therapist insists is good for him. As usual, he stalled, and resisted, and walked at a snail's pace. When my husband returned from synagogue after his morning prayers, I went to greet him with a report about my frustrating morning. Somewhere between my bedroom and the front door, I realized: This is complaining! Rav Sheinberger's words flashed through my mind. I turned my frown into a wide smile, and greeted my husband with an enthusiastic, "Good morning! Isn't it a wonderful morning to be alive? *Kol haneshamah tehallel Kah, Hallelukah!*"

Five minutes later I found the rat, dead behind our refrigerator.

The Perks of Depression

I had not realized how much I complained. I thought I was simply reporting: my frustrations with the children; how difficult it was to find a parking space; how the new cordless telephone, one week after the warranty expired, stopped working. My newly-installed, post-rat complaint radar, however, detected an incessant habit of framing experiences negatively.

I asked myself, Why? Since how we perceive situations is a choice we make, why would anyone choose misery?

The answer is part ego, part culture. In stories and novels, a character's cleverness/resourcefulness/heroism stands out only in relation to the difficulty of the problem he/she faces.

My ego must have internalized this point early on: If I wanted to be regarded as clever/resourceful/heroic, I was compelled to emphasize the difficulty of the situation facing me. After all, how would my husband know what an expert and sensitive mother I am if I didn't apprise him of the child-rearing calamities I had to deal with today? How would my friend know what a forbearing and saintly person I am if I didn't tell her how a neighbor (without mentioning names, of course) gratuitously insulted me?

In addition, my cultural indoctrination insists that people who always smile are somehow shallow. Don't they keep up with current events — with current wars, famines, and epidemics? What could they possibly be happy about?

As a college student in the 60's, studying melancholic poets from Baudelaire to Ezra Pound, I somehow assimilated the notion that people who are depressed are deep. In fact, on our Brandeis campus, if you weren't depressed, there was something wrong with you.

Joy and Judaism

*J*udaism has a diametrically opposite approach. Many think that the Jewish emphasis on joy dates back to the 18th-century advent of Chassidism. In fact, the Torah itself makes a startling pronouncement. After prophesying terrible punishments that the Jewish people will have to suffer, the Torah proclaims that all this will come upon us "because you did not serve Hashem, your Lord, with joy ..." [*Deuteronomy* 28:47]

Why should the Torah consider the greatest detriment to Divine service to be sadness rather than sin?

Imagine that your spouse surprises you with a getaway to a paradisiacal place. Brightly colored parrots are squawking in the palm trees. A crimson sun is setting into a crystal blue ocean. Your spouse presents you with a bouquet of roses — no — orchids! Then he/she places before you a basket filled with ripe fruit: pineapples, mangoes, papayas, figs. Sitting atop the fruit is a large box of Belgian chocolates. (Don't forget, this is *my* fantasy!) Let's say that you sat there morosely complaining because he/she didn't serve you steak. What does that indicate about the relationship?

But this is precisely the world Hashem has conjured up for us! Sunsets and orchids and daisies and mountains and butterflies and parrots and kittens and mangoes and strawberries and, yes, cocoa beans! Every complaint about what we don't have is a slap in the Divine face, a failure of perception more grievous than any failure of action. If we don't perceive, from moment to moment, how much Hashem loves us and how much He is giving us *as an expression of that love,* then we are relinquishing the relationship with Him, for which purpose, according to Judaism, He created the world.

Learning to Praise Hashem

Praising Hashem for every breath is a prescription not only against rat infestation, but against every sort of sadness. The process has four steps:

> *1. Look for the good in the thing or situation facing you. Set your mind to noticing the details.*
>
> *2. Recognize that everything comes from Hashem, Who animates the entire creation — every muscle, neural impulse, and atom at every millisecond.*
>
> *3. Recognize that Hashem has given this thing or situation specifically to you, because He loves you — individually.*
>
> *4. Let the joy well up in your heart, and praise Hashem!*

My post-rat life has a different hue; somber tones have given way to bright splashes of color. Now when people ask me how I am, I reply, "Terrific!" and mean it, without worrying if they'll think I'm shallow or vacuous. I'm not embarrassed to be happy.

On a day-to-day level this translates into:

> - *Instead of grumbling about having to fold the laundry, I appreciate every garment. My husband's T-shirts? I praise Hashem for cotton, that wonderful breathing fabric that grows from the ground, and for giving my husband T-shirts to wear that I didn't have to weave or sew, and that I have a husband at all. Contour sheets? I praise Hashem for clean sheets, which feel so fresh and inviting at bedtime, and for the contours, which, even though they're hard to fold, enable me to make the bed in a jiffy. And while I'm sitting there folding laundry and praising Hashem, I don't forget to thank Him for the washing machine, that I don't have to bend over a washboard like my grandmother did.*

> *Instead of complaining that the bedroom phone doesn't work, I praise Hashem that the kitchen phone does. And I thank Him for the thousands of conversations I had on that phone before it was dropped once too often. And I praise Hashem that telephones exist, so that I don't have to run to a friend every time I want to tell her something.*

Rav Shlomo Wolbe, *zt"l*, recommended the following exercise: Several times a day, before you eat a fruit, hold the fruit in your hand and contemplate the process Hashem initiated in order for you to have that particular fruit. For example, hold a tangerine in your hand, and reflect on how from a tiny tangerine seed, a sapling grew. Over the span of a few years, Hashem provided lots of sunshine and water so that the sapling would grow into a tree. Then, last spring, hundreds of flowers — with an intoxicating fragrance — bloomed on the tree. Gradually the flowers fell away and a tiny, green fruit emerged. Over a period of eight months, the fruit grew larger and larger. Then it turned a bright orange color. Then someone picked it, and packed it, and shipped it to the store where you bought it. And Hashem was behind this whole process, just to present you with this tangerine. Then say the blessing, "Blessed are You, Hashem our God, King of the universe, Who creates the fruit of the tree." Then, with your eyes closed, bite into a section of tangerine. Relish its sweetness, its texture, its juiciness, its vitamin C, coming just when you need it in winter, and the way each tiny packet of juice is individually packaged. Then relish Hashem's love for you that is expressed in this gift.

You'll never be depressed again.

Friend or F.O.E.

Persistent long-term trends suggest a steady weakening of marriage as a lasting union. ... Young people's pessimism about their chances for marital success ... also do not bode well for marriage.
— State of Our Unions: The Social Health of Marriage in America, 1999

Although many singles would jump at the opportunity to marry, many others are "single by choice," opting for the apparent "freedom" of singlehood over the complexities and self-sacrifice of a committed lifetime relationship. A recent *New York Times* article on relationships quotes 16-year-old Brian: "Being in a real relationship just complicates everything." Brian's ingenuous admission may speak for more adults than would care to admit it.

In the Jewish worldview, the eclipse of relationships, which are defined by caring and giving, is not just another lamentable symptom of post-modern society gone awry. Rather, genuine relationships — with Hashem, with other human beings, and with oneself — are the *raison d'etre* of human existence. To spurn relationships is not only to lose the game, but to negate the very purpose of playing.

The Force of Disconnection

The Torah repeatedly warns against submission to the *"el zar."* *El zar* is usually translated as "strange god," but, as Rav Shlomo Wolbe, z"l, writes, it can also mean, "god of estrangement." The *el zar* is the force of disconnection and alienation. Declares Rav Wolbe: "What a frightening force is the *el zar*, which transforms a person into being a stranger to himself, to others, and to his Creator — truly a stranger, without emotion, without understanding, without connection, without love!" [*Alei Shur*, vol. 2][1]

The *el zar* or Force of Estrangement (F.O.E.) is counter juxtaposed to the true God, the God of Oneness. The credo of Judaism, "Hashem is One," means something more profound than "one" in the sense of "not two or three." Hashem's "Oneness" is pure monism, the ultimate unification of everything in reality and beyond.

Human beings are as binary as computers. At any given moment, a human being is either serving Hashem by moving toward oneness or serving the F.O.E. by moving toward disconnection and estrangement.

When a husband and wife argue, the F.O.E. rejoices. When adult siblings become estranged from each other, the F.O.E. scores a victory. When co-workers gossip about each other, the F.O.E. smirks and rubs its hands. When different groups of Jews hurl invectives at one another, the F.O.E. dances in glee.

---

1. Rav Wolbe, z"l, wrote his *sefer Alei Shur* for men, and neither intended nor wanted women to learn it. However, he did give permission for some of his disciples to conduct *middos* workshops for women, occasionally including photocopied passages from the *Alei Shur*, always under the supervision of the Rav. All of the quotes from the *Alei Shur* that I cite, as well as any of Rav Wolbe's other writings, were taught to me in a *middos* workshop by one of the Rav's disciples, who had received explicit permission from Rav Wolbe to do so. In keeping with the Rav's wishes, I must strongly discourage any woman from picking up the *Alei Shur* and reading it on her own.

Of course, the F.O.E. itself is a creation of the One God, Who, in granting human beings free choice, offers the polarities of good and evil, love and hate, connection and disconnection. Like everything else in creation (except for human beings), the F.O.E. is a servant of Hashem, entirely under His control. Hashem unleashed the F.O.E. in the world in order to maximize the free choice of human beings. The Talmud refers to this world as *"olam yedidus,"* a world of closeness or intimacy, a world of relationships. The choice, however, between relationship and estrangement is entirely ours.

We all know how to worship Hashem: *bentching* after meals, learning Torah, keeping Shabbos, eating kosher, etc. What does it look like to worship the *el zar*? Criticizing other people, judging them negatively, or speaking *lashon hara* are all consummate ways to worship the *el zar*, because they always create distance. Next time you criticize your spouse or children, say to yourself: "Congratulations! You've just prostrated yourself to the *el zar*." Then consider: Is that whom I want to worship?

Judaism also calls the *el zar* the *"yetzer hara"* [evil inclination] and "the *satan*" [accuser]. It is a wily force, which disguises itself as righteous indignation, adherence to principles, and a multitude of other lofty claims. Whatever its costume, the F.O.E. can always be recognized by its effect: it creates distance.

Anti-Relationships

A scowling repudiation of other people obviously destroys relationships. Sometimes, however, the F.O.E.

comes disguised as relationship itself. Such "relationships" are really anti-relationships, for, in the process of forming a bond, they destroy a potentially closer bond.

For example, a parent who spends hours a week helping the poor, but has insufficient time for his or her own children is partaking of an "anti-relationship." (The average American teenager speaks 7 minutes a day with his mother and 5 minutes a day with his father.) A Jew whose heart bleeds for the Palestinians but who feels no anguish when a fellow Jew is murdered is also in the grips of the F.O.E.

To understand how different relationships have different inherent potentials for bonding, we can assign a numerical "bonding value" to various relationships. For example, you could form a relationship of love (=giving) with a drug addict in your city. I did that. Nonetheless, with all my involvement with Mayan, the differences between us were too huge to allow a bond — deeper than, let's say, 5 out of 100 — to form. Let's say your relationship with your neighbors (after all, you've chosen to live on the same street or in the same building) could potentially reach 20 out of 100. Let's say your relationship with your cousins, aunts, uncles, etc. could reach 40, and your relationship with your friends could reach 60. Relatively speaking, your relationship with your parents and your children would have a potential of 100. And your relationship with your spouse would have a potential of 10,000, because it's the sole relationship with a potential for total bonding — spiritually, emotionally, intellectually, and physically.

Whenever you opt to devote yourself to a relationship with a lower potential value *at the expense of* a higher value relationship, you're really choosing *against* relationship. If I spend so much time tending to my children that I never have quality time alone with my husband, I'm serving the F.O.E. in its possibly most cunning disguise.

Sadly, a society that fails to recognize "anti-relationship relationships" as a disguise of the F.O.E. is a society likely to end up with a 60 percent divorce rate.

In the House of Mirrors

*I*t's obvious that bad character traits such as anger, jealousy, and pride estrange a person from others. Rav Wolbe reveals that bad character traits also estrange a person from himself.

One who lacks positive relationships with other people is locked into a house of mirrors. These mirrors, however, are not the narcissistic reflecting glasses that treat an egotist to her favorite view: herself. Instead, they are like the "house of mirrors" (usually located next to the "haunted house") in an amusement park. They distort the image they reflect — this one short and fat, that one tall and skinny, and all of them wavy and warped. Bad character traits give a person a distorted image of herself, until she becomes as estranged from her true self as she is from others.

This self-estrangement is most apparent with the trait of anger. After people calm down from an angry outburst, they often say, "I'm sorry. I lost myself." This is literally true.

According to Rav Wolbe, the power of jealousy and pride to estrange one from oneself is more subtle. It works like this: Let's say Shifra is jealous of Mindy. She thinks, "Mindy is so thin, has a gorgeous house right out of a magazine, and always knows the right thing to say." In focusing on Mindy's advantages, Shifra becomes oblivious to her own good points:

her sense of humor, her affability, and her compassion. By seeing herself only in terms of what she lacks that others have, Shifra acquires a distorted self-image. Jealousy has locked her into the house of mirrors.

Pride works in a similar way. If Ezra is swelled up with pride because he graduated with honors from Harvard Business School and succeeded in becoming the CFO of a Forbes 500 company just three years later, he is focusing on part of himself — his intelligence and business acumen. He is apt to be oblivious to many of his other qualities, such as his abruptness and stinginess. And he may blame his bad temper on the ineptitude of his co-workers. Clearly, Ezra does not know himself. The F.O.E. has him by the throat.

Across the Board

Rav Wolbe makes a startling revelation: People are consistent in all their relationships. A person who serves the F.O.E., the force of estrangement, will be disconnected from Hashem, from other people, and from himself. There is no such thing as a person who loves Hashem, but has a troubled relationship with his wife.

This explains a surprising statement by the 16th-century sage, Rabbi Chaim Vital. In his *Kuntres L'Chassanim* [p. 11], Rav Wolbe cites Rav Chaim Vital that *"Midosav shel adam nimdedos ach v'rak k'fi yachaso el ishto* — A man's character traits are measured *exclusively* by his relationship with his wife."

Rav Wolbe comments on this:

> *A person who is involved in performing chesed for many other people — he gives loans and gifts, visits the sick, comforts the mourners, gladdens chassan and kallah — will certainly celebrate at the end of his life when he goes on to receive his reward, for he has many merits because of the chesed he performed. However, know with certainty that in the Heavens they examine how he related to his wife — whether he also treated her with chesed. If he behaved with chesed toward his wife, he is fortunate and things will be good for him. However, if he angered and ignored his wife, if in his home there was anger and insistence without mercy, without chesed or empathy — that will completely determine his judgment, and the Heavenly court will not remember one drop of all the chesed he did for others.*

This means that a married man's entire portion in the Next World is determined by his relationship to his wife. And, we can infer, a married woman's entire portion in the Next World is determined by her relationship to her husband.

But what of the person who is devoutly religious and performs major works of charity notwithstanding his/her embattled relationship with his/her spouse? Why is all the good one does "erased" by one's negative relationship with one's spouse? According to Rabbi Wolbe's principle of consistency in relationships, such a person's piety and charity is not motivated by love (=giving), but by selfish interests. We cannot know what goes on in another person's heart, but alienation from one's spouse — the quintessential human relationship — is a telling sign of fealty to the Force of Estrangement.

The F.O.E. is vanquished by the development of good character traits. The more one practices (not just talks about) generosity, forgiveness, and love, the more one serves the God of Oneness. The result is improved relationships in all spheres.

The essence of relationship is love, or, more accurately, *ahavah*. While the Hebrew word *ahavah* is translated as "love," it literally means "I will give." True love is giving.

While a healthy relationship usually consists of mutual love or mutual giving, the contemporary insistence on mutuality ("I'll make dinner if you do the dishes.") is the reverse of love; it's a symptom of mutual taking.

All human babies are born takers. To learn to love, or give, requires tremendous effort and dedication to spiritual growth. The optimum laboratory for such inner work is close relationships. Inner growth is both the prerequisite and the product of successful relationships.

Working on becoming a giver is difficult and demanding. No wonder so many Americans are loathe to undertake the challenge. As the *Times* article quoted above summarized the prevailing attitude toward relationships: "They are complicated, messy and invariably painful."

The F.O.E. is having a field day.

Gabbing About Goodness

The day was rainy, the bus was late, and the atmosphere at the bus stop, where I was impatiently waiting with several other people, was tense. A woman in her late 60's wearing a brown raincoat scurried by. Just as she passed the bus shelter, she slid on the wet pavement and fell. I rushed toward her. Helping her up, I asked, "Are you okay?"

She nodded and commented: "It says that a person who falls in front of other people is *gaivadic* [prideful]."

I smiled, thinking, "If you were really *gaivadic*, you wouldn't be quoting that." But I said nothing.

The woman continued on her way. As I returned to the protection of the bus shelter, another woman there remarked out loud: "What a special person! She falls and she uses it as a opportunity to admonish herself spiritually! What a remarkable, humble person!"

With that comment, the atmosphere in the bus shelter palpably changed. Goodness hung in the air like a presence. We all smiled at each other and nodded.

How to Love Your Neighbor

The mitzvah, "Love your neighbor as yourself," is considered by the sages to be a fundamental mitzvah of the Torah. Like all mitzvos, it requires us to do something concrete and specific. Vague sentiments of affection for others could delude a person into thinking that he/she is fulfilling this mitzvah, but the Torah insists that we ground our sentiments in concrete actions.

The Rambam in *Mishneh Torah* writes that "Love your neighbor as yourself" is fulfilled in three ways: (1) by speaking well about others; (2) by fulfilling their physical lacks; and (3) by treating them with honor.

Thus, although I had had the same positive thoughts about the woman who slipped at the bus stop, only the person who actually voiced her praise was fulfilling the mitzvah, "Love your neighbor as yourself." And because every mitzvah connects a person to Hashem, the atmosphere in our damp bus shelter reflected that spiritual transformation.

In the Jewish world today, much focus is given to not speaking *lashon hara*. To refrain from speaking *lashon hara* is an exalted spiritual accomplishment. Much less emphasis is given to the other side of the coin: speaking well about others. Of course, if you praise A to B, who dislikes A, B is likely to respond with a litany of pejorative *lashon hara:* "She's not really so great. Why, I've seen her do _____." As always, you must be circumspect regarding to whom you say what. With that caution in mind, however, each of us could probably triple the amount of good we speak about every day.

Reinforcing Goodness

*I*n fact, this is an important principle in educating children. The experts instruct us to give our children more positive feedback than negative feedback. Thus, they tell us, don't wait till your toddler misbehaves to comment on his behavior. Notice when your toddler is playing nicely, and say out loud, "How nicely you're sharing that toy with your sister." This reinforces good behavior.

Even those who have acquired the skill of praising young children probably pass up manifold opportunities to voice goodness about those they live and work with. How about:

- **Every night at dinnertime or bedtime, telling your spouse one positive thing about each of your children:**

    "When Rachel spoke on the phone with her grandmother today, she showed her a lot of love and respect."

    "When I told Eli he couldn't use the car tonight, he accepted it graciously."

- **Pointing out your spouse's good points to your children:**

    "You know, Tatty was really tired tonight, but he helped you with your homework anyway."

    "Even though Mommy was super busy today, notice how she took time to call Aunt Mimi so she wouldn't be lonely."

- **Not just thinking well about your friends, but actually mentioning their good traits:**

"Devorah is so reliable. She said she'd do me a favor, and then even though her schedule changed, she still went out of her way to do it."

"Binyamin is so devoted to his learning. He just got back from a business trip, and half an hour later he was at the shiur."

- **Looking for positive things to say about your fellow workers:**

"My secretary has a bad cold, but she still came in today because she knew I needed her."

"My boss is under a lot of pressure right now, but he took the time to mention the good job I did on that recent project."

With each of these simple statements, you fulfill that most glorious of all mitzvos: Loving your neighbor as yourself.

Rabbi Abraham J. Twerski M.D. points out that the morning prayer service begins with the words, *"Baruch she'amar v'hayah haolam* — Blessed is He Who spoke and the world came into being." He explains that, at the outset of our prayers, we have to remind ourselves that words create worlds.

At the outset of every day we should remind ourselves that good words create good worlds.

True Riches

Seventy-five orphan girls in Calcutta taught me the real meaning of gratitude. It took me ten years to figure out the lesson.

Although it was my second extended period helping out at this Calcutta orphanage, I still marveled at the standard of living of the girls. Growing up, I had had my own room; these girls didn't even have their own beds. They slept on thin mattresses spread on the floor, two girls to a mattress, sharing a blanket and a mosquito net. During the day the mattresses were piled up in a corner, and the room was used for play and doing homework.

Their only private space amounted to a box the size of a large shoe box. In this box each girl kept all her worldly possessions: the one of her two cotton frocks she was not currently wearing, two pencils, and a copy book. About twenty-five of the girls owned a pair of sandals, in which they trotted out on special occasions. About a dozen girls owned a pretty dress, a gift from an impoverished grandmother. That was it. No other garments. No toothbrush. No crayons. Not one girl owned enough to fill her box. Yet they were the most cheerful and loving group of people I knew. I adored them.

The girls prevailed on me to teach them English. One day we tackled the lesson about opposites: tall-short, thin-fat, rich-poor. After explaining the words in simple English, I would have one girl stand in front of the class and ask, "Is Bhavani thin, fat, or medium?"

The girls would raise their hands, and the one I picked would answer: "Bhavani is thin."

The girls were smart and highly motivated. The lesson was proceeding well until I summoned Lakshmi to stand in front of the class. Pointing to the scrawny, barefoot girl in her plain white frock, I asked, "Is Lakshmi rich, poor, or medium?"

Two dozen hands flew up. I called on one girl. In loud and perfect English she answered: "Lakshmi is medium."

Obviously she didn't understand the words. Lakshmi, like all the girls, was abjectly destitute, a reality they all accepted with cheerful fortitude. I called on another girl. Eagerly, she replied, "Lakshmi is medium."

I again explained the meaning of the words "rich" and "poor," this time using their Bengali translations so there would be no further misunderstanding. Then I asked the whole class: "Is Lakshmi rich, poor, or medium?"

In joyful unison they all cried out: "Lakshmi is medium."

I was confounded. By what mental gyrations did these girls consider Lakshmi — and by extension themselves — as anything other than poor?

After the class, I repaired to my room (my own private room) and tried to figure it out. After all, the girls knew that most children, even in poverty-stricken Calcutta, had more than they did. They attended school with "normal" girls — girls who had parents and shoes and pretty colored ribbons in their hair.

Carefully I analyzed what exactly they *did* have. I came up with a list of just four items: a *rudimentary* level of shelter, food, education, and friends. That was it.

But what about all they *didn't* have? Not one of them had a dowry, without which prospects of marriage were slim.

None of them owned a book or a toy. None of them had money to buy a treat or a trinket — ever. By what stretch of their imaginations — or their hearts — did they not define themselves as poor? The question simmered in my mind for a decade.

Just Desserts

Ten years later I was learning Torah in Jerusalem. The rabbi was explaining why the matriarch Leah named her fourth son Yehudah, a name derived from the root "to thank." Since the word "Jew" derives from the name "Yehudah," thanking is somehow integral to being Jewish.

But why did Leah wait until her fourth child to use this name? Wasn't she more grateful for her first child than her fourth?

The rabbi, citing classical commentators, explained that Yaakov knew he would have the twelve sons. Since there were four wives, each expected to have three sons.

With the birth of this, her fourth son, Leah felt that she had received more than her fair share. So she named him Yehudah, saying, "This time I will thank Hashem."

This teaches us something essential about gratitude. Gratitude is a function not of how much we have, but rather of how much we have *relative to how much we feel we deserve*.

When you have worked hard at your job, you usually do not feel flooded with gratitude when you pick up your paycheck. Even a holiday bonus may come to be expected as your just desserts and not elicit a great surge of gratitude — unless it is a far bigger sum than you feel you deserve.

The opposite of gratitude is a feeling of entitlement. The attitude of "I deserve it" turns every gift into a paycheck.

Recognizing Good

The Hebrew term for gratitude is *"hakaras hatov,"* which literally means "recognizing the good." The secret embedded in the Hebrew is that gratitude depends not on getting something good, but on recognizing the good that is already yours.

Thus, gratitude is totally a feat of consciousness. It requires a "back to basics" mentality, becoming cognizant of all the rudimentary things we usually take for granted. No matter how much we lack, no matter what difficult times we are passing through, every one of us can find a myriad of things to be grateful for.

If you've lost money in the stock market, but you still have your children, you can be grateful.

If you've lost your job, but you still have your health, you can be grateful.

If you can't move your legs, but you can move your arms, you can be grateful.

The Object of Gratitude

In addition to recognizing the good and experiencing what you have as a gift rather than a paycheck, gratitude requires one more ingredient.

There is a fallacy that prevents many people from experiencing true thankfulness. Some think that thankfulness, like love, is a warm, fuzzy feeling inside, the way you feel when you've downed the second dessert of your Shabbos dinner. That good feeling, however, is not thankfulness, but satiation. It becomes thankfulness only when you realize that your mother or wife toiled to make that mousse pie, and you direct your appreciation to her.

Both thankfulness and love must have an object. True gratitude implies that I am grateful *to the giver of what I have received.* Gratitude without an object is like one hand clapping.

From a Torah perspective, all human beings are creatures. Life — and every part of it from the tiny hairs inside our noses to our thousands of enzymes — is a gift from our Creator. We are entitled to nothing. We are grateful to Hashem for everything.

A Recipe for Gratitude

Here, then, are the four steps to gratitude:

1. *Recognize the good that you possess.*

2. *Acknowledge that it is a gift, not something you deserve.*

> 3. *Identify the source of the gift*: Hashem or a human being.
>
> 4. *Express your thanks.*

According to Judaism, gratitude is the basis of everything: faith, joy, awe, and love of Hashem. Only when we recognize how much Hashem has given us and how little we deserve it, can we come to a place of faith and love.

Little wonder that a Jew is supposed to start every day with an expression of thankfulness for life itself, the recitation of the *Modeh Ani*. "Thankful am I before You, living and eternal King, that You have returned my soul within me with compassion — abundant is Your faithfulness."

You will notice that this single sentence incorporates all the ingredients of gratitude. It expresses thanks for the most elemental gift of all, life itself, to the Divine source of life. There is no better way to start one's day.

Once we are washed and dressed, a Jew continues to thank Hashem for things that might otherwise go unnoticed. The fourteen "Morning Blessings" of one line each focus our consciousness, in gratitude, on such elemental capacities as the ability to see, to stretch our muscles, to stand erect, and to walk. Some of these blessings are easy to feel genuine gratitude for. We may, however, be so oblivious to other of our "gifts" that we must be jolted into appreciation.

I personally could not relate to one particular blessing until the morning after I had emergency abdominal surgery. I was lying in my hospital bed groaning in pain when the nurse told me to get up and walk a little. I thought she was insane. Only when her gentle persuasion gave way to insistence, did I force myself to sit up and gingerly get out of bed, wrenching with agony at every movement. Finally standing up, the most I could manage was a stooped shuffle across the room. The nurse kept saying, "Stand up straight," but my abdomen hurt too much.

Then it was time for my morning prayers. Standing next to my bed like a hunched over nonagenarian, when I got to the blessing, "Blessed are You, Hashem our God, King of universe, Who straightens the bent [over]," I almost cried. How had I never related to this blessing before? How had I so taken for granted the "simple" faculty of standing erect? Why did I have to lose this ability before I could appreciate it?

It took me a long time to unravel the mystery of my Indian orphans' definition of themselves as "medium," rather than "poor." They knew the secret of gratitude; they saw what little they had as a gift, rather than thinking they deserved anything. They exemplified the teaching of *Pirkei Avos:* "Who is rich? The one who is happy with his portion."

Testing ... 1,2,3, Testing

My friend Tzippy owned an antique diamond ring that had belonged to her grandmother. The ring was Tzippy's only family heirloom. When she washed her hands, she sometimes put the ring next to the soap dish in the bathroom.

One day Tzippy's husband David flushed the toilet and reached for the soap. As he did so, he saw a small, shiny object fly in an arc directly into the flushing toilet. He hurriedly found Tzippy in the kitchen and asked her if she had left her grandmother's ring by the soap dish. Tzippy glanced down at her finger and answered, "I suppose I did. Why?"

"Because I just flushed it down the toilet," was David's alarming answer.

Tzippy felt like screaming, "YOU WHAT? MY GRANDMOTHER'S RING!! IT'S IRREPLACEABLE!! HOW COULD YOU BE SO CARELESS?!!"

Instead, she stopped herself. She knew she was facing a test, an arduous, grueling test. And she knew the only way to pass it.

Tzippy took a deep breath, and in soft, measured tones asked, "O-kay, soooo what should we doooo now?"

David, feeling dreadfully guilty, had been ready to defend himself against his wife's attack with a self-righteous counter-attack: "HOW CAN YOU BE SO CARELESS AS TO LEAVE

YOUR VALUABLE RING IN A PLACE LIKE THAT? I'VE TOLD YOU A THOUSAND TIMES NOT TO LEAVE YOUR GRANDMOTHER'S RING THERE."

Since Tzippy did not attack, however, David did not counter-attack. Instead, he answered humbly, "I'm really sorry. I guess we should call the plumber and ask him to check inside the pipes, but it's a real long shot."

Tzippy suggested that before they called the plumber, they should take a look in the bathroom. Perhaps the ring had fallen next to the toilet, not in it. "I saw it fly into the flushing toilet," David insisted, but he went with her to satisfy her doubts.

They scrutinized the floor all around the toilet. They found nothing. Then they looked into the toilet bowl. They could not believe their eyes. Poised perfectly in the middle of a narrow porcelain shelf just above the bottom of the bowl was her grandmother's ring.

"If I had screamed at my husband," Tzippy told me at the conclusion of her story, "I know the ring wouldn't have been there."

Divine Tests

The concept of Hashem testing human beings is as old as Judaism itself. According to the Midrash, Hashem tested the Patriarch Avraham ten times, each test more difficult than the one before. The ultimate test was Hashem's command to Avraham to sacrifice his beloved son Yitzchak. The Torah explicitly introduces this account with the words, "Hashem tested Avraham." [*Genesis* 22:1]

What is the purpose of a Divinely ordained test? A student is tested in school so that the teacher can find out how much the student has learned. The omniscient God, by contrast, is already aware of a person's capacity before the test. The purpose of a Divine test, therefore, cannot be to reveal any new information to Hashem.

The Midrash points out that the Hebrew word "tested," *nisah,* is derived from the word *neis,* meaning flag. As a banner flies high above and identifies an army or ship, so a test is meant to elevate and reveal the innate potential of the person being tested.

A test is always a choice at the upper limit of a person's capacity. Passing the test actually changes the person. Potential becomes actualized. A rose bud contains all the petals of the opened rose, but a rose in full bloom is far more beautiful than a bud. Avraham standing with a knife in his hand on Mount Moriah was a greater Avraham than he had been at the approach to the mountain.

Recognizing Tests

When we fail our tests, it's usually because we didn't recognize the situation as a test. Tests come in many disguises: someone else's ineptitude, a traffic jam, an unexpected (and unwanted) guest, a computer malfunction, a telephone call just as you're falling asleep, a financial loss, a child throwing a tantrum (usually in the middle of a store), a gratuitous insult, suggestions from your mother (or better yet, your mother-in-law) on how to raise your children, etc., etc.

If only we could see a neon sign flashing in front of our mind's eye, "THIS IS A TEST!" all of us could muster enough patience, forgiveness, kindness, self-discipline, calmness, or whatever other character trait is called for, to pass the test. How tragically often it is only afterward that we realize the test beneath the disguise, as we hit our foreheads in frustration and regret at a squandered opportunity to grow.

The key to recognizing a test is to remember that everything, *everything*, EVERYTHING, comes from the One God. Hashem is the ultimate Source of every occurrence, every financial loss, every traffic jam, every tantrum. Although humans have free will to choose between good and evil, what happens to any individual is determined by Hashem. A thief can choose to mug a passerby at midnight, at the corner of Broadway and 86th where you walk every night, but if it isn't Hashem's will for you to be mugged, you'll be delayed a block away, or a policeman will show up just at that moment, or the thief will run into an old pal who owes him money. That your 2-year-old throws his tantrum in the middle of an upscale department store surrounded by well-dressed singles shaking their heads and clicking their tongues is a deliberately scheduled Divine test for you.

The trick is to insert Hashem into the picture in two places: as the Source of the test and as the Director signaling which path to choose. Hashem, through His Torah, has given us definite instructions on how to respond to an unexpected visitor, a gratuitous insult, and child-rearing advice from our mother-in-law. The more Torah we learn, the better equipped we'll be to pass our tests.

The Rewards

*I*n the above story, Tzippy perceived that the ring was still there, in seeming defiance of the natural scheme of things, as a Divine reward for her passing her test. But surely Hashem does not reward humans in the same way that a parent rewards a child who brings home a good grade.

Rewards for tests are similar to prayers fulfilled. When Hashem grants our prayer, it's not because we have succeeded in convincing the Almighty to give us what we want. Rather, earnest prayer transforms us and makes us into bigger vessels, able to contain the blessings that Hashem is always eager to bestow on us. Similarly, tests passed make us into bigger vessels, more able to contain even "supernatural" levels of Divine beneficence.

Several years ago, my family was vacationing on the Golan Heights, near the Sea of Galilee. One day we found an isolated stretch of shoreline, pulled our car over, and went swimming.

"Isn't this relaxing?" I luxuriated.

"Well, I'm kind of nervous," my husband replied. "I have the car key in my bathing suit pocket, and I'm worried that it'll float out."

"Are you kidding?" I upbraided him. "Your pocket is no place for the car key. Give it to me." I was wearing my modest "swimming dress," with two zippered pockets, and safely inserted the key.

The next day, we drove off the highway, over dirt roads winding through orchards and fields, to do the "Madrasa," a hike through one of the streams that feeds into the Sea of Galilee. This hike, popular in the heat of the Israeli summer, involves walking in ankle-high water past lush, overhanging vegetation. At intervals, the stream forms delicious waist-high pools, where the hiker can dunk down and cool off.

I was walking ahead with one of our children. Suddenly my husband, pale and distraught, caught up with us and announced, "I lost the car key."

"What do you mean you lost the car key?" I replied in horror.

"It was in my bathing suit pocket, and I just felt for it, and it isn't there. It must have floated out when I dunked down a way's back."

"Well, let's go back and look for it," I suggested with dawning desperation.

"No, we'll never find it. The bottom here is all mud, and I don't even remember exactly where I dunked."

I stood there staring at him, my mind quickly calculating the ramifications of his carelessness. My set of car keys was in my purse, locked inside the car. To open the car, we'd need to call a locksmith from Tiberias, but the cell phone was also locked inside the car. And even if a fellow hiker lent us a cell phone, how would we find a locksmith? And if we found a locksmith, would he be willing to come all the way out here into the wilderness? And if he were willing to come all the way out here, how much would he charge us?

I felt like screaming, "HOW COULD YOU? JUST YESTERDAY I TOLD YOU NOT TO PUT THE CAR KEY INTO YOUR BATHING SUIT POCKET! I'M WEARING MY SWIMMING DRESS WITH ZIPPERED POCKETS! HOW COULD YOU HAVE BEEN SO CARELESS?!!!"

Then I remembered Tzippy and her ring. I knew, in a flash of clarity, that I was being tested. And that the only way to pass my test was to not lose my temper.

So I took a deep breath and said in measured tones, "O-kay, let's just enjoy the rest of the hike. And let's pray that, when we get back to the parking lot, one of the other hikers will be a car thief who's done *teshuvah*."

An hour later, we emerged from the stream onto the bank. Two trails led back to the parking lot. Normally, I would have just forged ahead, but I was in total surrender mode. "Which way would you like to go, dear?" I asked my husband.

He chose the trail through the eucalyptus grove. As we walked, I could see, on the far side of the grove, a circle of cars, where apparently a group had been having a barbeque. I saw the cars driving off, one at a time. One vehicle, however, was not moving. It was a Renault, with its hood up. The back doors were open to reveal some kind of technical equipment, but I couldn't make out what kind. Perhaps, I thought, he's a plumber or an electrician, and he might have a tool we can use to pry open the car door. As I approached, I saw that the Renault's owner was working on the engine, while his wife was standing beside the vehicle. In my best Hebrew, I explained to her what had happened, and asked if her husband had any tools that could help us.

She replied that their car wouldn't start, so her husband had been trying to fix it for the last 20 minutes. If he ever got the car to start, she would ask him to help us.

I decided to wait. After all, I had no place to go.

No more than 3 minutes passed when I heard the sound of the engine turning over and purring. The man shut the hood of the car and came to the rear, where his wife and I were standing. I reiterated our plight, that we had lost our car key, and asked if perhaps he had a crowbar or some kind of tool to pry open the car door. He looked at me as if I were crazy, stepped over to the Renault's rear doors, and slammed them shut, revealing a sign that read: "URI LOCKSMITH."

Two minutes later, he was at our car. We watched with fascination as he deftly used his state-of-the-art tools to open the car door. We paid him fifty shekels ($12). As he walked away, he called over his shoulder: "You folks sure are lucky. If my car hadn't broken down, I'd have been gone from here half an hour ago."

We don't get a revealed Divine reward every time we pass a test, but that time we sure did.

Challah: Kneading Our Spiritual Needs

"You're so lucky," Shanni was telling me. "You're a *baal teshuvah*, you've practiced meditation, you have a relationship with Hashem. I've been doing the mitzvos all my life. They're dry for me, routine. I don't feel the closeness."

Whenever I hear this mournful confession, I feel like I'm sitting in the passenger seat of a brand new Lexus and the driver doesn't know how to use half of the state-of-the-art features.

Is it possible that a religion that has produced such God-lovers as King David, the medieval poet Yehudah HaLevi, the 16th-century mystics of Safed, the Baal Shem Tov, and the women who pray daily at the Kosel can be lacking a route to closeness to Hashem?

Is it possible that a religion that inspired "The Song of Songs," and *"Yedid Nefesh"* ("Splendid, beautiful, radiance of the universe, my soul pines for Your love ….") can be considered dry?

What's missing here?

Union of Wills

The highest union with God that humans can achieve is union of will. Kabbalistically, the most lofty of the ten *Sephiros, Keser,* is characterized by joy, faith, and will. To unite one's will with the Divine will is ultimate closeness to God.

Even in human relationships, real love entails a uniting of wills, which often requires a submission of one's will to the will of the beloved. That is why real love, as opposed to Hollywood love, requires hard work and renunciation. If you want to go Italian, but your spouse wants Chinese, oneness will be achieved only if one of you loves enough to say (sincerely): "Whatever makes you happy is fine with me."

In this light, the greatest impediment to a relationship is not really knowing what the other wants. This problem crops up in our family every year on my husband's birthday, when my eagerness to give him what he wants is squelched by his not wanting anything in particular.

This year was different. My inquiry two weeks before his birthday elicited the definite response that he wanted an acclaimed four-volume set on the laws of Shabbos. Joyfully, I walked into our local Jewish bookstore and asked for the set.

It was out of print. The bookseller assured me that there wasn't a set to be had in all of Jerusalem, but the publisher was running off a new printing which should, with luck, be out in a month or two. I was crestfallen.

The day before my husband's birthday, I was shopping in Geulah when I passed a bookstore. A firm believer that it never hurts to try, I went in and asked for the set.

The Chassidic storeowner replied, "I have the very last set in all of Jerusalem. Someone ordered it months ago, and I kept it for him, but he hasn't returned from America. So I'm willing to sell it to you."

Jubilant, I purchased the formidable tomes, and set out to meet my husband, who had the car. We had arranged that he would wait for me at the top of the hill of Rechov Straus, some four blocks away. It was a hot day, and I was already schlepping a half-dozen heavy packages. The four-volume set weighed a whopping 10 pounds, but as I traipsed up the hill, I felt ecstatic that I could actually give my husband exactly what he wanted.

In the Torah, Hashem told the Jewish people exactly what He wants from us. Far from being "saddled with the burden of the mitzvos," we are privileged to have 613 ways to connect with Hashem. There is no greater demonstration of His love for us than the mitzvos: 613 channels of total connection.

Sliding Into Second

When *frum* Jews complain that they feel no sense of connection with Hashem while performing the mitzvos, they are admitting their own lack rather than the Torah's lack.

The sense of connection with Hashem that eludes these Jews does not come automatically. The pitfall of Jewish observance is that it's easy to fall into a mechanical performance of the mitzvos. Let me rephrase that. It's hard *not* to fall into a mechanical performance of mitzvos that are performed repeatedly, daily, sometimes many times a day. To perform the commandments as they are meant to be performed — consciously, joyfully, focused on the Commander — is a feat of mindfulness that requires consistent effort and a level of concentration enough to challenge a brain surgeon.

Rav Shlomo Wolbe has written: "Obviously, when performing the mitzvos mechanically, there is neither mindfulness nor love nor joy."

What does Rav Wolbe recommend as an antidote to such mechanical performance of a mitzvah? Not to enter the mitzvah suddenly. Rather, "let us contemplate that the Holy One, Blessed is He, Himself commanded us in this commandment, and that through it, we are connecting with Him." [*Alei Shur*, p. 327]

Life is busy. No one has time to do everything and do it right. Most of us perform mitzvos — pray, recite blessings over food, etc. — like a baseball player sliding into second base. We consider it commendable that we take the time to perform the mitzvah at all. The notion that we should take an extra couple of minutes and pause before fulfilling a commandment to reflect on the One Who has commanded us and to unite our will whole-heartedly with His may seem daunting, but this is the way the mitzvos are meant to be performed.

For example, the Rambam writes that before reciting the *Shemoneh Esrei* one is *obligated* to stop and reflect on the greatness of the God one is about to address. Given that it takes the average Jew anywhere from 5 to 15 minutes to recite the *Shemoneh Esrei,* isn't it a shame not to take the extra 2 minutes of reflection before beginning in order to reframe the whole prayer as an exercise of love and closeness?

Taking Challah

I have been religiously observant for eighteen years. Three months ago, a woman named Racheli Miller started giving a course in our neighborhood on the mitzvah of taking challah. In the Torah, Hashem commands that once we enter the Land of Israel, when we bake bread, we should separate a small piece of the dough and put it aside. This is one of the three mitzvos that are specifically given to women.

Not being the earthy type, I have never felt inclined to bake bread from scratch. With my breadmaker, yes. With my husband (a pianist who loves to exercise his fingers by kneading) making the dough, and me just saying the blessing and breaking off a piece of dough, yes. But to take a ten-week course in the single mitzvah of separating challah, no thanks.

When a friend asked me why I wasn't taking the challah course, I replied glibly that I'm not the earthy, bread-baking type. My friend looked at me aghast. "Don't you know that all the blessings of physical abundance come down into the world through the performance of the mitzvah of taking challah? The mitzvah also effects healing in fourteen different ways."

I enrolled in the course, wondering how there could be so much to say about a single mitzvah.

"The mitzvah of challah is cosmic in its effect," Mrs. Miller proclaimed. Every week my jaw dropped lower as she expatiated on the profound ramifications of this one mitzvah.

Then she announced that the following week Rabbi Elozor Barclay would be coming in to teach us about the halachic specifics of the mitzvah. This would take two hours.

Two hours? I couldn't imagine how the rabbi could fill up two hours. And, of course, I already knew how to do the mitzvah.

I went to the class anyway. I discovered that I had been doing the mitzvah wrong.

The following week, Mrs. Miller announced, she would be demonstrating how to make challah. I came prepared for a Pillsbury lesson that I didn't need because my husband has the world's best recipe for whole-wheat challah.

The demonstration was a life-changing event.

Now I make challah once a month, and it's the spiritual highpoint of my month. I start by turning off the phone and announcing that no one is permitted into the kitchen until I've finished; this mitzvah requires total concentration. Then I give *tzedakah,* so that all my prayers will be favorably accepted. Then I say a chapter of *Tehillim,* to open up the gates of heaven. While sifting the flour, I sing, because joy is the foundation of all spiritual success. Then I add each ingredient consciously: sugar for the sweetness I hope to see in my family's life; yeast so that each member of my family will grow and expand; water represents Torah; when measuring salt, which represents rebuke, I fill two tablespoons, then shake some back into the salt container, because we should always give less rebuke than we think we should; and as I slowly pour in the oil, I "anoint" each member of my family by name, praying for his or her specific needs.

Kneading is the time to pray. My teenage daughter Pliyah Esther and I take turns, each of us thinking of people to pray for by name: single friends that they should get married; childless friends that they should have babies; sick people and terror victims that they should have a speedy and complete recovery; people struggling financially that they should have livelihood; people experiencing marital conflict that they should have *shalom bayis.* Pliyah Esther reminds me to add the names of Israel's missing soldiers and of Jonathan Pollard. On and on we knead and pray, with such spiritual focus and intensity that the kitchen becomes charged.

Now the dough is ready for challah to be taken, but the spiritual preparations to perform the mitzvah properly continue. Reading from a laminated sheet prepared and distributed by two Israeli sisters, I pray fervently that my performance of the mitzvah of challah will repair the sin of Eve. That just as she brought death into the world, I will bring life into the world, nullifying death, erasing the tears from every face.

Now I am ready to perform the mitzvah. I break off a small piece of dough, recite the blessing over the mitzvah, and with both hands lift the piece of dough aloft and proclaim: "Behold, this is challah!"

My hands are quivering with the spiritual intensity of the moment, and Pliyah Esther's face is awe-struck. With my hands still raised, I utter two more prayers — one that my taking challah should be considered as if I had brought an offering in the Holy Temple, that it should atone for all my sins and be as if I am born anew, and the other for the complete and final redemption of the whole world.

It has taken me over an hour to perform this one mitzvah. I feel exalted, tremulous, ecstatic as I used to feel after hours of meditation.

For seventeen years, I sporadically (and incorrectly) performed the mitzvah of challah, while having no idea of the profundity and spiritual potential of the mitzvah. I slid into second base, recited the blessing, broke off a piece of dough — and felt nothing. It did not connect me to Hashem, except on the most rudimentary level.

The lack was not in the mitzvah. The lack was not in Judaism. The lack was in me.

The mitzvos are an unparalleled spiritual feast. Most Jews, even most Orthodox Jews, have barely tasted their sumptuousness. Connoisseurs know the difference between eating and dining. The latter takes time — and concentration on the taste of every bite. A connoisseur dining in a five-star restaurant will not complain at how long it takes to prepare the food. Nor will he assess the quality of the restaurant by how full he feels when he leaves.

Connecting to Hashem through the mitzvos takes time, constant learning, and a commitment to moving ever deeper. Judaism is not a fast-food religion.

Not So Small Miracles

On Sarah Apel's 5th birthday, her grandfather Jacob presented her with an olivewood-covered *siddur* that his father had acquired decades before during a pilgrimage from White Russia to Palestine. In the front of the *siddur*, he wrote: "Always be proud that you are a Jew, and know that you have a holy land."

Sarah, whose family was non-observant, could not read Hebrew and had no idea how to use a *siddur*. So she put the precious gift under her pillow and kept it there for the next seven years. Apparently the *siddur* seeped into her dreams. Although she lived in Upland, a small town in central California, her dreams were of a faraway Golden City. In a recurrent dream, repeated hundreds of times, she saw herself walking on a narrow bridge toward the Golden City. Then she heard a voice from heaven saying, "If you look only at the light coming from the Golden City, you will get to the Golden City."

But as she walked, she heard other voices, coming from beneath the bridge. There she saw beautiful people dressed in beautiful clothes, singing beautiful songs. They called to her to come and join them, but when she moved toward them, she would fall off the bridge and be in "Nowhereland forever, like an empty shopping center, with nothing real inside."

One day in her 12th year, Sarah's father announced that he had bought a bigger house in an adjacent town, and soon they would be moving. Sarah loved her house, especially the big elm tree in the yard, where she would spend hours yearning to come closer to her Creator. "You may be moving," she told her father sadly, "but I'm not."

One night a few weeks later, while Sarah was sleeping soundly, her father lifted her up and put her into the family car. The next morning, she awoke in a different house in a different town. Appalled, Sarah jumped onto her bicycle and cycled for half an hour until she reached her old house. There a horrifying scene greeted her. A moving van was parked in front of her house, and a strange family with three sons was moving in. She watched them, disconsolate. Finally, wretched, she got back onto her bike and pedaled away.

The Beautiful People

The dreams of the Golden City vanished. Instead of heeding the heavenly voice to focus on the light emanating from the Golden City, Sarah responded to the siren call of the "beautiful people." By the time she graduated high school, the 60's were in full swing. Beautiful people abounded: hippies with their free-flowing clothes and soulful folksongs, meditators with their religion of universality and love, and native Americans with their exotic culture and bond to nature. The Golden City was forgotten.

In 1965, Sarah was studying art at U.C.L.A. A non-Jewish friend said to her, "I always knew you were a Jew because there is such trust in your eyes. I recently met a young man who also has trust in his eyes. You should meet him." The friend introduced her to Dana Fox, a tall young man who had not known he was Jewish until he was 18 years old, when someone cracked a derisive Jewish joke in Dana's living room. When Dana laughed, his mother upbraided him, "Don't laugh. You're also a Jew."

Sarah and Dana discovered that they were astonishingly compatible. One day, their conversation drifted to their childhoods. Dana told her that he had grown up in the small town of Upland. Sarah was amazed.

"I grew up there, too, until I was 12 years old. What street did you live on?"

"Sixth Street," Dana replied. "I lived at 554 North Sixth Street."

Sarah turned white. That was her house. Dana was one of the three boys she had seen moving into her house.

The Wedding

Eventually, Dana and Sarah decided to get married. Her mother, ecstatic, planned a wedding in their Reform temple for a Sunday afternoon in July.

On the morning of her wedding day, Sarah woke up frantic. She had had a horrific dream of the Golden City of her childhood. This time, however, the Golden City was burning. All its residents were screaming in anguish.

Sarah phoned Dana and told him, "We can't get married today. I don't know why, but it's a terrible day to get married." When Dana reached her side, he realized that she was intractable. But why?

They decided that a rabbi might solve the foreboding mystery of her dream. They looked in the Los Angeles yellow pages under "Rabbis, Orthodox," and found a name and nearby address. Quickly they drove to the rabbi's house and knocked on his door. When the rabbi opened the door, Sarah blurted out plaintively, "Why can't we get married today?"

The rabbi gazed at them and replied, "Because it's Tishah B'Av, the calamitous day of the burning of the Holy Temple in Jerusalem."

Dana, Sarah, and the rabbi all stood there with tears streaming down their cheeks. The rabbi cried because these young Jews had planned to get married on a day of fasting and mourning. Dana cried because this rational explanation meant that he would have to postpone his wedding. Sarah cried tears of joy because she had finally discovered the name of her Golden City — Jerusalem! Suddenly she fathomed the meaning of all her dreams.

Much to their families' chagrin, Sarah and Dana postponed their wedding for two days. On Tuesday, the 11th of Av, the rabbi they had found married them in an Orthodox ceremony. "Our wedding meal was the first kosher food we ever ate," recalled Sarah years later.

The Backyard Miracle

Dana and Sarah moved to the San Francisco Bay Area. They rented a modest house at the bottom of a steep hill, with a lovely backyard surrounded by an eight-foot-high redwood fence. By the summer of 1970, they had two children, and Sarah was expecting their third soon. Dana worked as an elementary school teacher, and Sarah taught art.

One day, Sarah was working in the kitchen. Her two small children were playing in a little plastic swimming pool in the backyard.

Suddenly Sarah heard an urgent voice inside her head, commanding: "Run fast! Bring in the children! Quickly! Now!"

Sarah sprinted into the backyard, grabbed one child in each arm, and dashed back into the kitchen. As soon as the screen door slammed behind her, Sarah heard a deafening crash. She turned around to see a huge semitrailer truck filling up her entire backyard. The redwood fence was smashed like so many toothpicks. Under the wheels of the truck was the little pool.

Leaving the Desert

The Foxes' oldest daughter suffered from recurrent earaches. A doctor suggested that they move to the dry climate of Arizona. So, in 1971, the family drove their VW bus to Arizona. There, in a trailer on a hill in the desert near a dramatic cliff drop, they settled, among Mormons, Catholics, and native Americans.

Two years later, the Yom Kippur War struck Israel. One night Dana had a nightmare. He cried out, "They can't take my land away from me!" When he woke up in the morning, he told Sarah that he wanted to go to the nearest *aliyah* office to inquire about moving to Israel.

Dana, Sarah, and their three young children piled into their VW bus and drove to the *aliyah* office in Phoenix. The *aliyah* representative there asked them if they had ever been to Israel. They answered, "No."

"Well, do you know anything about Israel?" he queried.

"No," they replied.

"Are you part of a Jewish community?"

"No."

"So why do you want to move to Israel?" he asked them, baffled.

Sarah told him about her olivewood *siddur* from Palestine, and about her dreams of the Golden City, which on her wedding day she understood to be Jerusalem.

The *aliyah* representative was visibly moved. In a tone uncharacteristic of Israeli officials, he told them: "My children, my children, come home."

They hesitantly decided to make *aliyah*. They filled out all the forms, and arranged to leave in exactly one month. Then they drove back to their desert home on the cliff.

Sarah was scared. After all, a war was going on, which at that point Israel was not winning. When she and Dana alighted from the VW bus, with the children still playing inside, she told her husband, "If we go to Israel, our lives and our children's lives could be in danger."

No sooner had the words left her mouth than the VW bus started to roll, with the three children still inside. In seconds it picked up speed, until it was careening down the hill at 60 m.p.h., heading straight for the cliff. Dana, Sarah, and some dozen of their neighbors stood frozen in horror. Nothing could stop the vehicle. In moments, it hurtled over the cliff — then stopped in midair. Its back wheel had caught on a small bush. To everyone's amazement, the bus hung suspended in the air, held only by the bush.

All their neighbors started shouting, "A miracle for the Jews! God has done a miracle for the Jews!"

Everyone ran up to the vehicle and with ropes managed to pull it back onto the cliff. The children were uninjured.

Sarah and Dana, spent with horror and relief, walked with a Mormon friend back to their trailer. When they entered the trailer, they were greeted by a ghastly sight. Dozens of strange black insects were everywhere — on the floor, in the frying pan on the stove, even climbing up one of Dana's boots as they stood there. In two years living in the desert, they had never seen a single insect like these. "What are they?" Sarah asked their friend.

The friend quickly grabbed a towel and flitted the insect off of Dana's boot. Then he motioned them out the door. "They are deadly scorpions," he warned. "I have never in my life seen so many at one time."

Sarah and Dana understood that God was sending them a clear message. Suddenly Israel did not seem so dangerous. "We got the message," Sarah recalled years later. On the spot, they both resolved to follow through with their *aliyah* plans. That very afternoon, they began selling their furniture. As soon as they sold their first piece of furniture, the scorpions disappeared. Every last one of them.

A few months later, the Fox family arrived in Israel. As they descended the stairs from the airplane, Dana — now Shlomo — said, "We have come home to become Jews again."

Twenty-eight years later, Shlomo and Sarah Fox-Ashrei have eight children and eighteen grandchildren, all learning and living Torah in Jerusalem. Shlomo and his sons are respected *talmidei chachamin*. Sarah has a unique vocation. She spends hours each day praying at the Kosel and performs the service of "doing forty days of prayer at the Kosel" for those who live too far away to do it themselves.

❧

The Still Small Voice

*H*ashem is always communicating with human beings. While the messages we receive may not be as dramatic as the Foxes', most of us at one time or another experience Divine guidance — through intuition, dreams, or the uncanny unfolding of unlikely circumstances.

Most people, especially women, have at one time or another heard the quiet voice of intuition. Suddenly it occurs to you to phone a friend you haven't thought of in ages. You call and discover that the friend has recently suffered a tragedy and is so grateful for your call. Or you're debating about whether to book an earlier or later flight to your nephew's wedding. "Something" tells you to take the earlier flight. After you land, you find out that the later flight was canceled, and you would have missed the wedding.

One Friday morning as I was cooking for Shabbos, I suddenly got the idea, "Call Meir and invite him for Shabbos." Meir was the 25-year-old secular Israeli son of my Yemenite cleaning woman, Etty. Etty had told me that Meir had recently started to show a flickering of interest in Judaism. My rational mind tried to dismiss the idea: "Meir doesn't even know our family. He lives an hour's drive away. He'll never want to spend 26 hours with English-speaking, *chareidi* strangers. It's preposterous." But again I heard the whisper, "Invite Meir." I phoned Etty for Meir's number, invited him, and — wonder of wonders — he came for Shabbos!

That started a process that gradually led Meir to do complete *teshuvah*. Today he is married to a Bais Yaakov graduate and learns full-time in *kollel*. And periodically his proud mother asks me, "Whatever made you call Meir and invite him for Shabbos?"

When Can You Trust a "Message"?

How can one know if a "message" is really from Hashem rather than from that notorious ventriloquist, the ego?

The Torah specifically prohibits reading omens. Two white doves circling around the heads of you and your date should not be interpreted as a sign that you should get married. The sudden appearance of scorpions in your home is not an omen. Rather, it presents a clear, rational fact: life-threatening danger. If you were worried about following a certain course of action because of its prospective dangers, now you must weigh those possible dangers against the reality of your actual, present danger. Omens are open to diverse interpretations. Messages present facts; we may or may not want to draw the obvious conclusions.

From Sarah and Shlomo's story, we can garner three clues as to when to trust a "message":

1. If the message bids you to do something inconvenient, difficult, or downright

distasteful, it is probably not coming from your ego. *Sarah's message to postpone her wedding cost her the ire of her mother, who had spent months planning the event. Dana's dream-message to move to Israel in the middle of a war was a challenge that ran counter to all their preferences. Rebbetzin Hinda Adler used to say: "If it's difficult, that's a sign that it's good."*

2. **When in doubt, consult a rabbi.** *Sarah's dream convinced her that that was not the right day to get married, but she couldn't understand why. They intuited that an Orthodox rabbi would be able to shed light on her dream-message, which he did.*

3. **If it contradicts the Torah, then it is not a message from Hashem.** *The Torah is the ultimate Divine message: direct and irrevocable. The Torah specifically warns against false prophets. They are false, even if their prophecies come true or they can work miracles, if they bid you to do anything that contradicts the instructions of the Torah. The same principle applies to all kinds of "Divine messages." I believe that there has not been a single day since Sinai that Hashem has not communicated indirectly with human beings. However, there has not been a single Divine communication since Sinai that contradicts the message of Sinai.*

The more we see Hashem's hand in our lives, the more manifest His hand will be. And the more we obey His directives, however difficult, the more the flow of Divine communication will course through our daily lives. If Sarah had ignored her dream of the burning city, or decided that, in spite of the message, postponing the wedding was too difficult, one wonders whether she would have been able to hear the inner voice that warned her to save her children.

The key to understanding Hashem's messages is honesty. If you scrutinize such messages honestly, intelligently, and without prior agendas, and you seek guidance from a rabbi or rebbetzin who is committed to the will of Hashem above his or her own will, and you are willing to follow even directives that are scathingly difficult for you, then you can trust your inner guidance as having a Divine source. What the prophet Elijah called "the still, small voice" of Divine inspiration is always speaking to us. The more honestly we listen, the more clearly we'll hear.

Suffering: Interloper or Invited Guest?

"Those were amazing moments, exalted moments. They were moments of indescribable closeness to Hashem. If someone would offer me all his money in exchange for the love I experienced then, I would scorn his offer. It was the greatest gift I ever received in my life. It changed me; it changed my entire existence."

The reader is apt to assume that the young woman who enjoyed this beatific spiritual experience was seated in meditation either at the Kosel or in a serene natural setting. In fact, she was lying on the floor of a bus during a terror attack.

On the morning of Tuesday, July 16, 2002, 22-year-old Yehudis Weinberg, a Chassidic woman and mother of a 14-month-old baby, left her home in the village of Emanuel. She took a bus to Bnei Brak in order to take a test at a local teachers' college. After completing the test, she caught a bus back to Emanuel. Fifty passengers were on board the fortified, bulletproof bus.

One and a half minutes outside the gate to Emanuel, a blast shook the bus. A bomb planted on the road was not intended to decimate the bus, but just to stop it. Then the terrorists, stationed on a hill above the road, were able to direct their automatic weapons' fire through the chink in the bus' armor — the 6-inch-high ventilation windows that ran along the length of the bus, above the large, sealed, bulletproof windows. The terrorists shot hundreds of bullets into the trapped bus for 15 minutes, killing ten passengers and wounding dozens more, before the Israeli Defense Forces arrived and stopped them.

Yehudis Weinberg tried to find shelter on the floor of the bus, but it was already packed with the bodies of the living and the dying. Yehudis was hit by seven bullets. One bullet tore open a major artery in her left leg. As she recounts:

> *I decided not to think at all about the wound, about the blood I was losing, about when the rescuers would arrive, or why the security forces had not yet killed the terrorists. I said Psalm 61 word-by-word, letter-by-letter, with meaning as deep as the ocean. I had read in a book that the blessing "everything exists by His word" cancels evil decrees, so I started saying those words hundreds of times. ... Very quickly I sensed why this blessing cancels evil decrees. The words assert that "everything exists by His word." Hashem is watching over me. He determines exactly what will happen. I am completely in His hands, like an infant protected in his mother's clasp. I will experience only the events He decreed I will experience. And He loves me with such a strong love that it is impossible to describe it in words.*

The first rescuer to reach the scene was an I.D.F. medic named Eitan. Eitan does not know how he entered the bus. "After the blast, the doors were locked. We couldn't get in through the doors, and we couldn't get in through the bulletproof windows. The narrow upper window at the back of the bus had shattered, so I jumped in through that space. An adult cannot possibly fit through such a small opening. It didn't seem possible for me to get through, but somehow I did."

The sight that greeted Eitan was more horrific than anything he had ever seen in his more than twenty years of experience. A specialist in multiple-casualty incidents, Eitan was well trained in the principle that the most urgent cases are not those calling for help. He always obeyed the rule to approach first those who are silent.

This time, however, when he heard Yehudis screaming, "Come here! I can't breathe!" Eitan inexplicably went to her first. He saw the blood gushing from the wound in her left leg, and immediately stopped the bleeding.

Afterwards, in the hospital, the doctors ascertained that had the bleeding continued even a little longer, Yehudis would have died. As it was, she had to receive eighteen units of blood.

The Copasetic Life

I used to fear suffering. I don't mean just the devastating suffering of illness and loss. If my computer malfunctioned, if a brand-new blouse got a stain, if a can of tuna fish got knocked off the cupboard shelf and crashed down on my favorite handmade ceramic mug, it was enough to ruin my day — or at least my hour. Not only would I fret over the time, money, and effort it would take to fix the problem (schlep the computer to the shop downtown where there's no parking *and* lose two days' work; scrub the blouse with egg white or whatever else my *Hints for Housewives* advised; waste time shopping for another mug that I wouldn't like as much), but I would be irritated and resentful that *something that never should have happened happened.*

According to my worldview, life was supposed to run like a well-oiled machine, what I call the "copasetic life": As I drive down the boulevard, I sail through one green light after another; unavoidably delayed on my way to mail an important package, I get to the post office 5 minutes before it closes, not 5 minutes after; when I need two eggs to bake a Shabbos cake late Thursday night, my neighbor is still awake and has them.

The copasetic life does not mean ease. I was willing to work, even work very hard, to keep the machine running smoothly — but a glitch? A malfunction? A total breakdown? These were interlopers that offended my sense of how things should be. How dare they presume to crash the party that is my life?

Then one fine Wednesday afternoon, I walked into Dr. Cohen's office to get my biopsy results, and walked out with a diagnosis of cancer. Throughout the succeeding weeks of tests and treatment, three things were crystal clear to me:

1. *This tumor came from Hashem.*
2. *This tumor was a gift of Hashem's love.*
3. *This tumor was Hashem's invitation to me to change in a deep way.*

I did not figure out any of these points. They were not the product of philosophizing or theologizing. I just *knew* them with total clarity. Kabbalah speaks of the "arousal from below," meaning our own prodigious efforts to get close to Hashem, and "the arousal from Above," meaning when Hashem reaches down to us. Hashem's overwhelming love that Yehudis Weinberg felt while wounded on the floor of the bus, which she repeatedly described as "the greatest gift I ever received in my life," was just such an "arousal from Above."

This influx of Divine support explains why I, who could not gracefully endure being woken up late at night by a wrong number, felt periodically, during the weeks I was facing a life-threatening illness, serene, exalted, and privy to spiritual clarity. I was riding high on Hashem's love.

At the end of my treatment, I was left not only cancer-free, but also free of my mistaken worldview. If cancer was Hashem's loving gift, what about a computer crash? A stain on my new blouse? A shattered mug? If cancer was a golden opportunity to grow spiritually, then the computer crash must be a silver opportunity, and the stain must be a brass opportunity, and the shattered mug must be ...

I realized how much energy I had squandered fearing and resisting suffering in my addiction to the copasetic life. It's as if every challenging experience has two components: the pain itself and our fear/rejection of the pain. This second factor can multiply the first factor many times over.

For example, the fear that often precedes an appointment to have a cavity filled can cause days of apprehension and nervousness. Once seated in the dentist's chair, the pain of the Novocain shot itself lasts less than a minute, while the discomfort of the drilling is in direct proportion to the patient's level of tension.

My experience with cancer taught me to stop slamming the door against Suffering, desperately trying to lock him out with an armory's supply of latches and dead bolts. Once Suffering was standing in my living room, I realized that he had something to teach me.

I began to see that Suffering — both major afflictions and minor irritations — was not an interloper in life, but rather the personally invited guest of Hashem. And this guest came for a purpose.

What I Learned From My Hockey Career

I must have been the most unathletic girl in New Jersey when I was growing up. But during my freshman year of high school, I had one shining moment of glory.

I had joined the freshman field-hockey team. (They took anybody, without tryouts.) I spent most of the season on the bench, for good reason, but one afternoon, when our team was playing the freshman hockey team from Audubon, the coach put me in the game. By some fluke, I started to wield my hockey stick with real prowess. I even scored two goals.

The coach was pleasantly flabbergasted. "You're really on fire today," she told me incredulously. She decided to put me into the junior varsity game that immediately followed our freshman game.

I felt like Popeye after his dose of spinach. Suddenly I was a hockey star! I plunged into the game with vigor I never knew I had. I got that ball on the end of my hockey stick and roared down the field. I deftly hit the ball past the goalie and right into the goal. I was a champion!

But why was the Audubon team cheering? Why was my team groaning? Why was the coach pounding her forehead in remorse?

I had hit the ball into the wrong goal. I had scored a goal for the opposing team.

From this I learned that more important than playing the game well is identifying which is the right goal.

It seems simplistic, but this was precisely the flaw in my pre-cancer worldview. At the beginning of a workday, I thought the goal was to put in a productive day's work. When I bought a new blouse, I thought the goal was to look nice and neat. When I bought my handmade ceramic mug, I thought the goal was to use it to drink hundreds of cups of herbal tea over the next few years.

Judaism teaches that there is always only one overriding goal: to be in a relationship with Hashem. As the last line of the *Shema* states unequivocally: "I am Hashem, your God, Who brought you out of the land of Egypt, *to be for you a God."*

The whole Exodus — the plagues, the splitting of the sea, indeed, all the suffering in Egyptian slavery that preceded it — was for one purpose: to establish our relationship with Hashem as our God.

That's the goal. Sometimes that goal requires the cosmic drama of the Exodus. Sometimes that intense, loving relationship can be achieved through the horror of a terror attack, as Yehudis Weinberg experienced. Sometimes we can come closer to Hashem through cancer. Sometimes through a computer crash. Sometimes through a shattered mug.

Everything, *everything,* in life is an invited guest. Everything can serve the purpose of bringing us closer to Hashem.

The Right Tool

One Tuesday I noticed that my flowers from Shabbos were droopy — in fact downright dead. I took the vase off the dining-room table, discarded the flowers, and reached for my bottle brush to scrub the vase. The bottle brush was not in its usual place.

"No matter," I thought. "I can do fine without it." I filled the vase up with soapy water, swished the water around, and poured it out. The inside of the vase was still coated with slime.

I reached for the brush I use to scrub the dairy dishes. It was too big to fit through the narrow neck of the vase. I tried using my fingers; they weren't long enough.

Not to be thwarted by the lack of a bottle brush, I decided to improvise a replacement. I took a wooden ruler and covered it with a washcloth. Voila! It was narrow enough to fit through the neck and long enough to reach the bottom of the vase. But it wasn't flexible enough to get to the hard-to-reach places right below the neck, at the point where the vase flairs outward.

Standing there holding my slimy vase, I had a revelation: To do the job right requires the right tool, and no matter how clever and resourceful I am, there's no replacement for the humble bottle brush.

The Tool of Torah

That night I sat down to read my email and was almost knocked out of my chair by the vitriolic force of a scathing letter from my cousin. This cousin was insulted by something I had written in one of my articles. Her letter was like a bomb packed with poison-coated nails. She attacked not just my article, but my entire despicable self and my loathsome life. According to her, I was a contemptible cousin and a rotten human being, and had always been so.

I sat there in front of my computer at first flabbergasted, then hurt, then resentful. Even if I had been guilty of an indiscretion in my article, certainly I did not deserve all the insults she had fired at me.

Not one to be cowed, the warrior in me took up her sword and was about to launch a counter-offensive. My cousin was not such a sterling individual herself, and I knew just what to say in retaliation. My hands were poised on my trusty keyboard, a weapon I well knew how to wield, when I stopped short.

The Torah prohibits us from taking revenge. [*Leviticus* 19:18] The principle of "an eye for an eye" is meant to guide courts of law in adjudicating damages (i.e., the value of an eye). As for individuals embroiled in interpersonal clashes, we are prohibited from returning tit for tat.

My hands withdrew from the keyboard. Okay, I wouldn't write her back a scathing letter. I got up and went to unload the dishwasher, but inside I was still fuming. How dare she?! By the time I had finished unloading the glasses, I realized to my dismay that the Torah also enjoins us, "Do not hate your brother in your heart." [ibid. v. 17]

"Oh, no!" I thought. "I'm not even allowed to hate her?" I felt like I had been caught red-handed about to chomp into a cheeseburger. Prohibited thoughts and feelings are as unkosher as prohibited food.

I sat down at the kitchen table and decided to work this through. My feelings of outrage were bubbling up in my heart like a volcano, but the Torah expected me to control my thoughts and emotions as well as my actions. I knew that the way to change emotions is to change the thoughts that I was telling myself. By a gigantic act of will, I "changed the tape." I forced myself to remember good things about my cousin, times she had been loving to me, times she had been vulnerable.

Finally I stood up, calm enough to go to bed. I had followed the injunctions of the Torah. I hadn't taken revenge and I didn't hate her in my heart. I would not write her a nasty letter; in fact, I wouldn't write to her at all. If she finds me so abhorrent, then obviously the relationship is over. I don't need a relationship with her anyway, I thought as I fell asleep.

The next morning, it dawned on me: The "silent treatment" is also forbidden by the Torah. According to the Rambam, a Jew who does not greet his/her fellow for three consecutive days has transgressed the mitzvah to love your neighbor as yourself. The Torah was actually requiring me to communicate with my cousin.

It took me hours to work up to it, but that afternoon I sat down at my computer and wrote my cousin a letter. I humbly apologized for the offense in my article, told her how much I valued our relationship, and expressed my hope that this altercation would not create a rift in our family.

A few hours later I received a three-sentence email from my cousin. It said: "Sorry. I was having a bad day. Of course I love you and want to be friends with you."

I read her email in consternation. If it hadn't been for the Torah, her "bad day" would have led to a family feud that might have lasted a lifetime.

Torah is the irreplaceable tool that Hashem gave us for living in this world. Some people say that Torah is the "instruction manual for planet Earth." I tend to think of it as the bottle brush.

Choosing Up

The ballroom of Jerusalem's Plaza Hotel was filled with 250 well-dressed young Americans, Englishmen, South Africans, and Australians. The occasion was the 20th anniversary of Yeshivat Darche Noam. The attendees were all college graduates and professional people who had become observant and had relocated in Israel.

The guest speaker, Minister of Immigrant Absorption Yuli Edelstein, was shifting uncomfortably in his seat. As he surveyed the crowd, all of whom had moved to Israel from affluent English-speaking countries, he wondered what he would say to them. He himself had made *aliyah* from Russia, after years as a refusenik and three and a half years doing hard labor in the Gulag. What could he say to these spoiled Americans? When he finally did rise to speak, however, he surprised even himself.

Mr. Edelstein began by admitting his qualms in addressing a crowd whose background was not fraught with the hardships he had faced. He told how when he was first imprisoned by the K.G.B., he did not have with him his *tefillin*. His wife brought his *tefillin* to the prison every morning, but the K.G.B. refused to give them to him. When his official interrogation began, Yuli refused to talk. He explained to his K.G.B. interrogators that he could not speak because he had not recited his morning prayers properly because he did not have his *tefillin*. Within an hour, the *tefillin* were brought to his cell.

On the day the investigation ended, a group of K.G.B. thugs came to Yuli's cell, ransacked the place, and found his *tefillin*. While two men held him, a third broke apart his *tefillin*, tearing the sacred parchment scrolls to shreds in front of his anguished face.

"How could I *not* come to Israel?" Mr. Edelstein asked us in an impassioned tone. "They tore up my *tefillin*! I had no choice to stay in such a country. But *you*," he said looking directly at our rapt faces, "none of you had to make *aliyah*. You chose to leave countries where you were free. Nobody tore up your *tefillin*. Yet, you *chose* to make *aliyah*. You are much greater than I am. I consider it a privilege to be in your presence."

Real Freedom

According to Judaism, human beings have free choice, but only in a circumscribed area. Our only real freedom is in making moral choices. Every human being has a unique "choice box," explains Rav Eliyahu Dessler, a specific area of moral choice where he or she could truly go either way. This is the total locus of our freedom.

Most likely, the decision to murder or not to murder is not a viable choice for anyone reading this chapter. When we stand at the threshold of the next world, we will not be rewarded for our assiduous obedience to the mitzvah, "Do not murder." Given the society in which we were raised and the parents who trained us in basic values, murder is not a real option for us, even when someone cuts us off in traffic. In not murdering, we are not exercising free choice.

At the other end of the moral spectrum, few of us are on the exalted level of altruism where we would donate our entire life savings to pay for a lifesaving operation for a child we don't know. Nor would most of us seriously entertain the option of donating a kidney to a stranger. Such decisions are above our "choice box." They are not viable courses of action, given who we are today.

All true choice implies struggle. In exercising the difficult choices within one's unique "choice box," a person fulfills the very purpose for which he or she has come into this world: to change and grow.

This is what the sages mean when they say that at the end of life, we will be judged only according to our choices. A person born with an altruistic nature, raised in a family where doing for others was the norm, will not be rewarded for volunteering weekly at the local hospital. "Doing what comes naturally," to the extent that it means maintaining one's spiritual status quo, is a cop-out on one's life mission. We are here to struggle and stretch ourselves and become more than what we were when we started.

It is not how good we are, but how good we have become, that is the measure of the person.

The Tower Went Down, But the Person Went Up

The day after the collapse of the World Trade Center, the *New York Times* reported the story of a woman who could walk only with the aid of crutches who worked on the 64th floor of Tower Two. Fellow employees tried to carry her down the stairs. "They had me over their shoulder for 5 or 10 flights and just couldn't do it."

"Another co-worker she knew only as Louis," reported the *Times*, "came upon the struggling group, lifted the woman to his shoulder and carried her by himself, she said, adding that the temperature in the stairwell was at least 90 degrees."

Louis carried this woman down 54 flights of stairs, and did not leave her until she was safely inside an ambulance.

The Louis who fled from his office on the 64th floor was not the same man who emerged from the building. Somewhere between the 54th and the ground floor, Louis exercised his free choice and chose good. It may not have happened on the landing of the 54th floor when he picked up the woman and hoisted her over his shoulder. At that point, he may have been acting from an innately altruistic nature. He may have been constitutionally incapable of ignoring the incapacitated woman without at least trying to help her.

But somewhere in the smoky stairwell of the World Trade Center, when his muscles started to hurt, and the heat got to him, and the weight on his shoulder slowed him down more and more, and hundreds of panicked people pushed past him fleeing for their lives, somewhere — perhaps on the landing of the 34th floor or the 24th floor — instinct gave way to choice, and Louis chose to save this woman at whatever cost to himself.

The *Times* article related that around the 15th floor a rescue worker told Louis that the woman was out of danger, and suggested he leave her there and exit the building by himself. One of Louis' inner voices must have echoed the proposal: "Surely I've already done enough. No one else would have done half of what I did to save her. Even a professional fireman says it's good enough." Louis chose to heed the other voice that said:

"She's not safe until she's in a vehicle that can take her away from here."

The Louis who had arrived for work that morning was a man with the potential for greatness. The Louis who emerged, sweating and aching, from the World Trade Center was a great man. Only moral choices make us into the persons we can become.

Each one of us has the freedom to choose good. Our choices need not be on the scale of newsworthy deeds. Choosing beyond our comfort zone is intrinsically heroic.

So how do you "choose up"?

- *If you are a person who has no affinity with elderly relatives, right now call your great aunt who lives alone.*

- *If you have been nursing a grudge against friends or relatives who treated you badly, right now forgive them.*

- *If you have no time to learn more Torah, right now take a scalpel to your schedule and carve out one hour a week.*

- *If you are a person who tends to give more attention to building your capital than building your family, right now make a daring reversal of your priorities.*

Choosing up is ultimate freedom.

The Builder and the Terrorist

I approached Lior from the end of his hospital bed. The first thing I saw, protruding out from his blanket, was his grotesquely swollen foot. It looked like a 4-year-old's drawing of a foot — huge, boxlike toes, the skin stretched taut over the ballooned limb.

Not wanting to be caught staring, I looked up quickly to Lior's face at the other end of the bed. The 27-year-old was smiling broadly, glowing, radiant.

I looked back at his swollen foot, then again at his radiant face. How could they both belong to the same person?

Lior, who does building renovations, had been wounded in the terrorist attack in the Jerusalem neighborhood of Neve Yaakov two weeks before. He was in his apartment, and had been fasting all day for the Fast of Esther, on the eve of Purim. He was just breaking his fast with a glass of water when he heard the sound of machine-gun fire. He called the police, but the line was busy.

More shots. Lior did not own a gun. Suffering from a slipped disc, he had never served in the Israeli army. Nevertheless, propelled by the thought, "Maybe I can help," Lior charged out of his door in the direction of the terrorist. He took cover behind bushes and cars as he made his way closer to the terrorist, who was spraying bullets on every Jew within sight.

Lior saw a police jeep with three blood-spattered policemen splayed on the floor. Two of them were not moving, perhaps already dead. One policeman, injured, was trying to return fire.

Lior, approaching ever closer, saw the terrorist run up to the jeep and point the barrel of his gun directly at the head of one of the unconscious policemen. He pulled the trigger, but no bullet fired. He must have run out of ammunition. The terrorist dropped his gun, and grabbed the gun of one of the fallen policemen. The injured officer tried unsuccessfully to stop him.

At that moment, Lior sprinted toward the terrorist, jumped on him, grabbed him in a stranglehold, and dragged him 6 or 7 meters away from the stricken policemen. Lior and the terrorist wrestled on the ground. When police reinforcements arrived, they tried to shoot the terrorist. Suddenly Lior felt a sharp pain. A bullet had hit him in the hip. The terrorist was subdued and captured, and Lior was rushed to Hadassah Hospital.

Now, two weeks and five operations later, Lior's leg is badly infected. "I don't care," says Lior. "I was privileged to be able to do something for the Jewish people. The Jewish people are holy. It is the greatest thing to be able to help *Am Yisrael*."

One of the police officers died, and several civilians were wounded in the attack. But the other two policemen survived. One is already out of the hospital.

"You're a hero," I tell Lior.

"No, no, I'm an ordinary person," he protests, sincerely. Then he adds ingenuously, "Anyone would have done what I did."

"To run out, unarmed, in the direction of a terrorist attack? No way," I argue. "Weren't you afraid?"

"Yes, I was afraid," Lior answers simply.

I look at this man lying in his hospital bed, with his infected leg and his bad back, who was afraid to fight a terrorist with his bare hands. And who did it anyway. Because his impulse to help overpowered his impulse to hide. And I understand why he is radiant and happy.

Rebbetzin Tziporah Heller says: "If you want to feel good, do good."

And I, who have come to the hospital to distribute snacks and bottles of spring water to those wounded in recent terror attacks and their anguished families — because I couldn't stand sitting in my house and listening to the horrific news anymore — I also feel better. And the three women who came with me, as they hand out their boxes with tissues to catch tears, and straws and cups for the spring water, and *rugelach*, because all Yidden love *rugelach*, these women also find their mood lifting.

In front of one hospital room, where lies a 22-year-old girl injured in the Moment Cafe suicide bombing the night before, two tearful young women are eager to show us a photograph they are holding. "This is Sharona, who's in this room," they explain, pointing to one of the two smiling blondes kneeling on a grassy background, "and this is Ronit, five hours before she was killed."

We shake our heads, and embrace them, and cry with them, and hand them some *rugelach*. They are grateful we've come, and we are grateful we've come.

"If you want to feel good, do good."

Blake Nordstrom Speaking ...

Seattle resident Sarah Busch was chagrined when she opened her monthly Nordstrom statement. Instead of the concise, compact statement she had been receiving for decades, the 79-year-old retired bookkeeper unfolded a bulky 8x10 statement in a new format. She decided to complain.

She phoned Nordstrom's corporate headquarters right there in Seattle and asked to speak to someone in management. "Don't give me Customer Service," she instructed the operator. After a few rings, a masculine voice answered the phone. "First of all, I'd like to know to whom I'm speaking," Sarah Busch began.

"This is Blake Nordstrom," came the reply.

"Blake Nordstrom? You're the president!" a confounded Sarah Busch exclaimed.

"I am indeed," he responded.

"What are YOU doing answering the phone?"

"Well," Mr. Nordstrom explained in a bemused tone, "I was sitting here at my desk, and the phone rang, so I picked it up."

"You crack me up!" Mrs. Busch declared. She proceeded to tell Mr. Nordstrom that she had been a loyal customer since Nordstrom was nothing but a shoe store in downtown Seattle. "I still have the first credit card you issued when you merged with Best Apparel in 1963. It's all worn out and expired, but I keep it as a memento."

The corporate president and the retired bookkeeper enjoyed a convivial conversation for about 10 minutes, with Sarah Busch not forgetting to lodge her complaint about the new format of the monthly statement.

Two days later, she received a letter from Blake Nordstrom. Enclosed was a shiny new replica of her antiquated Nordstrom/Best credit card, obviously fabricated just for her. Mr. Nordstrom thought she would get a kick out of it, and indeed she did.

She called Blake (by now they were on first-name basis) to thank him. "Next time you're downtown," he invited her, "come up to the 6th floor to say hello."

A week later, a local *kollel* wife mentioned to Mrs. Busch that she had encountered some trouble while shopping at a Nordstrom branch. "No problem," Mrs. Busch responded, to the young woman's surprise. "Give me the specifics, and I'll tell my friend Blake Nordstrom about it."

The next day, Sarah Busch presented herself at the president's office. "Mr. Nordstrom is in a meeting," his secretary said politely. "He'll be finished in about an hour."

"Fine," the septuagenarian replied. "I'll do some errands and come back."

An hour later, she had the concierge phone from the first floor to see if Mr. Nordstrom was available now. The response was that she needn't take the trouble to come upstairs. Blake Nordstrom would come down to her.

She was standing with her back to the elevator when she heard a booming voice, "Is this the famous Sarah Busch?"

She turned to see a very tall, 40-something man with a wide smile approaching her. Blake Nordstrom greeted the short, elderly Jewish woman like a beloved relative. And, of course, he promised to look into her young friend's problem.

※

Waiting for Your Call

*T*his is a true story (related to me by Sarah Busch herself), and it is also a staggering metaphor. In earlier ages, Midrashim used the *mashal* of Hashem as a human king. In the modern age, it would be more apt to use the *mashal* of a corporate president. Recognizing the limitations of all such metaphors, what can we learn from Sarah Busch's surprising experience?

- *When we pray, how many of us actually expect that the Big Boss Himself will pick up the line?*

- *How many of us expect that Hashem, the Ruler of the entire universe, actually wants a personal relationship with us?*

- *When we receive a gift (such as every day of life), how often do we appreciate that the Almighty fabricated it just for us, because He wants us to enjoy it?*

- *How heedless are we of the invitation to "come up," in order to forge a relationship with the Divine?*

- *When things go wrong, do we actually feel that we have Hashem's ear?*

- *How little do we perceive that the Master of the Universe "comes down" to us?*

- *While we may be insignificant in our own eyes, can we believe that to our Creator we are on par with "the famous Sarah Busch" — i.e., worthy of Divine attention and affection?*

As any lactation consultant will assure a new mother, the more the baby nurses, the more milk will be produced. Similarly, the more we perceive Hashem in our lives, the more Hashem reveals Himself to us. And the opposite is also true: the more we attribute what comes our way to "chance" and the blind workings of nature, the more hidden and apparently absent Hashem is from our lives.

Rabbi David Aaron had a student who became observant and was to be married in Jerusalem. The student's anti-religious mother came for the wedding. When she was introduced to Rabbi Aaron, she vociferously expressed her atheistic convictions, expecting the rabbi to try to refute her views. Instead, Rabbi Aaron replied, "If you want to live in a Godless world, then that's the world you'll live in."

The loss was hers. And every time we opt for a Godless day, hour, or incident, the loss is ours.

On the other hand, when we recognize that we are never alone, that the Creator loves us and wants a relationship with us, that He is, as it were, "sitting at His desk waiting for the phone to ring," then we live in a God-filled, light-filled, love-filled world. Then, even when things go wrong, we know we can depend on the Boss to listen to our plight. (Note that Blake Nordstrom did not change the new billing format in response to Sarah Busch's complaint, but he did forge an unlikely relationship with her.)

Hashem's Job Description

The day I left Israel for my recent American lecture tour was utterly hectic. Scheduled to speak in 17 cities, I had dozens of logistical details to which I needed to attend. Since my plane was due to land at JFK at 5:30 a.m., I had told my cousin in Cedarhurst that I would take a taxi to her house. I had carefully calculated that the $90 in American money I had put aside in my bedroom drawer months ago for this trip would suffice for my taxi fare and other expenses upon arrival in the United States. As I rushed around Jerusalem, I purposely disposed of all my Israeli shekels so I wouldn't have to carry them around in the United States.

Sitting at the gate in the Tel Aviv airport waiting to board my plane, I suddenly realized that I had forgotten to take along the American dollars. I was embarking on international travel with no money whatsoever in my purse.

My first reaction was exasperated self-reproach: How could I have forgotten something so important? No matter that I had exerted tremendous effort during the preceding weeks organizing a myriad of details. How could I have omitted this one crucial detail?

Then I felt a surge of reassurance: *Hashem would take care of me.* How did I know? Because that's what He's been doing all my life. In fact, that's high up on Hashem's job description: He takes care of human beings 24/7 — the circulation system, the nervous system, the endocrine system, etc. That's what He does; He takes care of us. After all, He is the President of the whole universe.

Wondering how Hashem would get me out of this mess, I got up and walked toward the drinking fountain. In the corridor, a woman stopped me. "Aren't you Sara Rigler?" she asked. "I heard you speak last June in America."

We conversed for several minutes. It turned out that she and I were on the same flight. "Where are you going in the States?" she asked.

"My first speaking engagement is in Woodmere," I replied. "From the airport I'm going to my cousin's house in Cedarhurst."

"How are you getting there?" she asked.

"I'm not sure," was my truthful reply.

"Well, I live in Cedarhurst," she said. "I'm traveling with my husband and daughter. My son is coming to pick us up. If he brings the van, there'll be enough room for you, too. We can give you a ride."

Her son did indeed come with the van, and it turned out that they lived just a few hundred yards from my cousin's house. I didn't need taxi fare after all.

The Kotzker Rebbe's famous aphorism proved true yet again: "Where does Hashem dwell? Wherever you let Him in."

Alice's Cake

I was never before so happy to be up at night with a sick child.

It was last Monday [November 20, 2000], the night after an Arab terrorist bomb exploded beside a schoolbus carrying children from Kfar Darom. Two teachers were killed and ten passengers injured. Among the wounded were three children from the Cohen family. Twelve-year-old Orit's right foot was blown off. Seven-year-old Yisrael lost his right leg. Eight-and-a-half-year-old Tehilla lost two fingers and both legs. The doctors at Soroka Hospital made a valiant effort to sew her legs back on with a 17-hour-operation. The operation failed, leaving little Tehilla with no legs below the knee.

At 4:45 a.m., my 6-year-old son's cries woke me up for the second time that night. He was suffering from an earache and sinusitis, and the painkiller must have worn off.

Although being awoken from my always too few hours of sleep is my least favorite part of motherhood, that night was different. I groggily got out of bed and groped my way to the medicine chest. Squinting my eyes from the brightness of the bathroom lights, I measured out a dose of Acomol (the Israeli equivalent of children's Tylenol).

As I stumbled my way to my son's bed, my usually grumbling attitude to such sleep interruptions was suddenly replaced by a surge of intense gratitude. "Thank you, Hashem," I said out loud in a choked voice. "Thank you that unlike Noga Cohen, who tonight is running among three hospital rooms, in each one of which lies one of her permanently maimed children, my child has nothing worse than an earache, which will pass in a day or two, leaving no trace."

Gratitude, of course, always brings along its sidekick, joy. As I struggled to make my crying, half-asleep child sit up so he could swallow the medicine, a feeling of exultation welled up in my heart. My child was alive, with all his limbs intact. "How good is our portion!" The line from the Psalms flashed before my mind's eye, like a neon sign above Times Square. I had a reason for rejoicing.

Sitting on my son's bed trying to soothe him back to sleep, my two-chambered heart held within it agonizing sorrow for the Cohen family next to lilting joy for my son. The darker the former, the more brightly shone the latter. When, 10 minutes later, I had finally quieted him, I almost glided my way back to bed on a feeling of jubilation.

Itamar

The next morning my good friend Etty, who is a first cousin to Rabbi Ofir Cohen, the children's father, came to my apartment. Distraught and distracted, she told me she was on her way to Soroka Hospital. I asked her to gather the names and mothers' names of all the wounded. I needed the full names to give to my colleagues, a group of thirty-two women who weekly recite the Book of Psalms for the recovery of the sick.

At 4 p.m. that afternoon, the news on the Internet reported that an 18-year-old boy, while waiting to hitch a ride near the same intersection where the schoolbus had been bombed, had been shot in the head by an Arab sniper. He was being transported to Soroka Hospital by an army helicopter. A couple of hours later, the next bulletin informed us that the boy had died.

At 8:45 that night, Etty called me from Soroka Hospital and gave me the full names of all the wounded. At the end, she added, "And Itamar ben Rachel, who was shot in the head today."

"But I thought he had died!" I exclaimed.

"No," Etty answered somberly. *Baruch Hashem*, he's still alive. But after the operation, the doctor told his sister that he won't make it."

I hung up feeling, "Where there's life, there's hope." Armed with his name and his mother's name, I sprang into action. The religious women of Jerusalem have an emergency system which moves into high gear in drastic circumstances. One woman will call three, four, or five other women, tell them which psalms to say for whom, and bid them to call the same number of other women. In this way, thousands of women are reached in two or three hours.

I hurriedly called three women, asking them to say *Tehillim* for Itamar ben Rachel, and to pass the message on. Since I live in the Old City, near the Temple Mount, which is considered by our sages to be the "Gate of Prayer" from which all prayers in this world ascend to the higher realms, I determined to run to the Kosel, the retaining wall from the Temple Mount, to pray. I asked those women who could manage to drop everything to meet me there at 9:30.

A brigade of nine women met and fervently recited *Tehillim* for Itamar's recovery for half an hour. A few minutes after I returned to my apartment, the phone rang. It was one of the women I had called.

"Did you hear the 10:00 news?" I could hear the pain in her voice. "Itamar died. This time there's no mistake."

I went to bed that night distressed and disheartened.

Alice's Cake

The next morning, when I opened the refrigerator to take out orange juice for my children's breakfast, I noticed that the light was out and the food inside was barely cold. I listened for the hum of the refrigerator motor and heard only silence.

"Oh, no! A broken refrigerator!" I thought. "That means finding a repairman, paying at least 1,000 shekels, when we're already thousands of shekels in overdraft, and shlepping the food in the freezer around to find space in neighbors' freezers until the repairman finally gets here and replaces the parts."

No sooner had my mind emitted this burst of aggravation, than I stopped myself short: "Itamar's parents are arranging for their son's funeral today, and *you're* upset about a broken refrigerator? Are you crazy?"

The daily tragedies of this war are a slap in the face, waking me up from the somnambulant state in which I habitually bemoan any event that costs me time or money. I feel like Alice in Wonderland after she eats the cake which suddenly makes her grow so big that all the objects around her become tiny in comparison.

The life and death events of this war are that cake. All the irritations and annoyances of my life have suddenly assumed their true proportion: small and petty.

As I retrieved the orange juice, and quickly closed the refrigerator door to retain whatever coolness was left inside, I felt that same surge of gratitude and joy I had felt two nights before: Jewish mothers are burying their children today, and all I have to contend with is a broken refrigerator. How good is my portion!

With a heart full of equanimity and gratitude, I opened the yellow pages and started to search for a refrigerator repairman.

Moments later, I heard gagging sounds from my son's room. I ran in to see him spewing tangerine, bile, and phlegm all over the thick pile of the area rug in the middle of the room. I ran for a basin, held his head, and stroked him as he finished. Then I led him to his bed and went to fetch a damp washcloth to wipe his face.

This time my usual reaction (Oh, no! How will I ever clean up this mess?) barely managed to rear its head. I took care of my son, then tackled the rug. There I was on my hands and knees working away at the mess with wet rags, and feeling a wave of veritable bliss. "My husband and children are alive. Their bodies are intact. How fortunate am I! Just a badly soiled rug. Thank you, Hashem, that the tribulations You give me are so puny."

Pain and Gratitude

*I*n the summer of my 43rd year, my mother was diagnosed with stomach cancer. The doctors gave her three to six months to live. I was plunged into a dark world of sorrow and impending loss.

One day, shortly after receiving the terrible news, I had to go to our neighborhood grocery store to buy some butter and yogurt. As I walked through the square, I felt like an alien from another planet. The sky was blue, children were playing, and their mothers were chatting amiably. Only I was grief-stricken and burdened.

I picked out my butter and yogurt and took my place in line behind my friend Slotana. "Hi, how are you?" she greeted me warmly.

I told her about my mother's diagnosis.

"I know just how you feel," she said shaking her head. "My mother died of cancer when I was 21. I was in college when my father called me to come quickly. The whole experience was terrible, just terrible."

"I heard your mother has cancer, Sara." It was my friend Donna's grave voice behind me. "You know my mother died of cancer when I was 16. It was awful. I know just what you're going through."

For a few moments we stood there in silence, a camaraderie of pain and sorrow.

But when I left the grocery store and was again crossing the square, I was aware of a shift in my consciousness. Slotana had lost her mother at 21, Donna at 16. I had had my mother's loving presence in my life for forty-three years. She had lived to see me married (at the age of almost 39) and had lived to hold my first child in her arms. I had so much for which to be grateful. The sorrow at her impending death was still there, but now accompanied by a feeling of profound gratitude for all I had received during forty-three years of love and support.

More Than Pollyanna

This attitude of keeping gratitude uppermost in our consciousness is more than Pollyanna's "glad game." It is the essence of what it means to be a Jew.

The very word for "Jew" in Hebrew is *Yehudi*, which comes from the root word meaning, "to acknowledge, to thank." Acknowledging the reality of Hashem's infinite giving is synonymous with thanking Him.

Indeed, most people's stumbling block on the road to faith is suffering: the Holocaust, the death of children, etc. But focusing on suffering fails to acknowledge the truth that the world is filled with the goodness of Hashem, from the plenitude of air and fresh water to the tireless beating of our hearts and the intricacies of the immune system. Healthy children outnumber fatally ill children by thousands to one.

Once, years ago, I was traveling on a bus with Rebbetzin Tzipporah Heller. We were discussing the anguish of children's suffering, a subject that was my obsession at that time.

"Look at that tree," Rebbetzin Heller said, pointing to a cedar tree outside the bus window. "Its leaves, with nothing more than sunlight, air, and mud, manufacture food to sustain itself, and it also gives off vital oxygen into the air. If it were the only tree in the world, people would be lining up to see this wonder. But because there are zillions of trees in the world, it's commonplace and therefore ignored. The very multitude of Hashem's kindnesses conceals them from our awareness. The reason that we notice the tragedies is because there are relatively so few of them."

Rabbi Cohen's Lesson

Every Jew in Israel — right and left, religious and secular — shared the trauma of the Cohen family's tragedy. Etty told me that after the bombing, hundreds of visitors, many of them total strangers, thronged the corridors of Soroka Hospital. In each child's room, a veritable mountain of gifts and toys appeared. When the nurses cleared them away, within a couple hours a new mountain would appear. In the streets of Israel, everyone's face was tortured with the horror of the Cohen family's triple catastrophe.

The day after the bombing, the father, Rabbi Ofir Cohen, stunned the nation. In a televised interview, he loudly proclaimed the prayer which is the first words out of the mouth of every religious Jew every morning: "I give thanks before You, O living and eternal King, for You have returned my soul within me with compassion — abundant is Your faithfulness." For those who didn't get the point, he added simply, "I am grateful to Hashem that my children are alive."

Rabbi Cohen was not teaching us that the glass should be seen as half full. He was teaching us that the glass should be seen as 99 percent full. His children will never run or dance again. With the help of prostheses, they will walk again only with great difficulty. But they can see and hear, feel and think.

They can talk and sing. They can move their hands, feed themselves, learn to play a musical instrument, learn to operate a computer, and eventually learn a trade by which they can support themselves. They can show kindness to others and serve Hashem with what they have.

Rabbi Cohen, while facing a future in which every day and hour will be fraught with struggle for his family, was making the statement that life, even a life of disfigurement and difficulty, is precious and wonderful and something for which to thank Hashem.

How good is everyone's portion!

Growing and Not Just Older

Ninety-year-old Lorie Zeller flew from Los Angeles to Israel for her grandson's Bar Mitzvah. At the *seudah*, I approached the sprightly, white-haired nonagenarian and told her, "Mazel tov. I hear that your grandson read the Torah beautifully on Shabbos."

"Oh, yes, he was splendid," Mrs. Zeller replied. "But I couldn't follow the whole portion. I've just begun learning Hebrew."

"You've just begun learning Hebrew?!" I exclaimed.

At that point her son Dovid walked by. "I'm in awe of your mother," I told him. "At 90 she's just begun learning Hebrew!"

"Don't be in awe of her," Dovid responded with a joking smile. "She didn't just begin learning Hebrew. She began three years ago."

Personal Change in the Golden Age

Many of us regard youth as the time for growth, change, and personal transformation. While people in their 40's and 50's have been known to make major career or life changes, the period after 60 is often regarded as a stage of enjoying the fruits, but not planting anew. While pensioners enjoy traveling to new places, they rarely work at developing new skills, or, an even more formidable task, becoming new people. Is it really possible to make radical changes later in life?

Leah Abramowitz, founder of Israel's Geriatric Institute, maintains that while many people face old age clinging tenaciously to every detail of their lives, from their morning routines to the dilapidated couch they refuse to replace, others regard their later years as a golden opportunity to do all the things they never had time to do before. For example, Mrs. Lorie Zeller, the nonagenarian cited above, started working four days a week in a book center at the age of 64 and "took early retirement" at the age of 89.

Some exceptional people regard the post-60 years as an ideal time to work on improving themselves. Free of the pressures of career and raising children, they turn to the task of fixing character flaws that have plagued them for decades.

My friend Suzanne, for example, was chronically late, by an hour or more, for her entire life until a "revelation" at the age of 60 broke her tardiness habit. At 63, she tackled her inveterate disorderliness. After forty years of feeling helpless to keep her house neat despite the gentle importuning of her husband

and grown children, she finally transformed herself — and her house — into a paragon of order.

Spiritual Growth

Gerontologists have identified three factors that account for what they call "successful aging":

1. *good health*
2. *ample social contacts*
3. *a sense of a meaningful existence*

While "a meaningful existence" can be achieved through taking care of a spouse or volunteering for a good cause, ultimate meaning — with eternal, cosmic significance — is achieved through spiritual pursuits.

"It's known," claims Leah Abramowitz, "that the older generation has the greatest interest in spirituality." She notes that even on kibbutzim founded by staunch Socialists who had eschewed all religion, when these erstwhile Socialists retire, they love to sit and learn *Chumash* and Talmud.

"They're cramming for the next stage of life," Mrs. Abramowitz explains. "In every stage of life, there's a next stage. In youth, we study and prepare for higher study. Then, we prepare for a career. During our working life, we prepare for retirement. When you get into old age, the next stage is the Next World. Even non-believers unconsciously intuit that they're going to meet their Maker, and they have to get ready."

My friend's father started putting on *tefillin* daily at the age of 68 and my mother-in-law started lighting Shabbos candles at the age of 70.

༄

Bubby Irma and Her Cowboy

Even more courageous and adventuresome are those rare souls who transform their whole existence to God-centered lives in their seventh decade. Nate and Irma Charles, who had made *aliyah* from America, moved into Jerusalem's Old City when they were in their early 60's. Nate began studying with various rabbis there, and discovered that he had a lot to learn about Judaism. Religiously, Nate and Irma were Conservative Jews. "Once I started learning Torah," Nate recounts, "I got a whole new perspective on what it means to be a Jew."

Nate and Irma's three children were already grown. The single black spot in their lives was that one daughter, married for twelve years, had not succeeded in having children. When Nate consulted Rabbi Noach Weinberg, the Rosh Yeshivah of Aish HaTorah, about this, Rabbi Weinberg suggested that it might help if their daughter were to accept upon herself the *halachos* pertinent to a committed Jewish marriage.

Nate phoned his daughter back in America and passed on the rabbi's advice. Her terse reply was: "You've been in Israel so long you sound like the Moonies."

After several more months, and a failed adoption attempt, she decided to take Rabbi Weinberg's advice. Seven weeks later she phoned her parents. Nate picked up the phone and heard only silence. "Hello? Hello?" he kept asking. Finally came their daughter's choked voice: "I'm going to have a baby."

Nate looked at Irma. Two emotions surged up in both their hearts: exuberant joy and overwhelming gratitude to Hashem. "At that moment," Nate recalls, "it was clear to both of us that we had to give something back to Hashem. We decided to keep Shabbos and kashrus and the other mitzvos."

It was a total change of lifestyle for Nate, 63, and Irma, 62. Nate started to wear a *kippah* and to learn Torah every day — a practice he has continued for the last twenty years. Irma became the devoted "Bubby" of an entire community of yeshivah students and young couples. Her cooking skills — in her newly-kashered kitchen — became legendary as she routinely fed a dozen Shabbos guests every Friday night. More than twenty-five young people filled "the House of Charles" for *Kiddush* every Shabbos morning. On the eve of her 70th birthday, Irma published a popular cookbook-cum-memoir, *Adventures in Bubby Irma's Kitchen*. The book begins with the words, "I am thankful to Hashem, Who has allowed me, even after all these years, to enter into His world and has given me the opportunity to learn about Torah and mitzvos."

Changing lifetime habits is difficult, not only because the force of inertia hampers such efforts, but also because adopting a new action subtly incriminates one's previous actions, instigating the defensive response, "What was wrong with the way I was doing it before?" In her book, Bubby Irma describes the conflicting inner voices that beset her after she had learned that an egg must be cracked into a glass and checked for bloodspots before being considered kosher:

> *One day, I was baking my famous Babka, and as I always did, I started to break the eggs into the dough. A little voice inside said, "No, no, I have to crack the eggs into a glass and check that there's no blood."* ...

I walked away from the dough and got a glass into which to crack the egg. But I couldn't crack it. I heard a voice again: "Irma, you've been cooking for thirty-nine years and never cracked an egg into a glass. It's ridiculous. Don't do it!" So I walked back to the dough and started to crack the egg.

Again I was stopped by a voice that said, "Irma, if you are going to do something, do it right." So I cracked it into the glass, and what I saw and smelled put me into a state of shock. Not only was the egg rotten, but it was full of blood and even had a part of the beak formed. I dropped it and stood there in awe of Hashem. He had found a way to get His message across to me.

Change later in life also requires a good measure of humility. To admit that the practices of a lifetime can be improved upon is a challenge to the ego. Bubby Irma's humility is as legendary as her cooking. Fannie Schwartz recalls one pre-Pesach period when Irma was becoming observant. Twenty-two-year-old Fannie looked around Bubby's kitchen and informed her that she would have to cover two more surfaces. Irma grimaced. Did she really have to heed the instructions of someone forty-five years her junior? Bubby gave Fannie a look, but she did it. And when she was finished, she flashed Fannie her trademark smile.

For Irma and Nate, inner transformation became not a one-time feat, but a way of life. They both constantly strive to learn and to grow. At the age of 66, Nate learned from Irma how to make challah. Every Thursday night, a band of young American students from a local Jewish-learning program would crowd into the Charles' kitchen to watch Nate demonstrate how to make challah dough and Irma demonstrate how to braid it. While in his 70's, Nate adopted the practice of carrying a notepad with him wherever he goes. When he hears an interesting lesson about the week's Torah portion, he jots it down. At the Shabbos table, he pulls out the notepad and delivers his *dvar Torah*.

For some two decades, Irma also regularly attended Torah classes where frequently a half-century separated her from the other students. Even after developing a heart condition when well into her 70's, she would struggle up two flights of steps to Rebbetzin Tziporah Heller's class on improving one's character traits. When diagnosed with cancer at the age of 82, Bubby Irma told me: "I'm trying to figure out what Hashem wants me to learn."

For those of us a few or many years younger than Nate and Irma, their example of flexibility, perseverance, and good cheer in the face of adversity is a constant inspiration. Rabbi Shmuel Schwartz relates that when he was a 25-year-old neophyte studying in the yeshivah of Aish HaTorah and he would get discouraged, he would look over at Natie sitting there plugging away learning the *aleph beis* [the letters of the Hebrew alphabet] and be galvanized to keep trying.

In the Midrash [*Shemos Rabbah*], Hashem proclaims: "Because Israel is young and I love him." The rabbis explain that "young" refers to the ability to grow and change. How much Hashem must love Nate and Bubby Irma!

For the aliyas neshamah of Bubby Irma —
Chaya Rivka bas Leibel

Breaking the Comfort Barrier

"There are only two kinds of Jews in the world." The rabbi was addressing a group of Canadian teenagers in Jerusalem. "Those who are moving forward and those who aren't."

His pronouncement resonated with me. As a college student, I had abandoned the Conservative Judaism I was raised with because I considered it totally static. I set out in search of a spiritual path. A path, by definition, takes you somewhere.

After seventeen years immersed in Eastern practices, I attended a lecture by Rabbi Dovid Din, z"l. He said that *halachah,* or Torah law, came from the root word meaning, "to walk, to go." "*Halachah* is a path," he asserted. "You move along it."

That revelation hit me like a thunderbolt. If Torah was really a dynamic spiritual path, I was willing to take my first tentative steps along it.

Shedding Our Old Skin

*I*n fact, the metaphor of a path is not quite correct. I can traverse thousands of miles of path, amass 100,000 frequent-flier miles, and still be the same person I was when I set out. On a real spiritual path, it is the person, not the scenery, who changes. I know I am "moving forward" if I am not the same person I was a year ago. A spiritual odometer tracks inner changes, not outer mileage.

Many paths are level and straight. A real spiritual path is steep and occasionally has sudden turns. The Torah term for change is *teshuvah,* which means returning, changing direction. One's values, actions, and priorities experience a radical shift. One who treads the path in comfort is on a holiday hike, not a spiritual path.

And herein lies the rub. Human beings are not snakes. Snakes shed their skins painlessly as they grow. When humans grow, they must perforce shed some aspect of their former selves. This demands a painful renunciation, a renunciation of a little bit of who I was last month, of the comfortable skin I am used to calling myself.

For example, if a person with a volatile temper aspires to be less angry, she must change her knee-jerk reaction to events that set her off. In the process of overcoming this negative trait, she must speak and act differently than she has been used to doing her whole life. Such effort to break habitual patterns requires not only hard work, but also the desire to be different, to shed the familiar persona.

In fact, Rabbi Zelig Pliskin suggests that one way to become a more patient person is to see oneself as a patient person. The implication is profound: I lose my temper because I see myself as someone who loses her temper. Willingness to change my self-perception is a key to real change. The obstacle is my comfort with who I already am.

For a human being to really grow spiritually, he or she must break the comfort barrier.

This can be frightening, and at times exhilarating.

The Copernicum Revolution

This is not to say that a person who aspires to grow in Judaism must change every aspect of his or her life. Only one change is necessary, but it is absolutely essential: An aspirant must take himself or herself out of the director's seat, and put Hashem there. In every large and small decision, the Divine will, rather than one's own will, must be the deciding factor.

Of course, for those of us raised on secular humanism, this requires a Copernicum revolution. We have been conditioned to believe that the individual is the center of the universe. To abdicate *my* will to anyone, even or especially God, is the ultimate heresy in the religion of secular humanism.

National Review editor David Klinghoffer, in his articulate and thought-provoking book, *The Lord Will Gather Me In*, writes about his visit, as an adult, with the Reform rabbi at the temple where he grew up. Mr. Klinghoffer was seeking to clarify the Reform position on the obligatory nature of Torah. He recounts, quoting the rabbi: "… the choice to obey the Torah or not 'is based on what I find meaningful and relevant. The Reform movement interprets Jewish tradition to say that the Covenant allows for informed individual choice.'" Mr. Klinghoffer sums it up: "In other words, Reform means doing what you want."

Growing, in any spiritual path, entails sometimes or often doing what you don't want. This is the comfort barrier that must be broken en route to any serious spiritual growth.

For a Jew who believes that Hashem revealed His will in the Torah, this means:

- *Swallowing a clever wisecrack you were about to make about a co-worker, even though your listeners would have thought you were extremely witty.*

- *Finding a beautiful, stylish dress on sale, and not buying it because it doesn't meet the Torah's standards of modesty.*

- *Visiting your mother on her birthday, even though wealthy friends had invited you out to dinner that night in an exclusive restaurant where they would have picked up the tab.*

- *Walking back two blocks to return to the cashier at WalMart the extra $5 bill she inadvertently gave you as change, even though you need the money more than WalMart does.*

- *Not killing a mosquito that is buzzing around your head all Shabbos night.*

- *Giving a smile and a gracious "Good Morning" to your neighbor who always studiously ignores you.*

Every day, sometimes every hour, poses challenges and opportunities for growth. For religious and non-religious Jews alike, the imperative is to take the next step, beyond one's comfort zone. The opposite of being a good Jew is being a complacent one.

Teshuvah Again

The imperative to grow and change applies to all of us, including those who have been Torah observant for decades or who were born into observant families. *Teshuvah*, the process of turning around, is incumbent upon every Jew, every day. The Mishnah says: "Do *teshuvah* the day before you die." Since obviously no one knows which day he will die, the implication is that one should do *teshuvah* every day.

I remember a Yom Kippur about four years after I had become a *"baalas teshuvah,"* that is, started living a Torah observant life in Jerusalem. The whole theme of Yom Kippur is to do *teshuvah*, to change our ways, so that Hashem can grant us the gift of atonement. That Yom Kippur I suddenly woke up and realized that I had to do *teshuvah* AGAIN. I had been coasting, resting on my laurels after the great exertion of changing my whole lifestyle. I had already *done teshuvah,* I felt, so what were these 400 pages of the Yom Kippur *machzor* all about? I was comfortable in my new lifestyle.

Suddenly I experienced that same queasy feeling as my first day in college, when I realized, after working like a Trojan for four years of high school so that I would be admitted to a top university, that now I had to start studying hard all over again so I could get into a top grad school. Standing there in synagogue that Yom Kippur, I realized that the struggle to be better, kinder, more modest, more patient, more accepting of Hashem's will, is never ending. The path has its plateaus, but its endpoint recedes like the horizon.

Courage and Consistency

A story is told about William James, who was a professor of psychology at Harvard almost a century ago. At the end of one of Prof. James' public lectures, a man from the audience approached him.

"Professor James," the man began. "I was a student of yours ten years ago, and I heard you lecture on the exact same subject. But what you said tonight totally contradicted what you said then."

"My good man," Prof. James replied. "Do you think I've been standing still?"

Every one of us must grow, change, push ourselves to become a better person and a better Jew than we were last month. In these difficult times, we can afford to be only one kind of Jew: the kind who is moving forward.

Other People's Shoes

Before I left for my college year in India in 1968, my friends warned me not to act like a Western imperialist and impose my lifestyle on the Indians. "Don't worry," I joked. "I won't buy shoes for the natives."

But four months later, I found myself doing precisely that.

Twelve-year-old Mundju was the daughter of the family of servants who attended on the International Ladies' Hostel, where I lived. While the rest of the women and girls in her family were congenial and beautiful, Mundju was morose, taciturn, and homely. She rarely spoke and never smiled.

Like everyone else in her family, she went barefoot. Unlike everyone else, she had deep cracks in her feet. One day she came to my room limping. When I asked her what was wrong, she silently showed me a deep gash in her left foot.

I whisked her off to a doctor in the nearby clinic. He pronounced her foot infected. He prescribed some antiseptic cream and ... a pair of shoes. "If she doesn't wear shoes to protect her feet," he warned, "the infection will never heal. She'll be crippled."

"Do you want shoes?" I asked in simple Hindi.

Mundju's eyes lit up and she grinned.

I hailed a bicycle rickshaw and took Mundju to the Bata shoe store in the center of the city. (Banaras in those days had a population of 800,000, one traffic light, and less than two dozen automobiles.)

She happily picked out a pair of patent leather Mary Janes, which cost twice what I had expected to spend. Remembering my mother's dictum, "No use buying you something you don't like, because you won't wear it," I forked over the price of the Mary Janes from my meager student allowance, and handed the shoebox to Mundju. "Wash your feet when you get home, and put them on," I instructed her. "I never want to see you without them."

We took a bicycle rickshaw back to the university campus. I felt good. I had helped this poor girl. She was happy and on her way to good health.

The next day, she came to my room barefoot. I was exasperated. How could she be so heedless?! "Why aren't you wearing your new shoes?" I scolded her.

She lifted up her heel and showed me a huge blister. It had not occurred to me that a girl who has no shoes has no socks. I dropped what I was doing, found a rickshaw, and took Mundju back into the center of town. I bought her two pairs of white socks. Now we were "all systems go."

I didn't see Mundju for the next few days. Then, riding home one day, I saw her in the distance. She was walking barefoot.

I felt indignant. Here I had spent time, money, and energy trying to help her, and she was flaunting the doctor's orders and not wearing her shoes. How ungrateful! How reckless! How inconsiderate of my efforts!

I went straight to the servants' quarters and accosted Mundju's mother. When I finished my tirade, she looked at me sadly and said, "Don't you understand? These are the only pair of shoes Mundju will ever own. She's saving them for special occasions."

Before We Condemn ...

Several decades later I learned about one of the Torah's most intriguing mitzvos, the obligation to judge other people favorably. The Torah enjoins us: "Judge your fellowman justly." [*Leviticus* 19:15] The classic commentators explain this to mean: "Judge your fellowman favorably and interpret his actions and words only to the good." [*Sefer HaChinuch* 235]

Three thousand years before the advent of Cognitive Psychology, the Torah recognized that our attitudes (and consequently our words and actions) are formed not by what the other person said or did, but rather by our interpretation of what the other person said or did. Therefore, the Torah obligates us, whenever possible, to find or devise a favorable interpretation.

This mitzvah pulls the rug out from under the critical, condemning attitude that characterizes much of our interpersonal relations. In practice it looks like this:

- *Instead of faulting a friend for not calling you back when she said she would, you could think: "She may have tried to call me back, but my line was busy," or "She may have received an important call just when she was about to dial my number."*

- *Instead of faulting your spouse for being late (again!), you could think: "I'm not time-challenged like he/she is, but how much have I really changed my own ingrained bad habits?"*

- *Instead of faulting a repairman for not showing-up when he said he would (leaving you sitting at home all afternoon waiting), you could think: "His previous client may have had a more complicated job than expected,"* or *"When he went to phone me that he'd be late, he couldn't find my number or his cellphone battery was low."*

The result of judging others favorably is that we cultivate a positive, sympathetic attitude toward others. When we don't think badly about others, we don't speak badly about others, and we certainly don't act out angry, vengeful behaviors. We don't jump to conclusions. We don't condemn people who may be suffering circumstances far beyond our ken. We avoid a host of sins simply by putting our minds into the mode of favorable judgment.

Judging others favorably does not preclude self-protective actions or positive steps to redress wrongs. Judging others favorably doesn't mean to leave your $300 iPod on your desk when you go to the rest room. It does mean that if you don't find your iPod where you're sure you left it, check every drawer and pocket before you start suspecting your fellow workers. Often we are sure — and wrong!

Judging others favorably does not mean that when your child comes home in tears because her teacher yelled at and insulted her, you should refrain from taking measures to handle the situation. It does mean that before angrily calling the principal and demanding that the teacher be fired, you entertain the possibility that you haven't heard the full story and that, even if the teacher did act or react improperly, extenuating circumstances may have caused a usually fair teacher to act out of character.

Strategies for Judging Favorably

One of my favorite books, *The Other Side of the Story*, by Yehudit Samet, offers strategies for judging others favorably. Here is a sampling:

- *Stop applying a double standard. Many of us judge others severely while we have a host of excuses for our own reprehensible behavior. For example, we grumble about other drivers who double-park their cars and thus block a whole lane, but when we double-park it's okay because our son is just jumping out of the car for one minute to pick up the dry-cleaning and we didn't know there'd be a line and ...*

- *"Don't judge your friend until you reach his place." [Ethics of the Fathers 2:5] This means that even when another person has done something culpable, consider the possibility that you would have done likewise if you had been in the same situation. Your employee or co-worker quits to take a better-paying job, showing no loyalty to the company that gave him his start. Before you say, "I wouldn't do that!" think: "But would I do that if I had his mortgage, his debts, his size family?"*

- *Admit that you don't know the whole story. No court would render a judgment based on insufficient evidence, but we do it all the time. We see someone do something reprehensible, and we immediately decide, "Guilty!" What do we know of the background of the situation or that person's circumstances or challenges? Conjuring up the humility to admit, "I don't know," can save us from judgments that are severe — and wrong.*

My Plumber's Story

Several years ago, we put in a new bathroom, complete with cabinets and new plumbing. A few hours after the workmen left, I turned on the new faucet. The water pressure was nil. The faucet was defective.

The next morning, I called the plumber. Yes, Rami assured me, the faucet was guaranteed. He would replace it. He couldn't come that day, but he would come the following afternoon.

I waited all afternoon, but Rami didn't show. At 4:30, I called his cellphone. He apologized, but said he couldn't come. "Why not? Where are you?" I asked, annoyed.

"I'm at home," he answered meekly. "In Kiryat Yovel."

"Well, then, just come. You can be here in half an hour."

Rami refused. In reply to my entreaties and accusations, he promised to come the next day.

The next day, no Rami. By now the water from the defective faucet was coming out in a trickle. It took 3 minutes to fill up a cup to brush my teeth. I was irate. What terrible service! But he was the only plumber who could make good on the guarantee. I called again. Again he promised to come and didn't. Over the next ten days, he failed to show up seven more times. By now we were filling up basins of water from the bathtub.

During that period, I was working on "judging others favorably," and studying *The Other Side of the Story* with a friend in a daily telephone *chavrusah* [study partnership]. One of the strategies the book teaches is to imagine extenuating circumstances that could account for a person's acting improperly. Since we have no way of knowing what the *real* story is behind the person's actions, the story we make up to judge him favorably is as likely to be true as the condemning version.

I decided to judge the plumber favorably. After all, I told myself, even the worst plumber doesn't fail to show up ten times in a row. Something must be very wrong in his family, I concluded. Perhaps, heaven forbid, one of his children is seriously ill. Perhaps the child is in the hospital and Rami's wife is sitting by his bedside all day, so Rami, worried and grieving, has to stay home to take care of the other children. Once I concocted this hypothetical story, my anger cooled. I could fill up a basin of water from the bathtub to use at the sink without fuming. I continued to call Rami every day, but the bark was gone from my voice.

One day the doorbell rang. There was Rami with the new faucet. I greeted him kindly, showed him to the bathroom, and stood there while he worked. Gently I asked him, "Is everything all right in your family?"

He shook his head. With a choked voice he told me his story: He had been previously married to a woman who was mentally ill. After their divorce, she was incarcerated in a mental hospital for many years. Rami, meanwhile, had remarried and had six children. A few weeks earlier, by court order, his ex-wife was released. She located Rami and threatened his new family. While I was fretting about my faucet, Rami was home protecting the lives of his wife and children.

One doesn't have to be highly creative in order to imagine a story that puts someone else in a good light. One just has to want to do the mitzvah of judging others favorably. In the end, their truth may be stranger than your fiction.

Bigger Than You Think

A week before Rosh Hashanah, my friend Batya phoned me. "Today is the twelfth anniversary of our making *aliyah*," she told me, "and I'm calling to thank you for the homemade vegetable soup and whole-wheat chocolate chip cookies."

"What vegetable soup? What chocolate chip cookies?" I had no idea what she was talking about. I hadn't sent over any food at all.

"Don't you remember? The day we arrived in Israel, you invited us over for a 'welcome home' dinner, and you made vegetable soup and whole-wheat herb bread in your bread maker and your specialty tahina-miso spread, and you baked whole-wheat chocolate chip cookies. I'll always be grateful to you for greeting us so warmly."

I vaguely remembered inviting them over, but I certainly had no recollection whatsoever of the menu. I was amazed that, twelve years after the fact, those whole-wheat chocolate chip cookies lived on in someone's memory.

I hung up the phone feeling freaked out. It was a week before Rosh Hashanah, also called Yom HaZikaron, the Day of Remembrance. If my friend Batya, a mere mortal, could remember in detail what I cooked for dinner twelve years ago, how much more did Hashem remember the details of what I did twelve years ago and twelve weeks ago and twelve days ago?

Rabbi Tzvi Meir Zilberberg says that the greatest mistake we human beings make is that we underestimate the immense significance of our actions — both our negative actions and our positive actions.

When someone thanks you for a kindness rendered, and you reply, "It was nothing," you're reinforcing a false concept of reality. No action, however minute, is nothing. The person standing in front of you in line at the supermarket dropped a penny, and you bent over and picked it up? You noticed an acquaintance in the elevator, and you smiled and said, "Have a nice day!" as you exited? You spent 5 minutes and 20 cents setting up and lighting Shabbos candles? The spiritual effect of all those deeds is infinite and eternal. There is simply no such thing as an insignificant action, only inadequate perception of the effect of every action.

Reward and Punishment

One of the Thirteen Principles of Faith delineated by the Rambam is the belief in reward and punishment. But what kind of reward and punishment?

Judaism insists that reward and punishment are not meted out in this finite, physical world but rather in the infinite, eternal world of pure spirit where the soul goes after the death of the body. To give a physical reward for spiritual feats (and every choice to do good is a spiritual feat) would be like rewarding a soldier who had risked his life to save his whole battalion with the prize of ... 100 free ice cream sundaes. Reward must be in consonance with the deed that earned it. Therefore, doing good, which means aligning oneself with Hashem's will or, in other words, performing a mitzvah, can be rewarded only with a spiritual prize. All notions of heaven that resemble the luxury hotels — or harems — of this physical world are patently false.

The great 18th-century Kabbalist, Rabbi Moshe Chaim Luzzatto, explained the nature of reward and punishment:

> *The Highest Wisdom decreed that every act of observing Hashem's commandments should bring a person closer to Hashem to a particular degree. The individual then attains a degree of Hashem's light corresponding to this degree of closeness, and this in turn causes a degree of perfection resulting from that enlightenment to become an integral part of him.*
>
> *The opposite is true of sin. Every sinful act removes an individual from Hashem by a corresponding degree. This results in bringing him to a certain degree of concealment away from Hashem's light, causing His presence to be correspondingly hidden. As a result of that concealment, a degree of deficiency becomes an integral part of that individual. [The Way of Hashem, translated by Rabbi Aryeh Kaplan, p. 73]*

In other words, the inexorable effect of every action, whether good or bad, is to bring the soul closer to or further from Hashem. This in turn causes the person who performed the action to become more enlightened or more deficient. And this is true of every single action, word, and thought. No action is neutral. Everything we do, say, or think brings us closer to Hashem and our own perfection or draws us further away.

As children we learned that "everything is recorded in a book." The adult truth is that everything is recorded on our own souls. I am the product of the sum of my actions, words, and thoughts. The chocolate chip cookies I baked for Batya's family, or rather the act of kindness in greeting new neighbors, has eternal significance, because the soul is eternal. Even more than you are what you eat, you are what you do.

Rabbi Eliyahu Dessler provides a description of the bliss of closeness to Hashem that is conferred as a reward in the Next World. He writes:

> Let us collect the scattered hours and minutes of pleasure and enjoyment of a whole lifetime and concentrate them all into one minute. ... Now let us collect all the hours of pleasure experienced by all a person's friends and acquaintances throughout all their lifetimes and imagine that we can concentrate them all into that same minute.

Rabbi Dessler continues, packing into that same minute all the joy experienced by all the people in one's city, then in one's country, then in the entire world during one generation, then "all the happiness experienced by all generations of men from the beginning of creation until the end of time." Even this concentration of joy, he explains, quoting the verse from *Ethics of the Fathers*, would not equal "the smallest possible reward allocated for the smallest mitzvah imaginable." [*Strive for Truth*, pp. 31-33]

So-Called Small Deeds

*I*magine that you're on your way to visit your mother, and you stop by the supermarket to buy three tomatoes she asked you to pick up. ("Don't get more, or they'll just go bad.") The glass doors open electronically, you step inside, and suddenly light bulbs flash, music blasts, and the store manager steps up to you, shakes your hand, and announces, "Congratulations! You are our store's one millionth customer. I'm proud to present you with a gift certificate for $10,000 worth of groceries and a lifetime discount of 20 percent."

You stand there stunned. When you're finally able to speak, you stutter, "B-b-but I only came in to buy three tomatoes."

According to Jewish tradition, this is how we will feel when we arrive in the Next World. "B-B-but I only bent down and picked up a penny." How can we enjoy such enormous, eternal rewards for such miniscule actions?

A much-told Jewish story reveals the answer: Two women would regularly collect charity for the poor of their community. The two friends agreed that whoever died first would come back and tell the other what the Next World was like. After some time, one of the women died. A short while later she appeared to her friend in a dream and reported: "Do you remember the time we were searching for the home of a certain rich man? Suddenly I saw the street number. I pointed at it and said, 'There's the address.' Well, here in this world I'm being rewarded for lifting my index finger and pointing to the address."

It is the will of the Compassionate God to give us infinite spiritual reward for every mitzvah. To do this, every good action of ours is divided up into its component nanoseconds, and reward is conferred for each one.

For lighting Shabbos candles, you are rewarded for:

- *Looking for the candles in the supermarket aisle*
- *Putting them into your shopping cart*
- *Lifting them out of your shopping cart onto the checkout counter*
- *Paying for the candles*

- *Carrying the candles home*
- *Taking out your candlesticks before Shabbos*
- *Putting your candlesticks on a tray or table*
- *Inserting the candles into the candlesticks*
- *Getting the box of matches from the drawer*
- *Lighting the match*
- *Lighting the candles with the match*
- *Saying the blessing*

An awareness of this can invest the most humdrum life with significance and turn the most mundane action into a spiritual experience.

And what about punishment for sins, for those actions that hurt others and/or distance us from our Creator? The good news is that good actions are recorded with indelible markers; no subsequent action can erase them. Sins, by contrast, are recorded with washable markers. They can be erased with a two-step process: doing *teshuvah* and *kapparah*. *Kapparah* is the solvent, in the form of some degree of suffering, that erases all traces of the sin. Next time you get a parking ticket, lose your wallet, burn your finger, or miss your train, remember that annoyance/pain/anguish accepted with love is a sure-fire stain-remover for the soul.

Big Mitzvahs

While reward is reserved for the Next World, the transformative effect of a mitzvah (mentioned by Rabbi Luzzatto above) can sometimes be seen even in this world.

Several years ago I received a phone call from a rebbetzin I knew in America. She asked me if her 19-year-old daughter Mandy, who was studying in a learning program in Israel, could come with a friend for Shabbos. Reading between the lines of our conversation, I understood that Mandy had been suffering from personal problems and they had shipped her off to Israel in the hope that it would straighten her out.

I happily agreed to let the girls come, and asked if they could arrive on Friday morning to help me cook, because we would be having many guests for the Shabbos meals. Ten o'clock Friday morning found me without a single dish completed and starting to lapse into frantic mode.

At that point the phone rang. It was Mayan, a former drug addict whom I had been trying to help (but that's a different story). Mayan was crying and mumbling into the telephone. She was suffering from an infection, was running a high fever, and needed medicine. Would I come and get her and take her to the doctor to get a prescription and then get the medicine for her?

I listened in horror. In the best of times, Mayan had trouble walking. Mayan, at 38, lived with her elderly parents, but I knew that they couldn't help her because her mother was ill and her father was mentally unbalanced. Mayan had been clean for barely six months. I feared that any crisis, such as her untreated infection, could drive her back to drugs.

On the other hand, I had myriads of guests coming for Shabbos dinner and I couldn't spare any time at all, let alone the two hours that I knew this mission would take. As I stood there at a loss, Mandy and her friend rang the doorbell.

I greeted them with, "I need one of you to help me in the kitchen and the other to do a big mitzvah."

The girls looked at each other. Mandy's friend volunteered, "I'm good in the kitchen." Mandy, having inherited the mission by default, asked uncertainly, "What do I have to do?"

"It's not easy, but it's a very big mitzvah," I told her. "Look, I'll write it all down, step by step. First you take my credit card, go to the automatic teller, and take out 200 shekels. Then you get a cab and go to this address. With the cab waiting, you walk up three flights to the door that says, 'Shetreet.' A former drug addict named Mayan will be waiting for you. She's sick and she needs medicine. You may have to help her get dressed. Then you help her down the stairs — she has trouble walking — and you put her into the cab and take her to the Kupat Cholim [HMO]. After the doctor gives her the prescription, you take another cab to the pharmacy. She doesn't have to come in with you. Just make sure you have her Kupat Cholim card. You get the medicine, take Mayan home, walk her back up the steps, and then you come back here. Any questions?"

I looked up from the paper where I was writing and saw Mandy, wide-eyed with terror. "I don't think I can do it," she said softly.

I sighed. "You have to. I have to stay here and cook, and there's no one else I can send. If Mayan doesn't get help, she could go back to drugs." Then I added, "It's a big mitzvah. You could be saving her life."

In trepidation, Mandy, looking like she was being slapped into an astronaut suit and sent to the moon with no qualifications whatsoever, took the paper and my credit card. I walked her out, giving her directions how to get to the automatic teller. Her last words were, "I'm not sure I can do this."

Two and a half hours later, Mandy returned. Smiling broadly, she walked in the door and announced, "I did it! I did it!"

I applauded and hugged her. "You did a tremendous mitzvah," I told her. "You probably saved Mayan's life."

Mandy now had a request: "I'm going to call my parents to say Good Shabbos. Would you get on the phone and tell my mother what I did?" I could see that this was extremely important to Mandy, and I was happy to oblige. A sad story with a happy ending, I thought.

Two years later, I got an invitation to Mandy's wedding. She had indeed straightened out, and was marrying a fine young man with all the qualities that she sought and her parents had dreamed of. At the wedding, when I wished Mandy's euphoric mother "Mazel tov," she stared at me and said, "You know, you had a big part in this."

"Me?" I said, confused. I hadn't even seen Mandy in the last two years.

"Yes!" she exclaimed. "When you sent Mandy to help the drug addict, and she saw that she was capable of doing something truly important, that was a turning point in her life."

I had told Mandy that what she did was a big mitzvah. The truth is: There are no small mitzvahs.

THE PROMISED LAND

My Home, My History, My Heart

I live in a 900-year-old house inside the walls of the Old City of Jerusalem. When we expanded our miniscule bathroom by tearing down its meter-thick wall, we found the capital of a pillar from the 6th century. We also found pottery shards from the First and Second Temple periods.

The shards now sit on our living room shelf, in front of our wedding picture. Sometimes I gaze at them and wonder about the Jews who lived in this place, a few meters below the level of our house, over 2,000 years ago. They were married by the same Jewish rituals that I was, although they had no wedding pictures.

Byzantines, not Jews, built the building that formerly stood here. By then, 1400 years ago, we were in exile, dispersed throughout the Roman Empire. Our conquerors plowed over Jewish Jerusalem and replaced it with a Roman city, Aelia Capitolina. Jews were not allowed to enter, except Jewish slaves, of course. The Romans built a grand, pillared thoroughfare, the Cardo, a minute's walk from my house. The

Romans were the greatest empire the world has ever known, and the Jews were a tiny, vanquished people. Today Jewish children play in the ruins of the Roman Cardo.

Our house itself was built by Muslims, not Jews. By then, 900 years ago, the Muslims had conquered Jerusalem and, except for a brief century's lapse, held it fast from the Christian Crusaders. The Muslims allowed Jews to live in Jerusalem. When the Crusaders conquered the city in 1099, they slaughtered all the Jewish residents. Jewish blood flowed in the streets of Jerusalem. The blood is gone, but several Crusader buildings remain around the corner from my house.

When the Muslims regained the city, a smattering of Jews returned. The Ramban arrived here from Spain in 1267; he found barely enough Jews to form a *minyan*. He requisitioned a Torah scroll from the city of Shechem and established a functioning synagogue. My husband Leib Yaacov prays daily in that synagogue.

Some of the Jews exiled from Spain in 1492 made their way to Jerusalem (which, until the 1860's, comprised only the Old City). By 1840, there were 5,000 Jews in Jerusalem, compared to 4,500 Muslims and 3,750 Christians. By 1870, the majority of the population of Jerusalem was Jewish.

Our house was owned by Jews, as evidenced by the indentations chiseled into the doorpost of our house where the sacred parchment of the *mezuzah* was inserted.

Yearning for Jerusalem

*B*anished countless times, Jews have always returned to Jerusalem, irrevocably drawn here by a mystical yearning almost coded into our DNA.

The Torah refers to Jerusalem as "the place that Hashem will choose to rest His Name there." Jerusalem is central to the Jewish people not because it's our home, but because it's Hashem's "home." And although the Jewish intellect knows that Hashem is infinite and cannot be confined to a particular space, the Jewish heart knows that Hashem dwells in Jerusalem.

This is why, no matter how many times we have been exiled from Jerusalem by a succession of foreign conquerors, we have always made our way home. This is why every Jewish child in Israel, religious or secular, knows that Jerusalem is worth fighting for.

The Last Stand of the Jews of the Old City

My neighbor Puah Shteiner certainly knew it. She grew up in the Jewish Quarter in the 1940's, when the British governed the land. Her parents, grandparents, and great-grandparents had been born in the Old City. In 1948, Puah, aged 7, lived with her father, a respected rabbi, and family in Batei Machse Square, in one of a row of domed rooms that now constitute my son's school.

For weeks in the spring of 1948, the Jewish Quarter had been under Arab artillery bombardment from the nearby Mount of Olives. As soon as the British Mandatory Authorities left, the Arabs imposed a total siege on the 1700 Jews living in the Jewish Quarter. A scant 150 Haganah "soldiers," boys and girls, some of them as young as 13 years of age, were assigned the defense of the Quarter. They had among them exactly 113 weapons.

My Home, My History, My Heart / 153

Artillery shells, mortars, and snipers on the rooftops claimed the lives of sixty-nine residents and defenders of the Jewish Quarter. In her soul-stirring memoir, *Forever My Jerusalem*, Puah Shteiner recounts her childhood memories of the last stand of the Jews of the Old City:

> *The shells which had been thundering away all this time ... suddenly stopped. And then, from the silence, a voice called on a loudspeaker. "Surrender! Surrender! Do you all want to die? Surrender now, before we slaughter you all."*
>
> *This proclamation was repeated over and over again. After that, the deluge of shells was resumed, and the terrible hail of machine-gun bullets was renewed. We sat frozen on the floor, not talking or playing ... A shiver ran up my back and my hands shook.*

The Jews held out for fourteen excruciating days. Cowering in a storeroom to protect themselves from the constant bombardment by the well-armed Arab Legion (the Jordanian Army), Puah's family and a dozen others finally ran out of food. Venturing outside was a risky move that had already claimed the lives of two of the fathers of Puah's friends. Nonetheless, Puah's father and another man volunteered to make a run to the bakery to get bread. Puah's 9-year-old sister Naomi screamed for him not to go.

> *The shrinking Jewish Quarter was being bombarded heavily, but my sister Naomi almost overwhelmed the noise of the gunfire destroying our homes and streets. We had no idea whether the Arabs had captured the bakery yet or not. My heart felt like a shell about to explode ...*

> *Each moment Abba was gone seemed like an eternity. The shells continued to fly. When would Abba return? ...*
>
> *Shouts and cries of joy suddenly filled the dark passageway. They were here! They had arrived! Baruch Hashem! Just at that moment a shell exploded in the courtyard nearby ...*
>
> *Each of us received a piece of pita, over which we recited the blessing for bread. The little ones ate heartily, but as for me, the fresh pita stuck in my throat. It was hard to swallow bread for which my father had risked his life.*

When their ammunition ran out, the Jewish Quarter surrendered.

> *For two weeks we had fought to keep the Jewish Quarter for the Jewish people. But during those two long weeks of fighting, the Quarter had lost its limbs, one by one. House after house, street after street, it was destroyed. For two long weeks it had defied the enemy heroically, refusing to surrender to superior strength. But now, Divine will had sealed its fate, and today we would surrender.*

"House after house, street after street." I walk those streets daily. Whenever I go to the library or bank, I pass a small memorial for those who fell in the battle for the Jewish Quarter. Drawn to remember them, I walk down three steps to a sunken stone room. One wall is covered by a metal relief map of the Jewish Quarter in 1948, with the great domes of its two magnificent synagogues (later destroyed) protruding above the welter of alleyways and buildings. Arrows of blinking red lights retrace the Arab advance, perpetually recreating the battle.

In a deep cavity on the left, white metal names stand out against the blackness: the sixty-nine Jews who fell defending the place where I now walk so freely. Thirty-nine of them were official members of the Haganah. The youngest of these fallen soldiers was Nissim Giny, who had volunteered as a messenger boy because he was too young to hold a gun (even had there been enough guns). He was 10 years old.

The Jews won the War of Independence. The State of Israel was born. But without the Old City, it was a body without a soul.

Returning Home

*N*ineteen years later, on June 7, 1967, the third day of the Six Day War, an Israeli paratroop division encircled the Old City. Its leader Mordechai Gur commanded his troops: "We are approaching the Old City. We are approaching the Temple Mount, the Western Wall. The Jewish nation has been praying for thousands of years for this historic moment … Go forward to success!"

The paratroopers charged up to the Lions' Gate. The ancient gate was made for carts and camels, not tanks. A tank got stuck in the gate; many of the conquering soldiers had to crawl on their bellies under the tank to enter the Old City. It was a day of triumph and tears, like the long-awaited reunion of a mother and her children. For a people who has suffered so many defeats, this was a moment of perfect victory.

The Israeli Army found the Jewish Quarter in a sorry state. The Jordanian occupiers had begun to raze the Jewish Quarter and turn its ancient alleyways and structures into a modern, high-rise apartment complex. The Jews set about reclaiming the buildings, such as ours, that could be rescued, and built new buildings where only rubble remained.

In 1988, we bought our ground-floor apartment. One afternoon several years later, I noticed an old woman peeking into my kitchen windows. When I asked her if I could help her, she replied, "I lived in this house until 1929."

I invited her in, and she told me her story: In those days each one of our three bedrooms had housed an entire family. They shared a common kitchen in the courtyard. There was no indoor plumbing; an outhouse stood in a corner of the courtyard. Her father was a pharmacist, and what is now our living room had served as the pharmacy of the Jewish Quarter. When the Arabs rioted in the Old City in 1929, they destroyed the pharmacy, and her family fled to the greater safety of Jerusalem's new city.

How strange! I thought. My father too was a pharmacist. We looked at each other — two Jewish women born decades apart, both the daughters of pharmacists, both living in these same premises during dramatically different periods of Jewish history.

Like every Jew, I am a link in the long, long chain of Jewish history. When I walk the streets of the Old City, I feel that chain tugging at my soul. All the links move in unison: the Jewish women of millennia ago whose pottery shards sit on my shelf, the Jews brutally exiled by the Romans, the Jews who fell to the Crusaders' swords, the Jewish exiles from Spain who repopulated the Jewish Quarter, the pharmacist's daughter who lived in my house until 1929, the 10-year-old messenger boy, and the soldiers who crawled on their bellies through Lions' Gate to reclaim the Old City for the Jewish people.

We are a singular people who belong to a singular place. Forever.

At Home, At Last

I grew up as a strongly identified Jew in a predominantly Christian America. This posed few problems ten and a half months a year. But every November, when the holiday decorations started to go up, so did my defenses. The annual holiday concert in my public school was a real identity crisis for me. Should I refuse to participate? Should I go up on the stage with the rest of my class and just mouth the words of the songs?

The concerts ended with elementary school, but not my sense of alienation every December. I felt like I was milling around in a party to which I was not invited. Ours was the only house on our street without decorations. Every decorated department store, as well as the avalanche of greeting cards from my friends, only accentuated my sense of not belonging.

The Jewish holidays were even more embarrassing. Staunch Conservative Jews, in my family the children did not attend public school on Jewish holidays. In the autumn, that meant missing seven days of school right at the beginning of the term. While some teachers were understanding, others were not. And it didn't help matters any that classmates with names like Schwartz and Goldman did attend school on Succos. Who ever heard of Succos anyway?

After thirty-five years of living in the United States, a Christian country, and two years of living in India, a Hindu country, I now live in a Jewish country. And the very best time of year here in Eretz Yisrael is the Yom Tov season — from Rosh Hashanah through Yom Kippur and Succos. (Here everyone's heard of Succos!) Finally it's my party.

The party starts a couple of weeks before Rosh Hashanah, when the electric, phone, and credit card bills arrive with their wishes for a "Sweet New Year for the Whole House of Israel." Then the New Year cards decorated with shofars, apples, and honey arrive from the accountant, the bank, and the dentist. All the supermarkets feature sales on honey.

Jewish tradition teaches that negative decrees for the New Year can be reversed by "prayer, charity, and repentance." The air throbs with all three during this period.

Special penitential prayers, ideally to be recited sometime between midnight and dawn, start before Rosh Hashanah and continue until Yom Kippur. In the predawn darkness, the narrow, cobbled streets of my neighborhood, Jerusalem's Old City, are filled with people scurrying to their synagogues, as well as groups from all over Israel making their way to the Kosel.

The sages of the Talmud promised that the Divine Presence would never leave the Western Wall. All day and all night thousands of Jews flock to the Kosel. While usually there's the hubbub of people meeting and greeting each other, during this period before Yom Kippur, when life or death will be decreed for every person, the only sound is of fervent prayer. All kinds of Jews throng to the Kosel — girls in long skirts and girls in jeans, women wearing tight kerchiefs and women with cascading long hair. All pray with intensity, like a person granted a private audience with the Judge right before his/her sentence is to be handed down. The atmosphere of ardent prayer is pierced only by the recurrent blast of a shofar — a clarion call to repentance.

At 11 p.m. on the night before Rosh Hashanah this year, my husband Leib Yaacov sits down to make his last-minute charity contributions. Taking advantage of the hi-tech option, he phones the toll-free numbers on a few charity appeals to donate by credit card. I tell him it's probably too late; Israel is a country that goes to sleep early. Much to my surprise, people are manning the lines at that late hour. The Israeli version of the last-minute holiday shopping rush is the last-minute Rosh Hashanah charity rush.

Of course, all the holidays — Rosh Hashanah, Yom Kippur, and the first and last day of Succos — are all official national holidays. No school, no banks, no stores, no offices, no public transportation.

On Yom Kippur, the country completely stops. No radio nor television stations broadcast. Ben Gurion (Tel Aviv) Airport is the only major airport in the world that shuts down one day a year.

Over 80 percent of Israeli Jews fast on Yom Kippur. In a country as famously fractured as Israel, it is astounding that over 80 percent of us could ever agree to do the same thing at the same time. To paraphrase the well-known quip, in a country of 6,000,000 Jews, there are 6,000,001 opinions. But on Yom Kippur, the only opinion that counts in Hashem's, and the vast majority of us know it.

Right after the fast, the somber gravity of Yom Kippur gives way to the ebullience of Succos, which starts five days later. Succos is the holiday of joy. After forty days of introspection and repentance, we are cleansed on Yom Kippur as if born anew. Our sins are not only forgiven, but erased, like a huge cloud disappearing into the blue sky. Sin distances us from Hashem. The atonement granted on Yom Kippur restores our closeness to Hashem. On Succos, we celebrate that closeness.

Celebration is everywhere in the air. Ace Hardware in Jerusalem sells easy-to-put-together succahs, prominently displayed outside the store. Home Center features sales on folding tables and beds, perfect for eating and sleeping in the succah. The malls are crowded with tables offering succah decorations.

The final day of the holiday season is Simchas Torah, the holiday of rejoicing with the Torah. Over 60 percent of Israeli Jews dance with the Torah. Many synagogues take their Torah scrolls out into the streets to dance with them. There's no sense of embarrassment or shyness. After all, it's our party.

Loving the Land of Israel

I have a confession to make: I'm in love with Eretz Yisrael. I am simply smitten with this land. After nearly eighteen years living here, through two intifadas, two Gulf Wars, the ups and downs (mostly downs) of Israel's turbulent economy, and a two-and-a-half-year wave of terror that fills me with dread and heartbreak, my ardor for Eretz Yisrael has not abated.

Why do I love Israel? Because only in Eretz Yisrael do I feel the palpable presence of Hashem when I'm looking for a parking space, when I'm cooking dinner, when I'm hanging laundry, when I'm caught in a traffic jam, when I'm wondering how we'll pay the phone bill.

This should come as no surprise. Hashem explicitly promised in the Torah that He would have a constant, 24/7 connection with the Land of Israel and those who dwell here: "A Land that Hashem your God scrutinizes constantly; the eyes of Hashem your God are on it from the beginning of the year until the end of the year." [*Deuteronomy* 11:12]

Divine Supervision

*M*ost Jerusalem residents and visitors have myriads of stories about how the constant, direct *hashgachah pratis* [Divine intervention] has revealed itself in their lives. Michael Margulies, a recent Shabbos guest, told us this story:

Visiting for two weeks from Florida, he brought with him his grandfather's *tefillin*, intending to have them checked to see if these very old, European *tefillin* were kosher. He brought them to Ezra, a scribe here in the Jewish Quarter. Ezra opened the *tefillin* and immediately announced, without even scrutinizing the parchments, that the boxes were *pasul* [unfit]. He explained that the parchments were extremely large, the largest parchments he had ever seen, and they had been stuffed into the boxes in a way that was not permissible.

"So I'll just buy boxes big enough for the parchments," Michael offered.

Ezra shook his head. In almost thirty years in the business, he had never seen boxes huge enough for these parchments. "Look," he suggested to a crestfallen Michael, "give me a day to check the parchments. Its probable that the parchments will also be *pasul*, and then you won't have a problem. Give me your phone number and I'll call you tomorrow."

The next day, Ezra called. The parchments were kosher.

"What do I do now?" Michael asked desperately. "I have kosher parchments and there are no boxes big enough for them!"

"Look, this is Jerusalelm," Ezra replied. "Let's see what happens. I've never seen huge enough boxes for your parchments, but you're here another week. In Jerusalem, anything can happen."

Two days later, an excited Ezra phoned Michael. "You won't believe what just happened. A Chassid came into my store with four pairs of huge boxes, a size I've never seen before. He says he needs only three pairs. You can have the extra pair."

Michael, awestruck, answered, "Wow! This is Jerusalem!"

I was impressed by Michael's story, but not surprised. I had many of my own stories of what we call, "Jerusalem moments." To relate just two:

When my husband (a musician) and I made *aliyah*, the law was that new immigrants were entitled to bring in three "lifts" tax-free. This meant that we could ship major appliances and furnishings from America without having to pay the usual 100 percent customs — an opportunity too good to pass up. For our third and final lift we bought a microwave, a Maytag dryer, a self-cleaning oven, and everything else we thought we might need for the rest of our lives. When, back in Israel, we calculated the cost of all we had bought plus the shipping charge and insurance, we were $2100 short.

I prayed to Hashem to cover the shortfall. After all, we had made the purchases for the sake of our life in Israel. Two weeks later, an envelope came in the mail from the American Federation of Musicians, Local 47, to which my husband had formerly belonged. The computer printout informed him that reruns from a show he had worked on ten years before had been sold to a broadcasting company. Enclosed was a check for $2100.

Another story: In Israeli apartments, space is always at a premium. When we moved into this apartment fourteen years ago, therefore, I considered myself fortunate that I found two clothes hampers which, in terms of size and shape, exactly fit into the narrow passage between my bedroom and the bathroom, where the washing machine is located. After many years of use, one of the two plastic hampers cracked, until it was barely holding together. Its twin was still in perfect condition.

One day I looked at the broken hamper and said to myself: "It's not befitting *tiferet Yerushalayim* [the splendor of Jerusalem] to have broken stuff in our apartment." But where was I to buy a replacement to match the good hamper? Certainly they weren't making the same hampers any more. Even the store where I had bought the hampers had gone out of business. And what was my chance of finding two new hampers to fit the narrow space?

The next day, it was my job to prune the vines in my courtyard garden so that they would not interfere with our succah that my husband was preparing to put up. I was left with a carton of debris to dispose of. Where I live in the Old City of Jerusalem, we put our garbage in closed garbage rooms, one for every several families. I had not been to our garbage room for many weeks, because my husband takes out the garbage. But this was my project and my trash. When I opened the door to the garbage room to dump my carton of prunings, I couldn't believe my eyes. Sitting there was a hamper identical to mine, in mint condition.

Do I mean to say that Hashem, Master of heaven and earth, involves Himself in my finances and my hampers? Absolutely yes! That is the quality of the Land of Israel: total engagement. Constant, immediate, detailed Divine supervision. Unrelenting intimacy with the Infinite.

No wonder it's so difficult to live here.

Go to Your True Self

*H*ashem loves the Land of Israel more than the most fervent Zionist. How do I know? He says so in His Book. Over and over again. No Government of Israel Ministry of Tourism brochure extols Israel as much as the Torah. According to the Torah, Israel isn't simply a great place to visit — or live, but a piece of earth inextricably bound up with the soul of the Jewish people.

Hashem's very first pronouncement to the first Jew, Avraham, is a command to move to Israel. "Go from your land, from your birthplace, from your father's house, to the Land that I will show you." [*Genesis* 12:1]

The Hebrew word for "go" — *lech* — is followed by the word *lecha*, meaning "to yourself." The *Kli Yakar* asserts that going to Eretz Yisrael entails moving toward one's self, one's truest, deepest self. And *Ohr HaChaim* on that verse quotes the *Sifre*: "The *Shechinah* doesn't dwell except amid the Jewish people when they are in the Land."

The covenant that Hashem made with Avraham, Yitzchak, and Yaakov promised two things to their descendants: the eternality of the Jewish people and the Land of Israel.

During Hashem's first revelation to Moshe, at the burning bush, He declares that He is aware of the pain of the Children of Israel in their Egyptian bondage. Then Hashem reveals to Moshe His plan of redemption: "I have come down to rescue them from the hand of Egypt and to bring them up from that land to a good and expansive Land, to a Land flowing with milk and honey ..." [*Exodus* 3:8]

The Exodus was not only from a state of slavery to a state of freedom, but from a place called Egypt to a place that would subsequently be known as Eretz Yisrael. Coming to Eretz Yisrael was an integral part of the Redemption. A people who had entered into a special relationship with Hashem and who had witnessed open miracles and who had been given the Torah could reside only in this particular location, the Land of Israel.

Throughout the Torah, Eretz Yisrael is referred to as an *"eretz rechavah,"* meaning a land that is spacious or expansive. This seems almost amusing, because Israel is a tiny land, about the size of the state of New Jersey. Even in ancient times, Eretz Yisrael was a sliver of land mass surrounded by large empires. Our rabbis tell us that *rechavah* is not meant as a geographical description, but rather as a spiritual description. Eretz Yisrael is "expansive" because it expands the person who lives there.

Only in Eretz Yisrael

Judaism is the only religion in the world connected to a specific country. Other religions have sacred sites, rivers, and springs, but Judaism maintains that every inch of Eretz Yisrael within the Biblical borders is holy.

This has immense practical ramifications for the practice of Judaism. For instance, all the agricultural mitzvos (the commandments to tithe produce, let the land lie fallow every seven years, etc.) apply only in Eretz Yisrael.

The *Kuzari* describes Hashem's plan to cultivate the Jewish people as a "kingdom of priests and a holy nation" as akin to planting a vineyard. A vineyard needs four things: vines, land, sun, and rain. The *Kuzari* explains that the vines are the Jewish people, the land is the Land of Israel, the sun is Divine Providence (*hashgachah pratis*), and the rain is the Torah. Clearly, if one plants French vines in the Napa valley, they will yield different grapes. Just so, the Jewish people anywhere outside of Israel cannot fulfill its Divine purpose and potential.

Many Jews from the Diaspora feel a soul-awakening when they come to Eretz Yisrael, or to Jerusalem, or to the Western

Wall. The Wall, which sits at the base of the Temple Mount and is the remaining vestige of the Second Temple, has not a single spiritual trapping. No frescos, no incense, no music, no awesome architecture. Yet the *Shechinah*, the Presence of Hashem, is so tangible there that few fail to feel it.

Hashem's Special Place

*I*magine a husband taking his new bride to his "special place." Carrying a basket packed with wine and bread, as they walk along he regales her with descriptions of his secret place. "It's so beautiful, so quiet, so remote, like another world. You'll love it."

Finally they reach the spot, an isolated clearing in the forest. She takes one look and sneers, "This? This is your special place? There's nothing here! There's not even a bench to sit on! Not even a picnic table! Do you expect me to sit on the ground and get my skirt dirty? And there are insects crawling on the grass. I hate insects!"

If the beloved rejects the loved one's special place, what are the prospects for their relationship?

The Torah recounts how in the second year after the Exodus, the Israelites arrived at the borders of the Promised Land. Ten of the twelve spies sent to reconnoiter the Land gave a negative report, and the people refused "to make *aliyah*." The sages say that this sin, the rejection of the Land of Israel, was in some ways more grievous than the sin of worshiping the Golden Calf. After the incident of the Golden Calf, Moshe returned to the summit of Mount Sinai and pleaded for Divine forgiveness, which was granted. However, we have never been forgiven for the sin of rejecting Eretz Yisrael.

If the beloved rejects the loved one's special place, what are the prospects for their relationship?

❧

So Much More Than Nationalism

One way to reject Israel is to choose not to live here. There is another, more pernicious way to reject Hashem's special place: to treat it as a piece of real estate like any other.

Imagine that the husband brings his new bride to his special place of rendezvous. She looks at it and exclaims: "It's beautiful! We can turn it into a real estate development. We could probably divide it into a dozen plots, 50 by 60 meters each."

Eretz Yisrael is not about nationalism. The goal of "making Israel a country like all other countries" violates its very essence. Imagine the city planners of Venice deciding to do away with the system of canals throughout the city in order to make Venice "a city like all other cities." The attraction of Israel is its unique spiritual power, its holiness.

Eretz Yisrael is not about having a refuge from anti-Semitism. That goal has backfired. Israel is the only country in the world today where many Jews are being killed because they are Jews.

Eretz Yisrael is not about having a place where Jews are in charge. Yes, Israel has a Jewish president, a Jewish prime minister, Jewish legislators, mayors, and bureaucrats. It also has Jewish criminals and Jewish addicts.

Eretz Yisrael is the place that Hashem has designated for His rendezvous with the Jewish people.

How can we spurn this opportunity?

The Jigsaw Puzzle

During these troubled times [November, 2000] here in Israel, when every day pounds us with more tragedies — murders, kidnapings, terrorist bombings, desecrations of our holy sites — one activity that soothes my over-wrought nerves is working on my daughter's 1,000-piece jigsaw puzzle.

The puzzle is a print of a 19th-century painting of two young women in flowing gowns arranging sunflowers by an open, sun-bathed window.

I hold a tiny piece in my hand and examine it: two brush strokes of shades of beige beside another color so indistinct there is no name for it. What could this piece possibly be? A part of a gown? The background wall? Perhaps the skin of her hand? I haven't a clue.

Then I notice that at the very tip there is a dark brown line. Perhaps it is the line of the windowsill. I move the piece along the windowsill, trying every notch, and suddenly it fits! A sense of satisfaction wells up in me, a joy at things finding their proper place, a mini-mystery solved.

Only now, seeing the piece as part of the rest of the picture, I realize that the beige brushstrokes are a nose. I never could have guessed.

Weighing Invitations

The phone rings. It's my friend Chana's husband, inviting me to a surprise party for Chana's 50th birthday. Of course, I'd love to come, but they live in Efrat, a 25-minute drive from Jerusalem. Just an hour ago the "breaking news" on the Internet reported "heavy machine-gun fire" on the road to Efrat. Do I have to choose between my life and my friend's 50th birthday party? Chana's husband senses my fear. "We'll understand if you don't come."

An hour later the army relieves me of the decision by closing the embattled road. I send Chana an email birthday card and breathe a sigh of relief.

It's not so easy when the children are involved. My 12-year-old daughter asks me if she can attend a classmate's bat mitzvah.

"Where is it?" I ask, unsuspectingly.

"Where they live, in Beit El."

"Beit El?" I recoil in horror. "To get to Beit El, you have to go through the Ayosh junction. Arab snipers shoot at the Ayosh junction every day. How can I let you go there?"

Her classmates, all from Israeli families, call my daughter a "scaredy cat," because I won't let her go. But they are a different breed of Jew. One classmate and her family spent Yom Kippur in the Gaza settlement of Netzarim, which was literally under siege by Arab terrorists. The family traveled there and back in an army helicopter.

Every Friday nowadays, at the behest of the police, my daughter's school lets out a half-hour early so that all the children can get home safely before the Arabs finish their prayers on the Temple Mount, where the sermon has recently exhorted them to "slaughter the Jews."

Plumber or Terrorist?

*L*ast Thursday, with police warning of an imminent terror attack (which in fact took place four hours later downtown), I came home from an errand to find an Arab youth digging in the lane at the entrance to our Old City house. He was fumbling with plumbing pipes, although I was unaware of any plumbing problems on our street.

"Who are you?" I demanded in Hebrew.

"I'm with the municipality," he answered, without stopping.

"The municipality?" I was suspicious. He was not wearing the blue uniform of municipal workers, and he looked too young to be entrusted with an official job. "Where are your identification papers from the municipality?"

"I left them in the truck."

Vehicles cannot enter the narrow lanes of the Old City. The truck must have been parked a good 5 minutes away, a convenient excuse for not producing his papers.

"I'm calling the police," I warned. In a panic, I ran into my apartment, yelled to my husband to watch the suspicious Arab at our entrance, and phoned the police, talking so fast and so breathlessly that I had to repeat myself three times before the police dispatcher understood what I was saying.

Five minutes later, Yitzi, the chief of our local police station, and another officer arrived at the scene. By now another, older Arab man was working alongside the youth. Yitzi spoke to them in Arabic, examined their identity cards, and told me they were bona-fide subcontractors doing a job for the municipality. I let out a long sigh.

"Don't hesitate to call the police again anytime you see something suspicious," Yitzi said to me. "And don't be afraid."

"Of course, I'm afraid," I shot back at him. "These days, everyone is afraid. How can we not be afraid?"

"Are you religious?" Yitzi asked. I was about to answer flippantly, for my headscarf identified me as religious, but I sensed he was asking the question on a deeper level.

"Yes," I answered simply, sincerely, more to myself than to him.

He pointed heavenward in a silent gesture, the final, authoritative statement of the Israeli police department on how to deal with the terrorist threat.

Hashem's Jigsaw Puzzle

As I sit puzzling over another unrecognizable piece in our 1,000 piece jigsaw, it occurs to me that our traumatic situation is a section of Hashem's multi-billion piece jigsaw puzzle called "Human History."

I look at any particular piece, such as the death of 28-year-old Ayelet HaShahar Levy from a terrorist bomb in downtown Jerusalem, and I cannot possibly understand what I'm looking at or how it fits into the larger picture. But as a believing Jew, I know that history is not haphazard. I know that Hashem runs the world, runs the Land of Israel, runs this mini-war. And Hashem's finished picture will not have paint splashed all over the canvas willy-nilly. No, Hashem's finished picture of human history will be perfect, precise, and enthralling.

Hashem's puzzle is a picture of exile and redemption. And every baffling piece fits into the puzzle ... perfectly.

How do we manage to put together a 1,000-piece puzzle? We look at the finished picture on the lid of the box, of course. Without it, the task would be virtually impossible. Although human history comes with no such lid, we do have a general picture of the finished product: the ultimate redemption of all mankind.

The prophet [*Isaiah* 11:9] describes the Messianic era: "The earth will be full of the knowledge of Hashem as the waters cover the seas."

Although the sages differ on many of the particulars of that time (such as whether the world will continue to function according to the laws of nature), all agree that the Age of Redemption will be characterized by universal God-consciousness. Everyone will realize that Hashem, not chance, not economic factors (as Marx claimed), not the political powers-that-be (the false god that most of us worship), not military superiority, but HASHEM is the ultimate causal Factor behind everything.

With this in mind, many of the puzzle pieces I am now looking at begin to reveal parts of the larger picture.

A majority of Israelis expect to be saved by our powerful army or by the government. But the government is in disarray, and the army is restrained by the prime minister to the point that it has become a de-clawed, de-fanged tiger, left only with its roar. This restraint, a groveling attempt to please Europe and the U.S., has riled me as I've watched Jews die when the army could have saved them. Now, however, as I reflect deeply, I am beginning to understand that perhaps the army's enforced impotence will lead us to realize that our salvation lies not in the army, but in Hashem.

The puzzle piece fits.

Laughter in a Time of War

It had been a harrowing week.

On Wednesday, a homicide bomber on a crowded Haifa bus killed fifteen Jews, most of them teenagers on their way home from school.

On Friday night, two Arab terrorists infiltrated the security fence around Kiryat Arba. First they sprayed bullets on a family walking on the street, injuring five. Then they forcibly entered an apartment where Rabbi Eli Horowitz and his wife Deena were enjoying a quiet Shabbos dinner. They murdered the middle-aged couple.

On Saturday night, Anatoly Brikov, aged 20, died of his wounds from the Haifa bombing.

On Sunday night, I went to a show.

It was no ordinary show. My daughter and I and most of the audience had to travel there in a bulletproof bus. The production was being staged in Gush Etzion, an archipelago of 23 communities (almost all of them religious) south of Jerusalem. Although Efrat, the largest of the communities with a population of 7,000, is a mere 20-minute drive from Jerusalem, the road, winding between Arab villages, was so treacherous that the Israeli government built a bypass road, cutting tunnels through two hills.

They needn't have bothered. In the first months of the Oslo War, the "tunnels road" became a popular target for Arab snipers. Ten Jews commuting from the bedroom communities of Gush Etzion to Jerusalem were murdered in their cars. Residents of Gush Etzion adapted by installing bulletproof glass on their car windows (armoring the car doors was prohibitively expensive and too heavy for most private cars), taking the hour-long alternative route to Jerusalem ... and staying home at night. Gush Etzion became an area under siege.

Gush Etzion

It wasn't the first time. Gush Etzion, perhaps more than any other place in Israel, embodies the tragedy and resilience of the Jewish people.

Between 1928 and 1943, three contingents of Jewish pioneers tried to settle the barren, rocky, waterless hills between Jerusalem and Hebron. Plagued by recurrent outbreaks of Arab violence, they all failed.

In 1934, a Jew named Shmuel Holtzman bought the bloc of land which would become known as Gush Etzion. (*Holtz* in Yiddish and *etz* in Hebrew both mean "wood.") In 1943, the religious kibbutz of Kfar Etzion was established. With much sacrifice and hard work, it thrived. By the autumn of 1947, the bloc comprised four villages with a total population of 450 Jews, including 142 women and 69 young children.

The United Nations vote, in November 1947, to partition the Land of Israel into a Jewish and an Arab state was furiously rejected by the Arabs, who launched a fierce war to drive out the Jews. On December 10, 1947, Arab militias attacked a convoy bringing food and water to Gush Etzion, and killed ten Jews. After that, Gush Etzion was effectively under siege. Only convoys escorted by British forces managed to safely reach the bloc of settlements.

On January 5, 1948, the mothers and children of Gush Etzion were evacuated to the safety of Jerusalem. The men, and women with vital skills such as nurses and radio operators, stayed behind, to protect their settlements and to defend the southern approach to the holy city. They were too few, with too few guns and too little ammunition.

On May 12, two days before the State of Israel was declared, Gush Etzion was attacked by the full strength of the Jordanian Army, known as the Arab Legion. The defenders fought — and died — until they ran out of ammunition.

The surviving fighters surrendered to the Arab Legion. Leaving behind their precious, now empty, guns, they came out waving white flags, and assembled in an empty lot next to the school building. An Arab photographer came and photographed them. Then the Arab forces massacred all the survivors, except three who managed to escape due to the aid of benevolent Arab individuals.

In the two-day battle, 151 Jews fell, including 21 women.

The Six-Day War in 1967 liberated the area of Gush Etzion. Immediately after the war, the orphaned children of Gush Etzion, now grown, approached the government of Israel and asked to be allowed to start again on the land for which their fathers had died. Although the Labor government was averse to any Jewish settlements in the newly liberated territories, Prime Minister Levi Eshkol could not resist the entreaties of the children of Gush Etzion. He gave them his consent with the words, "Children, you may return home."

Three months later, the new generation was ready to carry on the vision of their fathers. They visited their fathers' graves in Jerusalem, and directly from the cemetery a line of cars set out for Gush Etzion. The same armored car that had evacuated the children in 1948 led the cavalcade.

The Raise Your Spirits Company

Our bulletproof bus traced the same route through the hills of Gush Etzion on our way to the performance of "Esther." The show itself had been born out of a similar phoenix-like spirit.

After two Efrat residents were murdered on the tunnels road in May 2001, a stifling depression gripped the community. Even after the month-long mourning period for 20-year-old Esther Alvan and 53-year-old Sara Blaustein (who had made *aliyah* from New York less than a year before) had expired, the residents of Efrat found that they could not banish their tears and sense of hopelessness.

The terror was ongoing. An Arab construction worker who had been building a house in Efrat entered the local supermarket on a crowded Friday morning with an explosives belt under his coat. An alert shopper took out his gun and managed to shoot the terrorist before he could detonate his bomb. A short time later, another homicide bomber was caught making his way through the town.

Sharon Katz, an Efrat resident who had made *aliyah* from New York ten years before, decided that something had to be done to lift the morale of the local residents. She understood that redemption issues from prayer and repentance, but prayer and repentance cannot issue from depressed hearts. As the Talmud asserts: "The Divine Presence can dwell only in an atmosphere of joy." Sharon sent an email out to the women of Efrat announcing, "We're putting on a show."

The result was "The Gush Etzion Raise Your Spirits Summer Stock Company."

Their first production was a well-known musical based on the Biblical story of Yosef. The entire cast and production crew, as well as the audiences, were women. The once-a-week show (because most of the cast were busy mothers and working women) played eleven performances, plus a presentation for the Women's Caucus of the Knesset.

During that period Israel experienced a terror attack almost every day. The cast would literally race from funeral to stage. "We would cry our eyes out," Sharon recalls. "Everyone backstage would be crying and reciting *Tehillim*, then we'd have to go on stage and make the audience laugh."

The show's director, Toby Klein Greenwald, made *aliyah* from Cleveland thirty-eight years ago. Toby's experience with theater as a response to terrorism dates back to 1975, when she worked with teenagers who survived the P.L.O. attack on a school in the northern town of Maalot in which sixteen of their classmates were slaughtered. "It's frightening to think," reflects Toby, "that that was more than twenty-five years ago, and the necessity still exists to use drama to help people overcome the stress of living in terror."

Esther

A year later, the terror had not abated. The "Raise Your Spirits Company" decided to create their own original show. They chose as their theme the Book of Esther, because it is a true story of unexpected salvation from certain annihilation.

The Jews of the Persian Empire in 357 BCE were a comfortable and complacent minority. King Achashverosh's edict of extermination of every Jewish man, woman, and child filled them with shock, fear, and despondency. "In each and every land, wherever the king's word and decree reached," declares the Megillah, "there was great mourning among the Jews, with fasting, weeping, and wailing."

While summoning the Jews to pray and repent, Mordechai sent secret messages to his niece Esther. Five years earlier Esther had been selected from among the other (willing and unwilling) contestants in an extended competition, and had become the queen of Persia. She had not revealed to anyone her Jewish identity. Now Mordechai entreated her to go to the king and plead for the lives of her people.

Esther hesitated. To appear before the king unsolicited was courting death.

Mordechai's reply reveals an often overlooked key to redemption: "If you remain silent now, relief and salvation will come to the Jews from another place."

Mordechai believed absolutely that the Jewish people would not be eradicated. If Esther would not act to save them, Hashem would use a different avenue. Belief in redemption is the prerequisite for redemption, while despair breeds defeat.

This is why the central Jewish prayer, the *Shemoneh Esrei*, is preceded by the blessing, "Blessed are You, Hashem, Redeemer of Israel." The Talmud asserts that prayer for the future redemption must follow a reminder that Hashem has redeemed us in the past.

That is the essence of the "Esther" show: a vivid reminder that Hashem has redeemed us in the past in order to galvanize our faith that He will redeem us this time as well.

The women of Gush Etzion conceived, wrote, and choreographed "Esther"; they also composed, arranged, and played the thirty-four musical numbers that constitute the show. The cast of over 100 ranges in age from 6 to 60. Everyone who wanted to participate was given a job: from the onstage pianist to the women who sewed the capricious costumes, from the little girls who do cartwheels to the comics who act out the hilarious "beauty contest."

A huge side benefit of the show is the over $60,000 it has raised. All profits are donated to the Gush Etzion Foundation, which distributes the money to the families of terror victims and to local community projects to counteract the effects of the ongoing terrorism.

The Performance

On Sunday night, billed as the last performance, the show starts late. The funeral procession of Rabbi Eli and Deena Horowitz that afternoon wended its way through Gush Etzion en route to Jerusalem, tying up traffic. We wait for the latecomers.

The show is introduced by the director, Toby Klein Greenwald, whose daughter is a close friend of the daughter of Deena Horowitz. Lest any of the audience are wondering how to justify a musical comedy on a day when four terror victims are buried, Toby asserts: "At the very beginning, we decided that we would not cancel rehearsals or performances because of terrorist attacks or funerals. We are not politicians. We are not soldiers. This is our way of fighting back."

I am dubious. I understand theater as catharsis and theater as diversion, but theater as fighting back?

The musical unfolds: the gaily-clad citizens of Shushan, the self-aggrandizing King Achashverosh, the sassy Queen Vashti, the sage Mordechai, the ethereal Esther, the villain Haman in black leather portrayed like a Harlem gang leader.

The dramatic climax is Esther's moment of truth, when she summons the courage to risk her life for her people. Rachel Abelow, who plays Esther, made *aliyah* from New York at the height of last year's worse wave of terror. She sings plaintively:

> *Give me the courage, O Lord, I pray,*
> *Give me the strength, help me save the day,*
> *Though my heart trembles, I'll overcome my fear.*
> *For I know You are always near.*

Then the denouement proceeds topsy-turvy. Haman is exposed and hanged. Mordechai is elevated in his place. Messengers are dispatched with new edicts. The Jews of Shushan celebrate.

The production's most emphatic statement comes with the final scene. The full cast pours onto the stage singing:

> *They'll come down from the mountains,*
> *They'll come from the skies,*
> *They'll come up from the valleys,*
> *With music and with sighs,*
> *They'll walk across the desert,*
> *With laughter and with prayer.*
> *Their sisters and their brothers*
> *Will be waiting there.*

The scenery has shifted from the palace of Shushan to the hills of Gush Etzion, those fought-for, died-for, returned-to hills. And when the ensemble repeats the lilting refrain, they change the final line to:

Their sisters and their brothers
Will be waiting here.

Suddenly the performers are playing themselves: women who have faced down terrorism and death and their own fears, and who have remained steadfast for the sake of their ideals. Every one of them has lost a friend or a neighbor or the child of her friend or the friend of her child. Yet, instead of giving in to despair and depression, every one of them is standing on the stage, hands uplifted, belting out the finale culled from the Prophets and fulfilled in recent history. These women are not performers playing heroes. These women are heroes themselves.

The whole audience is clapping and crying. Because it's a true story. Just as Hashem redeemed us in the past, He will redeem us in the not so distant future.

Gush Katif: The Night After

*I*t started with a sign and it ended with a sign.

On Israeli Independence Day, May 2005, in a massive rally in Gush Katif, attended by tens of thousands from all over Israel, the sign behind the dais proclaimed: WE WILL BE HERE FOREVER!

It was a conviction shared by almost all Gush Katif residents as well as many other Israelis. As the political noose tightened around Gush Katif that spring, with the lynchpin party joining the coalition vote to approve the Disengagement, one Jerusalem resident, who was living out his optimism by moving his family to Gush Katif, explained to the press: "God will have to send His salvation in a different [non-political] way." A prominent Religious-Zionist rabbi rented out Jerusalem's largest hall for Sunday, August 21, immediately after the scheduled expulsion, for a celebration to thank Hashem for the miracle he was sure would come. Indeed, as the nation counted down to the date of the Disengagement, most Gush Katif residents refused to pack their belongings or make any plans for the day after. The ubiquitous sign on front doors in every Gush Katif community read: "Together we will prevail." Even once the evacuation had begun in villages in southern Gaza, further north in Netzarim, the rabbi and yeshivah students stayed up all night dancing in anticipation of the miracle they were sure would save them.

The miracle did not come. Families were taken out of their homes of decades amid tears and pleas. One palm-tree lined community after another was emptied, their glistening white houses slated for bulldozing the following week. Synagogues were stripped of their holy trappings and Torah scrolls. A traumatized nation watched scenes of soldiers crying together with the families they were uprooting.

Judaism is a religion conceived out of a miraculous redemption, the Exodus from Egypt. It is a mitzvah of the Torah to remember the Exodus every day, to remind ourselves every day that Hashem has redeemed us and can redeem us and will redeem us. The hope for redemption is programmed into the Jewish soul. That is why Jews on their way to the gas chambers sang, "I believe with perfect faith in the coming of the Mashiach." Ultimate redemption is our promise and our destiny.

When redemption will come, however, is up to the Divine. It did not come in time to save Gush Katif. The Jews who were evacuated from the settlement of Netzer Hazani on Thursday, August 18, were loaded onto buses to take them away. They had nowhere to go. They told the bus drivers, "Take us to the Kotel!"

Word spread throughout Jerusalem and its environs that the banished Jews of Gush Katif were on their way to the Kosel. By midnight several hundred people were gathered at the Dung Gate to greet the evacuees. By 1:30 a.m., when the buses finally arrived, the crowd had swelled to thousands.

People lined the access road singing the words from *Tehillim*: "Hashem will not abandon His people nor the Land of His inheritance." As the first busload descended outside of Dung Gate, weary, tearful mothers, fathers, children, and youth trudged toward the Kosel. They were greeted by girls handing them large, orange marigolds, women doling out homemade cakes, young people distributing packets of candy to the children, and hastily-made signs proclaiming: "We love you and are with you."

Then the cry went out to clear the street so the next buses could drive in closer to the Kosel. The scene that followed was both wrenching and lilting. Hundreds of men linked shoulders and, facing the buses that inched their way forward, danced the evacuees toward the Kosel in the same way that a bride and groom are danced to the wedding canopy. And the refrain sung loudly through the star-studded night was always: "Hashem will not abandon His people ..."

The Gush Katif residents who alighted from the buses made their way through the throng, in a cleared passage like the split sea, amid tears and song. For an hour, a huge mass surrounding a lone Torah scroll beside the Kosel sang and wept. When Netzer Hazani resident Mayan Yadai was approached by an Old City couple who invited her and her family to come and live with them, Mayan replied, "I've come to the Kotel. Now this is my home."

Amid the thousands who had gathered to receive the evacuees was a woman who had lost her daughter in a suicide bombing. Even she, who knew that miracles do not always happen, was incredulous that this calamity had befallen the Jews of Gush Katif. As the wrenching events had unfolded during the past days, her mother, a Holocaust survivor, told her that this is how it was during the *Shoah*: pious Jews were certain that Hashem would save them miraculously, but the miracle did not come.

So what do Jews do the night after? What do Jews do when the longed-for, prayed-for miracle does not occur? The final word of the night, the final word of the Disengagement, was emblazoned on a large sign brought by the evacuees and hung on a fence near the Kosel. It was a sheet painted on the corner with light green letters: "FROM THOSE BANISHED FROM NETZER HAZANI," and then in meter-high red letters: *"**HASHEM, HU HA'ELOKIM** — **HASHEM, ONLY HE IS GOD**"*

The Divine Name indicated by "Hashem" refers to His attribute of mercy. Elokim, the second Divine Name in the sign, refers to His attribute of strict judgment. The sign's bold statement, the identical credo of faith embodied in the *Shema*, is: The merciful God is the same God Who judges us strictly. This is the way, for millennia, that Jews have accepted upon themselves calamity, in the faith that even the harshest fate is dictated by a merciful, loving God.

That sign, and the faith behind it, is the true miracle of the Disengagement. That is the miracle that did happen.

CONTEMPORARY ISSUES

The Spiritual Roots of Anti-Semitism

Rising anti-Semitism is a hot topic. Recently the subject was blazoned across the covers of such disparate magazines as *U.S. News and World Report, Tikkun, Commentary,* and *Foreign Policy.* A recent poll in which 59 percent of Europeans labeled Israel as the primary threat to world peace and a subsequent Italian poll in which 17 percent thought Israel should cease to exist and 22 percent declared that Jewish Italians are "not real Italians" has set off an alarm — and a host of attempts to explain the source of "the world's longest hatred."

After all, anti-Semitism is more paradoxical than an Escher staircase. As the Aish HaTorah seminar "Why the Jews?" so aptly points out:

- *Jews are hated for being a lazy and inferior race — but also for dominating the economy and taking over the world.*

- *Jews are hated for being capitalist exploiters — but also for being socialists and communists.*

- *Jews are hated for their Chosen People mentality — but also for their cringing inferiority complex.*

To that we must add the newest flavor of anti-Semitism: Jews were hated for 2,000 years because they didn't have their own state; now they're hated because they do.

Natan Sharansky, writing an epic-length article in *Commentary*, traces the transmogrifications of anti-Semitism from ancient Rome to modern anti-Zionism. His theory for the root of anti-Semitism is that it is the result of Jewish rejectionism of the prevailing religion/morality/mores of the surrounding society. He quotes the Roman historian Tacitus:

> *Among the Jews, all things are profane that we hold sacred; on the other hand, they regard as permissible what seems to us immoral ... The rest of the world they confront with the hatred reserved for enemies. They will not feed or intermarry with gentiles ... They have introduced circumcision to show that they are different from others ... It is a crime among them to kill any newly born infant.*

And what of Jews who whole-heartedly embraced the prevailing ethos? After all, German Jewry in the century preceding the Holocaust was the most assimilated Jewish community in history (until the present American Jewish community). Before the passage of the Nuremburg laws, forbidding Jews to cohabit with Aryans, the intermarriage rate was 42 percent. Conversion to Christianity was also widespread, with cultural luminaries such as Heinrich Heine, Felix Mendelssohn, and Gustav Mahler the most prominent examples. This did not, however, prevent the Nazis from burning Heine's books and gassing his descendants.

Mr. Sharansky explains the phenomenon of targeting non-rejectionist Jews: "The modern Jew was seen as being born into a Jewish nation or race whose collective values were deeply embedded in the very fabric of his being. Assimilation, with or without conversion to the majority faith, might succeed in masking this bedrock taint; it could not expunge it."

The point is more profound than Mr. Sharansky may realize. What is so "embedded in the very fabric of his being" that a Jew can be sniffed out by anti-Semites even when he looks, dresses, and acts indistinguishably from non-Jews? What is this "bedrock" essence that cannot be expunged, denied, or eradicated even by conversion? Judaism would say: the Jewish soul.

The Chemistry of the Soul

The Jewish soul, which is but a cell of the collective soul of the Jewish people, is eternal and immutable. Once someone acquires a Jewish soul, either by inheritance from one's mother or by halachic conversion, one can no more renounce one's Jewish soul than one can renounce one's DNA.

Souls are not generic. The Jewish soul, like the soul of every nation, has its own specific properties. According to *Chazal*, the defining characteristics of the Jewish soul are compassion, shame, and altruism. The Talmud goes so far as to say that if you see a Jew devoid of compassion, you can legitimately doubt that he is Jewish.

One of the properties of the Jewish soul is that it cannot bond with any other type of soul. This is why intermarriage is ultimately a denial of one's essence. Marriage is a union of souls, not just bodies and hearts. A Jewish soul cannot unite with a non-Jewish soul any more than a helium atom can bond with any other atom. Not because helium is clannish or racist or snobbish — or considers itself better than a hydrogen atom — but because chemical inertness is simply one of its essential properties.

ஓ

The Covenant

Assimilation means forfeiting one's own unique Jewish identity and adopting the behavior and values of non-Jews, whether Catholic or communist, Protestant or secular humanist. According to the Torah, Hashem's design for the Jewish people is to be separate, discrete, "a nation that will dwell in solitude and not be reckoned among the nations." [*Numbers* 23:9]

Jews are bidden to be "a light unto the nations." [*Isaiah* 42:6] A light stands separate from that which it illuminates. The Divine charge to the Jewish people is to "be a kingdom of priests and a holy nation." [*Exodus* 19:1] This is a mission from which we cannot resign because it is embedded in the Covenant between Hashem and the nation of Israel.

The Covenant, which Hashem introduced in His promises to the Patriarchs, which was accepted by the entire Jewish nation at Sinai (where all Jewish souls were present), and which was renewed on two other occasions in Jewish history, stipulates the following:

    1. *Hashem promised:*

- *That the Jewish people will never cease to exist.* [*Genesis 17:7*]

- *That He will never totally abandon the Jewish people. [Leviticus 26:44]*
- *That the Jewish people will inherit the Land of Israel. [Genesis 12:7; ibid. 15:18]*

2. We promised:
- *That we will be faithful to Hashem and keep His Torah. [Exodus 24:7]*

Unlike most covenants, this one is unconditional. Even if Israel reneges on its obligation, Hashem, in the merit of the Patriarchs and Matriarchs, will never annul His Covenant with us.

In her recent book, *The New Anti-Semitism,* feminist author Phyllis Chesler writes:

> *My heart is broken by the cunning and purposeful silence of progressives and academics on the subject of anti-Semitism and terrorism. I write "silence" to be kind. What I'm really talking about is the betrayal of the Jews ... by western intellectuals, some of whom are also Jews themselves. Perhaps like me they do not want to give up the larger world in order to retain their religious, racial, and cultural identities as Jews. After all, who willingly wants to wear the yellow star?*

Ms. Chesler is not oblivious to the Covenantal mission of the Jews. A few pages later she describes the Jewish people as "an eternal translator between realms: God's messenger." However, her aversion to "the yellow star," combined with her attraction to "the larger world," defines the twin forces that have always drawn some Jews (in smaller or larger numbers) into the black hole of assimilation.

Since assimilation is antithetical to Hashem's design for the Jewish people, what can Hashem do to keep His promise that the Jews will never become extinct? A cornerstone of Jewish monotheism is the insistence that everything — *everything* — comes from Hashem, the one and only Source. At the same time, He has given human beings free choice in the moral realm. Humans may not be able to choose what happens to them, but they are always choosing between right and wrong, good and evil. So, what if all the Jews in any given generation choose to assimilate into extinction (as the Harvard Center for the Study of Populations predicts the American Jewish community will do)?

That's where anti-Semitism comes in. Anti-Semitism is the Divine equivalent of the parent of a diabetic child locking the cookie jar. A Jew in 15th-century Spain or 20th-century Germany or 21st-century America may want to blend in with the surrounding society, but anti-Semitism is a sealed door, strong and black as iron, which keeps him out — and separate. Anti-Semitism keeps the Jewish people from dissipating into oblivion.

The ubiquitous effort to trace the source of anti-Semitism to the Jews remaining different and aloof — implying that assimilation cures anti-Semitism — is an inversion of the truth. Assimilation is not the antidote to anti-Semitism; anti-Semitism is the Divine antidote to assimilation.

The Spanish Inquisition

The Spanish Expulsion is a case in point. The Expulsion of the Jews from Spain in 1492, after five centuries of Spanish Jews flourishing — professionally, politically, and economically — was the greatest catastrophe in European Jewish history prior to the Holocaust. As Rabbi Berel Wein described the Expulsion: "The disaster that befell the wealthiest, most sophisticated and stable section of world Jewry plunged the Jewish people everywhere into a state of depression."

The common understanding of the Expulsion is that Catholic antipathy toward the Jews in Spain grew until, in April 1492, King Ferdinand and Queen Isabella proclaimed the Edict of Expulsion: Jews had the choice to convert, leave, or be burned at the stake. Most people believe this was the start of the Inquisition.

The true story of Spanish Jewry is quite different. In 1391, a full century before the Expulsion, anti-Jewish violence erupted. The response of large numbers of Jews, including some of the leaders of Spanish Jewry, was to convert to Catholicism. ("After all, who willingly wants to wear the yellow star?") In the course of the next fifty years, *more than half* of Spain's Jews converted, many of them continuing to secretly practice Jewish rites. As historian Maurice Kriegel writes of the pre-Expulsion period:

> *The combination of intimidation with the promise of integration [into Spanish society] was indeed difficult to resist. Members of the Jewish intellectual elite, inclined to a certain philosophical indifference towards the external manifestations of religion, could thus justify their acceptance of baptism ... Thus, by the mid-15th century, New Christians outnumbered those who continued to profess Judaism despite persecution and temptation.*

Both the Inquisition and the Expulsion were meant to solve not the Jewish problem, but the problem of the assimilationists, the *conversos*, who were suspected of secretly adhering to their former religion. According to Paul Johnson's *History of the Jews,* the 700 people (some sources put the figure as high as 2,000) burned by the Inquisition between 1481 and 1489 were *conversos.* As Johnson writes: "A *marrano* was thus much more unpopular than a practicing Jew because he was an interloper in trade and craft, an economic threat; and, since he was probably a secret Jew, he was a hypocrite and a hidden subversive too." (p. 224)

The goal of the Expulsion was to eliminate the influence of practicing Jews on the *conversos.* Again to quote Kriegel: "So long as there was a large and active Jewish community on Spanish soil, they [the Spanish inquisitors] said, all the Inquisition's attempts to deter and punish Judaizing Christians would be of no avail." The *conversos* were the catalyst that led to the Expulsion, historically and spiritually.

The Expulsion obliterated the Jews in Spain, but saved Spanish (Sephardic) Jewry. Of the 200,000 overt Jews in Spain in 1492, 150,000 chose to leave. They set up new communities in North Africa, Turkey, Holland, and Palestine. These communities became thriving, creative, energetic centers of Jewish life. The mystic community of Safed in the 16th century, for example, was wholly comprised of descendants of Spanish exiles. What would have happened to those 150,000 Jews if they had been allowed to remain in Spain, a land where waves of conversion had already claimed most Jews, including rabbis and community leaders?

This is not to say that all the persecution Jews have suffered during our 2,000-year-long exile is the result of assimilation. Suffering can be caused, at times, by many kinds of spiritual lapses, beyond the ability of human beings to discern. The Talmud explicitly states that the destruction of the Second Temple and the concomitant exile, considered the central tragedy of Jewish history, was caused by unwarranted hatred among Jews. (A cautionary statement for our times as well.)

The concept that Hashem engineers anti-Semitism to ensure the survival of the Jewish people does not mean that anti-Semites are exonerated from the evil they perpetrate. Anti-Semites, like everyone else, have free choice to choose between good and evil, and they bear the responsibility for their choices. However, as the Midrash states, "Hashem has many bears and lions." If the Arabs decided not to vent their hatred on us, there would be no shortage of European leaders, left-wing academics, Holocaust deniers, etc. to fill their role.

Glowing in the Dark

I was recently walking home with my son Yisrael in Jerusalem's Jewish Quarter long after the darkness of night had driven most tourists back to their hotels. Just past the falafel shop, we were detoured by a sign that promised: "3D ART." By the side of the pedestrian walkway, we saw a table sporting a picture of a Jerusalem cityscape propped up on a wooden box. In the box was a special kind of fluorescent light that made the white paint in the picture glow in the dark, creating a three-dimensional effect.

"How do you do it?" Yisrael asked the young artist.

"I have special glow-in-the-dark paint," he replied.

The artist told us that he had just, two months before, made *aliyah* from South Africa. I could see that he needed a sale, but we had no money, and the young locals sitting around tables by the falafel shop were clearly not art patrons. I opened my mouth to advise him: If you want to sell pictures, you should really set up here during the day, when the tourists are out in full force. They're your natural clientele.

But before I uttered a word, I realized that these pictures could not be displayed to advantage in daytime. In the light, the special effect would be lost. The particular beauty of these pictures shows up only in the dark.

Anti-Semitism is an encircling darkness. When Jews view "Kill the Jews" signs at American peace rallies or read a respected academic in the *New York Review of Books* opining that the Jewish state has no right to exist, we feel fear in the pit of our stomachs. As Ms. Chesler so graphically expresses the dread we all feel: "Tis a season of blood that's upon us. I knew it from the moment the two Israeli reservists were lynched in Ramallah in the fall of 2000. ... I wept because I understood that Jewish history was, once more, repeating itself. How foolish I'd been to think that we had finally escaped it."

The Jewish soul, however, is coated with a special glow-in-the-dark paint. The darkness is not our foil, but our challenge, our opportunity to shine. The purpose of life, as Rabbi Leib Keleman puts it, is to dance in the dark. Only in the dark does the greatness of a soul manifest. And what of the light? It's there to show us where the stairs are, so we can learn to navigate them. But the soul's true test is when the lights go out.

Jews must not be intimidated by the venom, the hatred, the calumnies of our enemies. Being popular is not a Jewish value. Being true to Hashem's Covenant is.

Who's Minding the Bus?

Two items on last night's Voice of Israel news sent a chill through every spine in Israel.

The first concerned yesterday's suicide bombing on the #14 bus, which killed eight Jews, including teenagers on their way to school, and wounded and maimed thirty-five others. A highly-touted solution to the bus bombings has been to station security guards on the buses. Within an hour of the latest carnage, a spokesman for Egged, Israel's bus company, announced that it is "simply impossible to post a security guard on every bus all the time." Later, the startling truth emerged: Two security guards, one after the other, had boarded the bus and checked it *while the terrorist sat there with his bomb in a bag on his lap,* and found nothing suspicious. The second guard, having executed his duty, hopped off the bus meters before it exploded into an orgy of fire.

Another solution to the threat of terrorism has been to post guards at the entrance to every café, restaurant, department store, supermarket, and transportation depot in Israel.

The news item that cast doubt over the efficacy of this measure concerned Maxim's, a popular Haifa restaurant, where twenty-one people, including whole families, were murdered by a female suicide bomber several months ago. Yesterday an undercover policewoman, with a fake bomb belt strapped to her, approached Maxim's, was checked by the security guard at the entrance, was permitted to enter, and sailed her way into the midst of the crowded restaurant. Maxim's, the radio announced, has consequently been shut down for thirty days for "security violations."

If the security guards can't save us, who can? The very existence of the State of Israel, fighting a losing war with terrorism, hinges on the answer to this question.

"Only X Can Bring Peace"

Two years ago, with the Oslo War in full swing, hundreds of Israelis dead, and thousands wounded and maimed, the answer, according to many, was: Ariel Sharon. Banners strung across every major intersection in Israel proclaimed: "ONLY SHARON CAN BRING PEACE!"

Only Sharon? Last I looked, Hashem was running the world. A counter slogan (from Psalms) popped into my head: "It's better to take refuge in Hashem than to rely on man. It's better to take refuge in Hashem than to rely on princes."

This does not mean to trust in Hashem and do nothing. The Torah demands that human beings exert maximum effort in the physical realm. We have the responsibility to do as much as reason dictates. Passivity is not trust in Hashem; it's sheer carelessness.

At the same time, we must address the issue: "Who/what should we trust to save us?" It is our attitude, not necessarily our actions, that requires re-examination.

The second of the Ten Commandments enjoins: "You should have no other gods before Me." "Other gods" refers not only to idols of wood and stone. The Hebrew word for "other gods," — *elohim acheirim* — means "other powers." The Bible's message, over and over again, is: Don't trust in other powers. That includes:

- *Political power*
- *Military power*
- *Diplomatic power*
- *Physical strength (of impregnable walls)*
- *Treaties with foreign powers (against which the Prophets constantly railed)*

Rather, we must look to Hashem to save us, because Hashem alone is the ultimate causal force in the universe.

Now the latest greatest savior from terrorism is being constructed: the security fence. With its state-of-the-art electronic detection system, impregnable construction, and razor-edged rim, the security fence will surely save us from the nefarious terrorists. Or will it?

Another verse from Psalms pops into my head: "Unless Hashem builds the house, they who build it labor in vain." Does that apply to fences, too?

I am certainly not advocating that we cease our self-protective measures. I voted for Sharon, despite the campaign posters. I endorse stationing a guard at the entrance to every public place. I am a staunch advocate of the security fence. But do I believe that any of the above will ultimately save us? Not on your life. Not on my life. Not on the lives of my children.

Only Hashem. That is the sum and substance of Jewish monotheism. No other power, government, army, diplomatic process, military arsenal, security measure, or foreign nation can save us.

"ONLY HASHEM CAN BRING PEACE." How's that for a campaign slogan?

Universalism: Can Loving More Mean Loving Less?

My mother-in-law, an 85-year-old widow, fainted in the plane while flying from Florida to her home in Los Angeles. Suddenly she had felt dizzy and had risen to tell the stewardess. The next thing she knew, she was lying on the floor of the first-class compartment being worked on by two doctors. The plane made an emergency landing in Austin, Texas. She was taken by ambulance to South Austin Hospital.

Three hours later she was still lying in a cubicle in the emergency department when we, calling frantically from Jerusalem, caught up with her. Mom kept insisting she was okay and wanted to go home. The doctor, however, explained that they were doing blood tests at 8-hour intervals to determine whether she had had a heart attack.

Our greatest worry was that she was totally alone. Neither we nor Mom knew a soul in Austin, Texas. Since she might be deemed well enough to go home the next day, it seemed premature for Jamie, my husband's younger brother in Los Angeles, to board a plane for Austin. Bob, my husband's older brother, was on vacation in Mexico and incommunicado until he got around to checking his email. What she needed — of this I was sure — was a sympathetic woman to sit by her bed and hold her hand.

"There must be a Bikur Cholim Society in Austin," I told my husband. Since it is a mitzvah to visit the sick, every Orthodox Jewish community has a group that makes hospital visits on request — to friends or strangers.

It took three phone calls: One to a Jerusalem friend who grew up in Fort Worth. A second to his friend in Dallas. A third to Ofir and Elana Shavit in Austin. Ofir, we were told, is the president of Austin's tiny Orthodox congregation.

Elana, an Israeli in her late 30's, answered the phone. My husband explained the situation. He apologized; he knew it was Friday morning in Texas, and she was surely busy preparing for Shabbos. But would she mind visiting his mother, and perhaps bringing her candles to light for Shabbos?

Elana replied that she would be happy to visit. A few hours later she crossed the threshold of Mom's hospital room like a sunburst. She brought two bags full of kosher food: grape juice to make *Kiddush*, challahs, a virtual smorgasbord of goodies, and — this was Texas, after all — a juicy, kosher steak.

Elana came back the next night, after Shabbos, before the angioplasty that placed five stents into Mom's two blocked arteries. She waved Mom off as the orderlies rolled her gurney out of the room for the procedure.

She came again on Sunday, even after Jamie arrived from Los Angeles. She called on Monday, when Bob flew in from Mexico. She visited again on Tuesday, with her husband and two of her children. She came for a farewell visit on Wednesday, before the procedure to install a pacemaker in Mom's chest. On Thursday, Mom flew home to Los Angeles.

Every day when we phoned Mom, she enthused about how wonderful Elana was. "I wish I could take her home with me,"

Mom effused again and again. Judaism maintains that visits to the sick are therapeutic. Elana's certainly were.

୨୦

Universalism and the Limits of Love

On Wednesday of that worrisome week, a friend of a friend came to see me. Gail was born Jewish, but was practicing an Eastern spiritual path.

When I described why I considered the Jewish path superior, Gail launched into a diatribe so vociferous it took my breath away. "I'm a universalist!" she exclaimed. "I could never buy into a religion which is so sectarian, so exclusionary, so tribal as Judaism. I believe in loving everyone!"

As her volume and her pitch rose, she continued for 10 minutes to inveigh against the evils of sectarianism.

Only after Gail left did I realize that without Judaism's "tribalism," Elana Shavit would not be visiting my mother-in-law in the South Austin Hospital that day. Only because we belong to the same group and subscribe to the same religious value system (after all, I volunteer to make hospital visits to "strangers" here in Jerusalem), did I feel free to call another *frum* woman and ask her to do me such a personal favor. Can you imagine me picking a stranger at random from the Austin telephone directory, and calling to ask her to visit my mother-in-law in the hospital?

The opposite of universalism is not sectarianism. The opposite of universalism, I realized with a start, is community. Defining a group according to religion, nationality, or shared goals creates a community. And a community takes responsibility for helping one another.

A community, by definition, includes some and excludes most. Its shared creed, convictions, or interests create a powerful centripetal force that bonds its members to each other. The particularism that defines a community is not its weakness, but its strength.

If one of the "adult communities" mushrooming in America today rejected the application of a family with small children, would it be considered "prejudice"? If a Zen monastery refused membership to a couple with a wailing infant, would it be stigmatized as "narrow-minded"?

I grew up in Haddonfield, New Jersey, with the feeling that all Jews everywhere in the world were one family. Many Jews still feel that way. They are the ones who experience every news report of a terror attack in Israel like a knife to the heart — and then go do something about it. Sadly, however, the more that traditional communities have given way to the consciousness of the Global Village, the more that deep feelings of love and empathy have given way to a sad shake of the head and on to the next item on the evening news.

A recent bestseller, *The Tipping Point* by Malcolm Gladwell, contends that when a group becomes too large, the bonds between its members break down. Gladwell found, for example, that successful companies operate in units not exceeding 150 people. Up to that number, there is a sense of mutual helping and teamwork, which dissipates when the group becomes larger.

In terms of interpersonal relationships, bigger does not mean better; bigger means more anonymous.

This is precisely the fatal flaw in Universalism. Universalism claims to foster more love than sectarian groups. In fact, Universalism delivers *less* love to *more* people, while community delivers *more* love to *less* people.

Gail railed that to subscribe to Judaism would be limiting. Yes, Judaism is as limiting as marriage. When one marries, one is in effect rejecting the possibility of forming an intimate relationship with everyone else in the world save this spouse. In a deeper sense, however, nothing is as expanding as marriage, which fosters a level of mutual caring and responsibility unattainable in any other same-generation relationship.

The day after Gail's visit, I sat down by my telephone to what I thought would be a daunting task: getting neighbors to cook for a family in our community whose mother is afflicted with a chronic illness. In our Old City community, as in every religious neighborhood, it is standard practice to supply meals to mothers for a week after childbirth and to mourners for the week of *shivah*. But this time, I had to ask women to commit to cooking a meal for a family of six *every* week or *every* second week ... indefinitely.

Eleven calls later, the cooking schedule was complete. Every woman I asked, including those who barely know the family, said, "Yes," with the exception of one woman whose daughter is about to give birth. That woman asked me to please call back in a month, and in the meantime, she'd be happy to go to the needy family a few times a week to fold laundry.

That's how community works. How does Universalism work? After all the rhetoric and lofty ideals, how many meals are delivered? How much laundry folded?

For those who aspire to universal love, a good place to begin would be visiting your mother. The next sure-fire step would be visiting someone else's mother — especially if she's elderly and alone.

The Every-Breath Solution

At 11:40 on Thursday night, May 24, 2001, I started to hear the sirens. Living inside the walls of Jerusalem's Old City, where narrow lanes take the place of trafficked streets, we only occasionally hear the wail of a distant siren. That night, however, siren followed siren, loud and close, one winding down only to hear the rising shriek of another.

"Something's going on out there," I told my husband, who had just gone to bed.

Fearing another terrorist attack, I called our local police station. "A building in Talpiot collapsed," the policeman on duty informed me.

Talpiot, a 10-minute drive from the Old City, has a large industrial and commercial district. "Was anyone in the building?" I queried, adding: "I want to know whether I should be saying *Tehillim* for the injured."

The policeman answered: "A Jew should always say *Tehillim*. Yes, a wedding was going on."

With a sense of dread exacerbated by the incessant wail of what I now knew were ambulance sirens, I roused my husband and our 13-year-old daughter. "We have to say *Tehillim*. A building collapsed in Talpiot in the middle of a wedding."

We had no idea whom we were praying for nor how many. It was a scene that has become too common: praying for the injured from bomb blasts, drive-by shootings, ambushes, kidnapings; praying for critically wounded children, young mothers, fathers of five, elderly immigrants. This time, however, our prayers were accompanied by the cacophony of sirens, one after another in a dirge of dire urgency.

Only after reciting our *Tehillim* did we turn on the radio to hear the news: 650 people had been in the hall at the time of the collapse. Jerusalem did not have enough ambulances nor hospital beds to accommodate the 350 injured. Ambulances were racing to the scene from as far away as Tel Aviv.

Somehow, sometime after 1 a.m., I managed to fall asleep, the sound of the sirens still perforating my ears and heart. I awoke to the 7 o'clock news: 19 dead (later to climb to 23), 350 injured — the worst civil disaster in the history of the State of Israel.

Israel is a small country where everyone feels like *mishpachah* — family. A contentious, bickering family to be sure, but family. That Friday morning every Jew in Israel felt scourged by a calamity so grievous, coming on the heels of so many tragedies, so many families shattered by terrorists' bullets, so many youths maimed by terrorists' bombs, that just as our eyes could no longer hold the tears, our hearts could no longer hold the pain.

Teshuvah

*I*t is axiomatic in Judaism that all physical effects have spiritual causes. Hashem runs the world. All of human history is moving toward the Final Redemption, the era of universal God consciousness. That process is fueled by individual and collective *teshuvah*, becoming conscious of our shortcomings and fixing them. The Talmud says that when one is beset with suffering, one should examine one's deeds and rectify whatever needs fixing. Suffering is not a punishment for wrongdoing, but a goad to rectification.

But where to begin? I could easily run off a list of two dozen areas that I personally need to fix; four dozen that the Jewish people could stand to work on.

On that tear-stained Friday morning, Israel's Chief Rabbi, Rabbi Yisrael Meir Lau, pointed to our national lackadaisicalness, a tendency toward carelessness and foolhardy optimism (*"Yihiyeh tov* — It'll be okay") that characterized not just the engineers and owners of the Versailles banquet hall, but much of Israeli society. The Maccabean bridge disaster that resulted in the deaths of four Australian athletes was another tragic outcome of this attitude.

Personally, this diagnosis did not speak to me. If Israel as a whole is plagued by calamity now, then we *all* have to do *teshuvah*, even those of us who are meticulous and painstaking in their professional and personal lives.

I called Rebbetzin Chaya Sara Kramer, the great, hidden *tzaddekes*. "We cannot do *teshuvah* on everything all at once," I complained, my voice desperate. "What *exactly* should we be doing *teshuvah* on?"

Without skipping a beat, she replied: "We have to love Hashem more."

That registered. Here was a *teshuvah* that every Jew, religious and secular, man and woman, exalted and lowly, could engage in.

"But how do we do that, practically speaking?" I asked.

"Thank Hashem for every single breath."

The Mosquito Principle

Love of Hashem, gratitude, and happiness are all intertwined, but we cannot set the process in motion if we fall prey to what Ken Keyes, Jr., calls "The Mosquito Principle": If there are 30 mosquitoes in your room at bedtime, and you kill 29 of them, the one remaining mosquito buzzing around your head is enough to keep you miserable all night. Similarly, if you have 29 of the 30 things you need to make you happy, you may think that you will be happy 29/30 of the time. Because of the Mosquito Principle, however, you are likely to be unhappy almost all the time, because your mind will focus on the one remaining thing you lack.

Rebbetzin Chaya Sara Kramer is both the advocate and the exemplar of the reverse of "The Mosquito Principle": **If you have even one thing to thank Hashem for, you can be happy.**

I call this approach the "Every-Breath Principle."

Rebbetzin Chaya Sara herself lost her entire family in Auschwitz, was experimented upon by the notorious "Angel of Death," Dr. Mengele, lived with her husband in absolute penury in a dilapidated shack in one of the hottest parts of Israel, never bore any children, and took care of numerous multiply handicapped children, without having running hot water or human help. Yet, her neighbors testified that she was always happy.

Once, I took several women from my neighborhood to Rebbetzin Chaya Sara to ask for blessings. She assured them that they would each get what they had come to ask for. Then one of our group piped up: "But how do we stay happy while we're waiting for the blessing to come down?"

Rebbetzin Chaya Sara looked at her uncomprehendingly. "How to be happy? You have eyes and they see. You have ears and they hear. You have feet and they take you where you want to go. How can you *not* be happy?" she rejoined, incredulous.

This is the "Every-Breath Principle." If you have eyes that see, you should thank Hashem and be happy. If you don't, but you have ears that hear, you can build your gratitude and happiness on that. If you can breathe, rejoice — and don't forget to thank your Creator for His largesse.

"The Every-Breath Principle" in Action

Just yesterday, Israel witnessed an incredible application of the "Every-Breath Principle." Gilad Zar, a 41-year-old father of eight, was shot and killed by Arabs as he was driving near his home in Samaria. Exactly sixty-seven days before, at nearly the same spot, Gilad was shot and seriously wounded in the chest and stomach. Miraculously, he survived and recovered, and, despite the protestations of his doctors, recently returned to work.

Yesterday, some time between her husband's murder and his funeral, his widow Hagar proclaimed: "I am grateful to Hashem for the two-month grace period He gave us to be together."

Not, as would have been fully justified: "How will I cope in the years and decades ahead without my husband?" Not: "How will I support, raise, take care of, and educate my eight children without their father?" But even at that moment of incalculable loss and devastation, Hagar Zar was able to find something for which to thank Hashem: sixty-seven days of life after her husband's first brush with death.

A person who has so internalized this principle of gratitude to Hashem for every day, every breath, cannot be routed. A nation that internalizes such gratitude and love of Hashem cannot be defeated.

Rebbetzin Chaya Sara's answer is the antidote for our seemingly insoluble national crisis. So far no one from the left or the right, from the political echelons or the military brass, has offered Israel a workable solution to the terror war which many now say threatens the very existence of the State of Israel. Rebbetzin Chaya Sara is instructing us that the fate of the nation depends not on military prowess nor diplomatic treaties, but on *teshuvah,* returning to the God Who originally gave us this Land in an eternal covenant.

So what do we have to do? You just did it. You breathed. Now thank Hashem for it.

Israel's Vital First Strike

If you were a Jew in Europe in 1940, and you actually knew that Hitler was developing the means to carry out his threat to exterminate the Jews, what would you do? Dismiss the danger as overstated? Try to arouse the nations of the world to stop him? Or take upon yourself to employ every radical means possible — both physically and spiritually — to avert the catastrophe?

If you are a Jew in 2007, and you actually know that Ahmadinejad is developing the means to carry out his threat to exterminate the Jews of Israel, what will you do?

The Jewish people today faces the greatest threat since the Holocaust. Islamofascism, which up to now has satisfied its murderous zeal with bus bombings in Israel and synagogue bombings in France, with beating up hapless Jews in London and New York, is soon to acquire a nuclear bomb.

Would it really use it to destroy Israel and its people? Despite the wishful thinking of those pundits who assure us that Iran would never push the button, every thinking Jew should take seriously the statement quoted by Benyamin Netanyahu in a recent CNN documentary on the threat of Islamofascism. Mr. Netanyahu had asked a Holocaust survivor what he had learned from the Holocaust. His reply: "When someone says he is going to exterminate you, believe him!"

The Three-Pronged Approach

*I*n a recent article, *Jerusalem Post* journalist Caroline Glick eloquently described the threat from Iran and argued that Israel should launch a pre-emptive strike against Iran's nuclear facilities.

Ms. Glick is correct in everything she said, but I was troubled by what she didn't say. A Jewish response to the threat of nuclear extinction that includes only physical and military solutions but omits spiritual solutions is doomed to failure, just as a test with 50 percent correct answers merits a failing grade.

When Yaakov Avinu and his family faced the danger of being slaughtered by Esav, who was rapidly approaching with 400 armed men, Yaakov responded in three ways: he sent gifts to Esav; he employed strategy by dividing his camp into two; and he prayed.

The Ramban wrote that Jews must employ this triple approach throughout the ages whenever danger looms:

- *Diplomacy*
- *Military strategy*
- *Spiritual response*

According to Rabbi Asher Weiss, Yaakov's "prayer" includes both prayer and *teshuvah,* which he defines as changing one's actions in order to come closer to Hashem.

Spiritual Causality

Many Jews equate spiritual response with "doing nothing." They fail to realize two of the most important principles underlying existence: (1) that the spiritual dimension is real and (2) that the spiritual dimension is causal.

The spiritual dimension includes Hashem, souls, and spiritual forces (angels). The materialistic approach to reality, which co-opted the Western mind over the last three centuries, holds that only the physical dimension is real; if something can't be seen, touched, or detected by scientific instruments, it doesn't exist.

Everyone who loves knows that this is untrue. We know that, even if neurobiologists can locate the site in the brain associated with feelings of love, love is a spiritual force that overrides the most basic physical instinct of self-preservation. And we recognize other attributes of the soul — courage, devotion to truth, and the seeking of meaning — as real, despite science's inability to measure them.

Yet even many people who believe in the existence of spiritual reality fail to understand that the spiritual dimension is causal. The universe, like any well-run corporation, operates by a chain of command from above to below.

A survivor of Hurricane Katrina standing on a rooftop in New Orleans waiting for hours to be rescued may blame the rescue workers manning the boats. Investigation, however, revealed that the failures of the rescue teams stemmed from the lack of preparedness in the pertinent municipal and state agencies. Further investigation revealed that the source of the failure went even higher — to the federal agencies responsible for dealing with the emergency.

Similarly, whatever happens anywhere in the cosmos is ultimately regulated by the highest cosmic authority: Hashem. If you want to change what happens here in the lowest world, the physical world, you would do well to address yourself to the top, to Hashem.

Once we acknowledge Hashem as the ultimate Source of everything that happens, the next step is to recognize that human beings have the power to influence Divine edicts. Rabbi Yaacov Haber likens the chain of cosmic causality to rain. Rain obviously comes from above to below, yet rain production is a cycle. The evaporation of water here below creates clouds, which in turn empty their moisture as rain.

Just as polluted water causes acid rain, so "polluted" actions in this world cycle up and cause harmful edicts to descend upon human beings. The converse is also true. Acts of *teshuvah* — of coming closer to Hashem — can reverse Divine decrees of annihilation for the Jewish people.

The Chafetz Chaim lived in the small town of Radin, Poland. Once some of his students asked him if they could help the world more by leaving the yeshivah and devoting themselves to political action. He answered: "The Torah that we study and the acts of kindness that we do in our small, unknown town of Radin are directly affecting the discussions taking place at this moment in the British parliament."

This is spiritual causality.

Soul Searching

The Talmud poses a seemingly rhetorical question: What caused the destruction of the Second Temple? The Talmudic sages, who still lived under Roman domination, should have known the obvious answer. The Roman Empire, which controlled the entire known world, dominated Judea. A large group of Jews rebelled against Rome, inciting the Great Rebellion. Two and a half Roman legions were dispatched to Judea to quell the rebellion. They encircled Jerusalem, put a siege on the city, and finally broke through the walls, decimated the city, and destroyed the Temple.

While these are the historical facts known to every child of that era, the Talmud ignores this chain of events as being causal. Instead, it answers its own question: The Temple was destroyed because of baseless hatred among Jews. Infighting among Jews was the water that evaporated and formed the destructive cloud that burst and washed away the Temple. The Roman legions were merely the instrument of the Divine edict of destruction caused by own our hateful behavior.

The present nuclear threat from Iran is not the first time that the threat of extermination of the Jews has issued from that country. How did the Jews of 2400 years ago respond to the contemporary Persian ruler's decree to exterminate every Jewish man, woman, and child? They did mass *teshuvah*. They fasted, repented, and cried out to Hashem. The Divinely orchestrated salvation of Purim was the result.

Rabbi Noach Weinberg, the Rosh Yeshivah of Aish HaTorah, has pointed out that the Persian Jews' choice to respond spiritually to the looming physical danger is significant. When Haman, the prime minister of Persia, issued a ruling that everyone must bow down to him as he passed on the street, Mordechai the Jew refused. The Jewish leaders of the time remonstrated with Mordechai not to provide a pretense for Haman to vent his anti-Semitism: "If you don't bow, we'll all be killed."

Nevertheless, Mordechai refused to bow. Haman became enraged, and convinced the king to issue an edict of extermination against all the Jews in the empire. At that point, the Jewish leaders, who had warned Mordechai not to resist Haman's authority, could have easily come back to Mordechai and blamed him for causing their collective doom.

Instead, they recognized that Hashem runs the world, and that Hashem would not wipe out the Jewish people because Mordechai refused to bow to Haman. They realized that the law of spiritual causality dictates that they must search their own souls for the spiritual cause of the edict of annihilation. They went to Mordechai and admitted: "You were right. This catastrophe has come upon us because we participated in the king's banquet [celebrating the destruction of the First Temple] nine years ago."

The spiritual response preceded the military response. The Jews' *teshuvah* brought down Divine clemency that foiled Haman's plot and wrought Haman's downfall. Nevertheless, the original royal edict could not be rescinded. Instead, Mordechai, the new prime minister of Persia, who now possessed the royal seal, issued a second edict empowering the Jews to battle their enemies. Although most of the non-Jews in the Empire understood that the tide had turned in favor of the Jews, many die-hard anti-Semites nevertheless rose up to kill Jews on the appointed day. They were met with a valiant Jewish self-defense, which left thousands of anti-Semites dead. The spiritual response did not preclude the military response, but it did precede it.

Our Response

We are living out a modern-day Purim story. Iran's developing of a nuclear bomb, coupled with Ahmadinejad's vociferous threats to destroy Israel, are nothing less than an edict of extermination. Even if Israel responds militarily, our first strike must be spiritual.

Teshuvah means changing course. It means doing something different than you've done before. It means coming closer to Hashem by accepting on yourself to do Hashem's will in some area of your life where previously you were ruled by your own will.

As in the events of Purim, our response to the looming holocaust from Iran must be mass *teshuvah*. This means that all Jewish men and women, whether they define themselves as religious, secular, or somewhere in between, must undertake a mitzvah that they were previously not performing, or improve their performance of a mitzvah in which they have been lax. The step must be big enough to be a real change, but not too big to successfully incorporate into one's life.

Some suggestions:

- *To stop putting down groups of Jews, no matter how much you disagree with their ways.*
- *To increase your Torah learning by one hour a week.*
- *To increase your level of tzniyus.*
- *To take the time to recite a berachah or to bentch with kavannah at least once a day.*
- *To honor your parents in a way you have not previously done.*
- *To learn mussar.*
- *To make peace with a relative or friend from whom you are estranged.*

And to do whatever you choose to do with the intention of drawing closer to the Divine will and averting "the severe decree."

This is Europe, 1940. I plead with you to commit yourself to some kind of specific *teshuvah* to ward off the looming destruction. As a Jew in Israel, I feel the lengthening shadow cast by Iran. My life and the lives of my children are at stake. And, because we are indeed one people with one destiny, all of our lives are at stake. Let us not be caught unawares this time.

holy days

Pesach: Born Free?

The day before my birthday, I had a furious fight with my husband Leib. In truth, we rarely argue, thanks to his calm and patient disposition. Leib is as tranquil as I am volatile, as mellow as I am quick-tempered. That day, however, realizing that our burgeoning overdraft allowed no money for him to take me out to dinner for my birthday, I found myself irately blaming him for our financial problems. I fired hurtful accusations that I never intended to utter. I was out of control.

It took an hour of working on myself to calm down, to change the inner tape, to realize the damage I had inflicted on the person I most care about, and to ask forgiveness. Leib readily forgave me. We made up, but the distance I had created with my invectives hung between us like a foul smell. Despite Leib's loving birthday card and sweet homemade gift, it was a miserable evening.

The next day, like every year, we planned to celebrate my birthday by going on a family excursion to see the wildflowers. This year we planned to make the hour-and-a-half drive across Israel to a hilltop near Rishon LeTzion where the rare *argamon* iris was in full bloom. As a special birthday dispensation, I asked Leib and my teenage daughter Pliyah Esther to prepare the picnic lunch, so I would have extra time to *daven Shacharis* at the Kosel.

I was still despondent about my outburst the previous day. I felt both trapped in a place I didn't want to be and helpless to break out. *Teshuvah* [repentance] in Judaism entails five steps, one of which is to take upon oneself not to repeat the sin. But how could I resolve not to lash out like that again when my hurtful words had tumbled out reflexively, without my conscious choice, almost beyond my control?

As I stood there praying beside the Kosel, an idea occurred to me. From now on, whenever I was about to say anything charged to my husband, I would take the ring I wear on my right hand, transfer it to my left hand, then transfer it back to my right hand. During the time it would take me to do this, I would ask myself the question: Will what I am about to say distance me from my husband or draw me closer? Since I never want to be distant from my beloved husband, if the answer is "distance," I would choose not to say it ... even if it's true, even if it's justified. I would simply *choose closeness*.

Revitalized and happy with this new tactic, I left the Kosel and jumped into our car as Leib and the children drove past the Kosel plaza. We were off to see the wildflowers.

Not having eaten breakfast, I was hungry. "What food did you pack?" I asked them.

"I don't know," Leib responded. "You asked Pliyah Esther to pack the lunch."

Pliyah Esther was taken aback. "I only packed tuna sandwiches. I thought *Abba* was supposed to pack the rest — the fruit and potato chips and cookies."

"Well, nobody told me anything about food," Leib answered dismissively.

I was about to say: "What? I certainly did tell you. I even told you where you could find the potato chips. Why don't you ever listen to me? Now what are we supposed to do with only half a lunch and no money to buy snacks? We'll all get hungry and cranky!"

That's what I wanted to say. Instead, I transferred my ring from my right hand to my left and back to my right while asking myself, "Will saying this distance me from my husband or draw us closer?" Clearly it would distance us, as mutual recriminations would give way to guilt and defensiveness and sweeping condemnations. So I kept my mouth shut.

That's when it happened. As I sat there in my self-chosen silence, I experienced a feeling of exaltation and freedom. I could do it! I could choose which course I wanted to follow according to where I wanted to end up. I was in control. I was free.

What Is Freedom?

On Pesach, every Jew is obligated to see himself or herself as if he/she personally had gone out of Egypt. This strains the imaginative powers of even the most fanciful of us. Back-breaking labor, massive bricks, the crack of the whip of the Egyptian taskmaster, the humiliations and torture of slavery are all so remote from our experience that, try as we may, the empirical sense of being enslaved eludes us. How, then, can each of us personally experience liberation from slavery?

If we look carefully at the Torah's account of the Exodus, we see that slavery to Pharaoh is juxtaposed not to "doing whatever you want," but rather to service of Hashem. To give one of many examples: "Hashem said to Moses: Come to Pharaoh and speak to him: So says Hashem, the Lord of the Hebrews: 'Send out My people that they may serve Me.'" [*Exodus* 9:1]

The opposite of Egyptian bondage was not a libertine free-for-all. The objective and culmination of the Exodus was the giving of the Torah at Mount Sinai. Hashem makes this clear the very first time He reveals Himself to Moses at the burning bush. "When you take the people out of Egypt, you will serve Hashem on this mountain." [ibid. 3:12]

The essential connection between freedom and Divine service is evident in the Hebrew calendar. From the second day of Pesach, Jews begin counting 49 days until Shavuos, the holiday that commemorates the giving of the Torah at Sinai. Shavuos is considered the culmination of Pesach. Ultimate freedom, by the Torah's definition, means serving Hashem.

This is surprising. The 613 commandments of the Torah are often regarded from the outside as 613 restrictions. How can they be synonymous with freedom?

Two Voices

According to cognitive psychology, all human actions are in response to an "inner tape" that plays nonstop in the human brain. This tape is most often recorded by heredity and environment. It tells us what to do, and, like automatons, we obey: "That person just insulted you. Insult him back!" "That driver just cut you off. Get angry!"

This is the Torah's definition of slavery. This is the voice of Pharaoh; it brooks no disobedience, nor does it even occur to us to disobey. There is no such thing as a bad slave, because a slave has no viable choices. For most of our waking hours, it does not even occur to us to disobey or change our inner tape.

In a world driven by the survival instinct and the pleasure principle, the Torah mandated an alternative way of life driven by holiness and spiritual values. The ethics of the Torah have become so imbued in Western civilization that we may not realize what a radical alternative they offered to ancient man — and continue to offer to us today. As historian Paul Johnson notes:

> *Most law codes of the ancient Near East are property-oriented, people themselves being forms of property whose value can be assessed. The Mosaic code is God-oriented ... In Mosaic theology, man is made in God's image, and so his life is not just valuable, it is sacred ... Whereas other codes provided the death penalty for offenses against property, such as looting during a fire, breaking into a house ... , in the Mosaic law no property offense is capital. Human life is too sacred where the rights of property alone are violated ...*
> [A History of the Jews, p. 33]

Mr. Johnson goes on to contrast the forbidden relations outlined in the Torah to the licentious practices of all other ancient civilizations.

With the giving of the Torah, a human being was no longer a slave to the imperatives of his/her desires. A second voice — the Divine voice — mandated a different, sacred course of action. The human being was free to choose. The exercise of choice itself is freedom.

That freedom entails choice is obvious when we observe the elections held in countries ruled by dictators. All the accouterments of free elections are there, such as voting booths and secret ballots. But if only one candidate is running, the election is clearly not "free." Freedom requires choice.

When Hashem gave the Jewish people the Torah, He gave us 613 choices. Observe Shabbos or not. Love your neighbor or not. Gossip or not. Unlike Pharaoh, Hashem, as you might have noticed, brooks a great deal of disobedience. That's why a person who violates a Divine commandment is not struck by lightning. Immediate punishment would limit our freedom of choice. The ability to make moral choices is a Divine gift. It's the only true freedom humans have.

The key phrase here is "moral choice." Your decision whether to eat *fleishig* or *milchig* tonight, or whether to wear your black dress or your blue suit is not an exercise of free will. Since there is no moral element present, they are mere preferences, not choices.

Only in the moral realm do you have free choice. When your inner tape says to give tit for tat, to respond to an insult with an even more lethal barb, you have the power to change the tape. You have the power to ask yourself, "Is this who I really want to be?" The very act of choosing between your knee-jerk response and the Divine imperative to be kind is freedom.

Each of us at every moment is heeding the voice of Pharaoh or the voice of Hashem. The voice of Pharaoh commands us to do what is instinctive, automatic, reflexive. "Doing what comes naturally" is ultimate bondage because we exercise no power of choice.

The voice of Hashem, on the other hand, offers an alternative to instinct. For example, by commanding us not to take revenge [*Leviticus* 19:18], Hashem in effect is saying: "Your instinct is to hurt those who hurt you. By commanding you to act otherwise, I'm offering you the ability to choose a different course."

The exercise of choice is the essence of freedom. Forget the taskmaster's whip and the massive bricks. Each of us is enslaved every time we act on automatic pilot, every time we react according to our instinctual programming.

To experience liberation this Pesach, we need only to break the bonds of instinct, to learn to deliberate and decide what we shall do or what we shall say, based on who we want to become — a slave of Pharaoh or a servant of Hashem.

Pesach: Chomping the Big Apple

Ancient Egypt was the Big Apple of its time. In terms of technology, art, architecture, literature, wealth, and highly organized bureaucracy, Egypt was a consummate civilization. It had been so for many centuries when a small group of seventy Semitic herdsmen arrived there 3,528 years ago.

No wonder that the second and third generations of that Semitic family, the grandchildren of Yaakov, were enthralled by Egyptian society. Its grandeur, its power, and its cosmopolitan air were enough to dazzle any immigrant child.

Imagine an Israelite youth peering at the imposing line of towering pyramids that started at the Nile Delta and extended for 1500 miles southward. The largest of them, the Great Pyramid of Khufu, stood 481 feet high; its base covered an area of 13 acres. The monumental structure contained 2.3 million blocks of limestone, each averaging 2½ tons. Gazing at this centuries-old pyramid, our immigrant youth would not have known — or cared — that its construction took 100,000 laborers twenty years of toil. Who would not want to be part of a society that produced such wonders?

Thus, the succeeding generations of Israelites gravitated to the majority culture, hobnobbed with its elite, and eventually worshiped its pantheon of gods.

Yet, like the next three millennia of their descendants, these proto-Jews were caught in an identity crisis. As much as they longed to become part of the glamorous and successful society that surrounded them, they also felt a fealty to their progenitors, Yaakov, Yitzchak, and Avraham, as well as to the unique worldview that they had espoused. Thus, the Talmud tells us, the Israelites in Egypt retained their distinctive Hebrew names, language, and dress. Their hearts longed to assimilate, but their souls clung to the outer vestiges of their ancestral identity.

Human Identity

For over a century, the Israelites in Egypt, as free and prosperous residents, were poised tenuously between two opposing worldviews. It's worth exploring the major differences in those worldviews.

Ancient Egypt was a society where animals, humans, and gods shared a fluid identity, with no definite distinctions between them. Many Egyptian gods bore the heads of animals, while sphinxes had the bodies of lions and human heads. Animals were venerated; bulls, cats, and crocodiles lived luxuriously in certain temples, and when they died they were mummified. Egyptian peasants lived in the same hovels as their beasts. Pharaoh was both a human king and a god, simultaneously Horus, the falcon god, and the son of Re, the sun god.

How different from the worldview of the patriarch Avraham! Avraham had believed in a Divine soul that distinguished humans from animals. God, Avraham taught, was a single, transcendent, non-corporeal existence Who had created human beings with a Divine constituent, the Divine soul. Thus, every human being was to be valued. Animals, while not to be mistreated, were essentially different than human beings because they lacked this higher order of soul. While bestiality was commonly practiced in the ancient Near East, the Torah of the Jews would categorically forbid it.

This is no minor distinction. The Torah relates that the first humans were vegetarians. Only after human society degenerated into rampant violence and promiscuity, which resulted in the Great Flood, did Hashem permit Noah and his descendants to eat meat. This was a deliberate step, the sages tell us, so that humans would experience their essential difference from animals.

Societies that have downplayed this distinction have always ended up valuing animals and devaluing human beings. The most notorious modern example of this is Nazi Germany. Hitler was a vegetarian and, at the height of the Holocaust, Germany supported an animal protection society that benignly rescued the pets abandoned when their Jewish owners were sent off to be slaughtered.

Morality and Magic

While the God of Avraham had — and demanded — a definite standard of right and wrong, Egyptian society was essentially amoral. It had no codified or written laws at all. Pharaoh's arbitrary judgments were the law of the land. Egyptian courts were merely the vicarious arm of Pharaoh's whims.

Integral to the Jewish concept of the soul is its ability to make moral choices. Morality was a novel concept introduced into antiquity by the Jews. While, unlike Egypt, ancient Mesopotamia produced many legal codes, these were utilitarian rather than ethical. Their aim was to protect property rights and preserve the efficacious functioning of society. According to such codes, murder was forbidden because a murderous society degenerates into chaos. According to the Torah, murder is forbidden because human beings are created in the image of Hashem and therefore human life has inherent value.

Ancient Egyptian religion sported a myriad of gods, and its practices were magical rites aimed at manipulating reality. Avraham insisted that there is one God, Who controlled the world and could not be controlled by the world. Avraham's God could, however, be related to with both awe and love. Avraham had, in fact, entered into a mutual Covenant with Hashem. Avraham promised to do His will (such as the rite of circumcision) and Hashem promised to bequeath to Avraham's descendants both a special providence and the inheritance of the land of Canaan.

Champions of Civic Duty

*T*he Israelites' wavering between their two warring identities ended dramatically 130 years into their Egyptian experience. The reigning Pharaoh of the Nineteenth Dynasty of the New Kingdom decided that the Israelites were becoming too numerous and would pose the danger of a fifth column during wartime. He decided to impound them into slavery.

The Midrash relates that the process of enslavement proceeded gradually and cunningly. At first, Pharaoh played on their identity as loyal Egyptians by summoning them as volunteers in a national construction enterprise. All the Israelites except the tribe of Levi rallied enthusiastically to their civic duty. Gradually the volunteerism turned into conscription, and finally slavery.

The slavery exposed the dark side of Egyptian civilization. The grand monuments that the Israelites themselves had admired had been built by human exploitation and torture. Pharaoh, worried by his astrologers' predictions of an Israelite redeemer, had the male babies thrown into the waiting jaws of Nile crocodiles. Unconstrained by any ethical imperative, the taskmasters were sadistic and cruel.

Yet, almost unbelievably, the Israelite infatuation with their adopted society was so tenacious that, according to Rashi, even at the height of the process of redemption, during the ninth of the Ten Plagues, some 80 percent of the Israelites declined to leave Egypt. Being a slave in the world's greatest civilization seemed preferable to the uncertain journey back to their archaic ancestral homeland. Even in the desert after their liberation, many of the former slaves pined for the amenities of Egypt.

Pesach: Chomping the Big Apple / 237

The Exile of Identity

Jewish history is a recurring process of exile and redemption. The first exile, the Egyptian exile, is considered the prototype of the four subsequent exiles: Babylonian, Persian, Greek, and Roman (in which we are ensconced to this day).

We think of "exile" as meaning the expulsion from our own land to a foreign land, and that was indeed the case with three of the above four exiles. The Greek exile, however, took place while the Jews lived in the land of Judea. In what sense, then, was it an "exile"?

The Greek exile was an exile of identity. While living in their own land, the majority of the Jews and almost the entirety of the upper classes chose to redefine themselves as Hellenists, aficionados of the prevailing Greek culture. Greek culture, like Egyptian culture a millennium before it, lured the Jews with its art, scientific advancements, and cultural sophistication. Like their ancestors in Egypt, the Jews of the Greek period thought they could juggle a dual identity. When two identities conflict, however, only one will ultimately prevail.

Every Jew alive today is the descendant of Jews who chose their Jewish identity as foremost. Two millennia ago, there were approximately 4.5 million Jews in the world, constituting 1.8 percent of the world's population. Today there are some 12.8 million Jews, constituting a mere 0.2 percent of the world's population. This decline in Jewish population relative to world population is due not only to repeated persecution and massacre, but also to the opting out of Jews in favor of the majority culture. Every Jew reading this essay is the descendant of Jews who repeatedly chose to identify as Jews rather than as Egyptians, Persians, Greeks, Christians, Muslims, or secularists.

Jewish identity is like gold. Gold virtually always occurs in combination with other substances. There are two primary methods of extracting the gold from the ore. The first, traditional method is to swirl it with water and allow the heavier gold to sink to the bottom. The more efficient modern method is to crush the rock in which gold occurs and then dissolve it in mercury or cyanide solutions. The dross dissolves and the gold is recovered.

Jewish identity can be recovered in both of these ways. In Jewish tradition, "water" is a metaphor for Torah. When a Jew is exposed to Torah, his or her Jewish identity separates itself from the amalgam that entrapped it.

The more extreme but effective method, akin to crushing the rock and dissolving it in a toxic solution, is the anti-Semitism that reveals the dark side of the majority civilization. The Maharal says that in order to know who you want to be, you have to first identify who you don't want to be. The Egyptian bondage taught those Jews willing to learn from it that they didn't want to be like the Egyptians. Rebbetzin Tziporah Heller points out that prior to 1933, the vast majority of German Jews wanted to be "Germans of the Mosaic persuasion," but after the Holocaust no amount of Goethe, Beethoven, or Kant could attract Jews to German identity.

Pesach is about the redemption of identity, the extraction of the gold from the ore. The Seder is a defining moment, in which each of us must come to the point of wanting our Jewish identity, our Covenant with Hashem, to be our primary identity.

The Haggadah speaks of "Four Sons." The "evil son" asks, "What is this service *to you*?" The Haggadah rejoins: "To *you*, and not to *him*. Because he has excluded himself from the [Jewish] community, he has denied Hashem." He is considered evil not because of his deeds, but because he has opted out of his Jewish identity.

The brilliant light of redemption, which first flashed into the world at the Exodus, is available every year at Pesach time. It is a gift from Above. All we have to do is want it. All we have to do is define who we really are.

Pesach: My Dayenu Ring

The diamond ring I inherited from my mother, a"h, is — or should I say *was* — my most beautiful possession. My father, a"h, had given the ring, a band of sixteen perfect diamonds, to my mother shortly after their wedding in 1944. As precious to me emotionally as materially, the ring adorned my hand every Shabbos. Every time I looked at its glistening perfection, my Shabbos joy soared.

Then, sitting at the Shabbos table six weeks ago, I glanced down at my ring and was horrified to see a gaping, black hole. A prong of the white gold setting had broken, and one diamond had fallen out. My horror gave way to a frantic search, with all members of the family on hands and knees searching the floors in the kitchen and living room, then sweeping, and finally giving up. The diamond was gone.

Every time I looked at my ring, all I saw was the gaping, black hole, like a beautiful woman smiling to reveal a missing front tooth. My gorgeous ring had become a toothless hag. Bitterly, I took it off and put it in its box. I could not bear to look at it.

Replacing the diamond would be an expensive and complicated procedure, as the setting itself had to be repaired. We were not in a position to undertake the expense. The ring remained in its place of exile every Shabbos, and whenever I, by force of habit, reached for it, I was poignantly reminded of my bitter loss.

Then one Friday evening two weeks ago, I missed the ring so much that I decided to wear it. After all, I reminded myself, there were still fifteen perfect diamonds there for me to enjoy. Why focus on what wasn't there when I could choose to focus on what was there? A ring is round, I told myself, and whenever the black hole faces me, all I have to do is turn it to reveal the still-perfect other side.

This turned out to be a potent spiritual exercise. Whenever I glanced down and saw the ugly hole, I said to myself, "I will choose what I will look at and what I won't look at," and I turned the ring until all I saw was the sparkling, perfect diamonds.

Then something strange happened. At one point, I looked down and saw the gaping hole. Instead of turning the ring, I chose, by an act of will, to look at the diamond adjacent to the hole. I gazed at it intently, noticing its clear-almost-blue color, its exquisite cut, and its happy sparkle. Then I realized with a start that in the fifteen years I have owned the ring, while I loved the ring as a whole, I never really bothered to look at the individual diamonds. Losing one diamond made me begin to appreciate the beauty of the remaining diamonds.

Dayenu

One of the favorite parts of the Pesach Seder is the song, "*Dayenu.*" The fifteen verses of this song enumerate the various kindnesses Hashem bestowed on *Am Yisrael* during the Exodus, such as delivering us from Egypt, splitting the sea for us, taking us through it on dry land, bringing us to Mount Sinai, giving us the Torah, etc. The refrain *"dayenu"* means: "It would have been enough for us."

Anyone who stops to consider the lyrics would find them enigmatic. After all, it seems outlandish to proclaim that if Hashem had split the sea for us and not led us through it on dry land, "it would have been enough for us." If Hashem had not led us through it on dry land, we would have all been slain by the pursuing Egyptian army. And what good would it have served us to be led to Mount Sinai and not to be given the Torah? In what sense is any of these individual steps "enough for us"?

The song teaches the same lesson as my no-longer-perfect diamond ring: Stop and notice the greatness of each and every part. The splitting of the sea itself was a tremendous miracle. Appreciate it for what it was, regardless of the next step in the progression.

The Torah requires us to remember the Exodus from Egypt every day. Such remembrance leads to gratitude, the core characteristic of the Jewish people. The very name "Jew" derives from the Hebrew name "Yehudah," which means "thank" or "acknowledge." In the midst of the Seder, which is a process of spiritual elevation consisting of fifteen steps, the song *"Dayenu"* teaches us how to achieve that quintessential virtue of gratitude: Focus, really focus, on each individual blessing you are given. Regardless of what came before or after it.

Every blessing is a stand-alone gift, just as every diamond is its own treasure.

Shavuos: Hashem's Greatest Gift

 meditation for Shavuos:

Hashem loves humanity so much that He gave us:

- *Butterflies*
- *Waterfalls*
- *Sunsets*
- *Mountains (for viewing, climbing, photographing, rappelling, and contemplating)*
- *Ladybugs*
- *Horses (to carry us)*
- *Donkeys (to carry our stuff)*
- *Cool breezes*
- *Sweat glands*
- *Sunshine (and just enough of it to warm the planet without burning it up)*

- *Photosynthesis*
- *Soil microbes*
- *Praying mantises (not only do they eat aphids, but they are a great parody of professors)*
- *Tropical fish*
- *More varieties of tropical fish*
- *Even more varieties of tropical fish*
- *Forests*
- *Gravity (an anti-gravity chamber looks like fun, but I'd rather eat my dinner from a plate)*
- *Grass*
- *Poignancy*
- *The color blue (not to mention fuchsia and chartreuse)*
- *Wildflowers (in all of their myriad varieties)*
- *Our immune system (which works even when we don't)*
- *Beating hearts (the ultimate perpetual motion machine)*
- *Hair (which some don't appreciate until they lose it)*
- *Saliva (imagine swallowing a cracker without it)*
- *Moonlight*
- *Moss*
- *Herbs (which teach us that every weed can heal)*
- *Snow (in all its various shapes: flakes, drifts, men, and caps on mountains)*
- *Physical pain (which alerts us when something is wrong)*

- *Opposable thumbs*
- *Eyelids (fill in your own reflection)*
- *Two 127,000,000-pixel cameras positioned in the front of our heads (our eyes)*
- *Oceans*
- *Waves (for swimming, painting, and proving the ephemeralness of sand castles)*
- *Buttercups*
- *Petunias (which are bigger and more colorful than buttercups)*
- *Irises and orchids (which are more intricately shaped)*
- *Jasmine and wisteria (with their divine fragrance)*
- *Roses (which need no commentary)*
- *Taste buds*
- *Mangoes*
- *Translucent cells in our corneas (and not over our intestines)*
- *Salmon (which inspire us by their example of swimming upstream)*
- *Cotton*
- *Giant sequoia trees*
- *Silk (this product of lowly worms should humble us)*
- *The Grand Canyon (should humble us even more)*

- *Our liver (which performs over 500 functions and manufactures more than 1,000 different chemicals)*
- *DNA*
- *Chocolate (need I say more?)*
- *Lizards (which eat mosquitoes)*
- *Mosquitoes (I'm not sure why)*
- *Asparagus*
- *Songbirds*
- *The hairs in our nostrils (an under-appreciated gift if ever there was one)*
- *Parrots*
- *Coffee beans*
- *Giraffes (and the special valve in their necks that enables them to bend to drink water and then straighten up without blacking out from the pressure change)*
- *Our circulatory system (that reaches every one of the three trillion cells in our body, and that knows exactly what to deliver to every one of them, putting the postal system to shame)*
- *Dolphins*
- *Cashmere (who would have thought to put something so exquisite on the underbelly of Mongolian goats?)*
- *Peacocks (even with their tail feathers not displayed; take a look at their iridescent necks)*
- *Our digestive system (that knows what to do with pizza)*

- *The sound of crickets*
- *The silence of cats*
- *Our sense of smell (and thousands of different fragrances to titillate it, from peonies to roasted coffee, from freshly-mowed grass to freshly-baked bread)*
- *Lightning*
- *Cows (without which we would not have ice cream)*
- *Rain*
- *Feet (with their intricate shock absorbers)*
- *Apples (in their perfect packaging)*
- *Stars (for navigating, astronomy, and a sense of how big is big)*
- *Shooting stars*
- *Seed pods (meditate for 60 seconds on this one)*
- *Grass with little pellets we can grind and make into bread and cake (wheat)*
- *Elephants*
- *Rivers*
- *Ears (that can distinguish the difference in tone between sincere and insincere)*
- *Teeth (custom-made to suit every species on the planet)*
- *Swans*
- *Babies (including the smell and softness of newborns)*
- *Skin*

- *The human brain (that has more connections than the New York City telephone system)*
- *Sleep (I often feel He didn't make enough of it!)*
- *Love*
- *Illness (that wakes us up from our spiritual sloth)*
- *Our stomachs (with their 36,000,000 acid-producing glands that digest a steak but don't touch the stomach's own lining)*
- *Smiles*
- *Cell division*
- *Several million other features of our own bodies that we will never notice or appreciate*

Hashem loves the Jewish people so much that He gave us the Torah, with its myriad mitzvos, which is:

- *A way to demonstrate our gratitude for all of the above*
- *A guideline of what He really wants from us, so we'll know*
- *613 ways to bond with Him as He wills*
- *A foolproof path to our own spiritual perfection*
- *The blueprint of creation*
- *A way to fix the world and ourselves*
- *The Jewish people's marriage contract with Hashem*
- *A Kabbalistic system that we can use and benefit from without understanding how it works*

- *An inexhaustible well of wisdom*
- *An eternal testimony to His love for us*

The Torah is a more precious gift than everything listed in Part One combined, because when we accept the gift of Torah, we receive the Giver Himself.

Tishah B'Av: Waking Up to a World Without Hashem's Presence

I remember with perfect clarity the sensation of waking up on the morning of March 9, 1990. In those first few fuzzy moments of consciousness, I oriented myself to where I was — in the spare bedroom of my parents' New Jersey apartment, and what day it was — two days after my father's death. As soon as I cognized that I had woken up into a world without my father, my heart plunged into a fathomless grief, like waking up into a nightmare that will never end.

The world without my father was not simply the same world minus one; it was a totally different world. This altered, diminished world lacked the stability and goodness that was my father. This world wobbled on its axis; its gravitational pull was heavier.

It took me a year to adapt to this new world, to learn to navigate its emotional byways. Now, more than fifteen years later, I've become proficient at maneuvering in this World-Without-My-Father, but it is not and will never be the same world in which he was so benevolently and lovingly present.

The ninth day of the Hebrew month of Av — Tishah B'Av — is to the Jewish people what March 9 was to me. We misrepresent the tragedy of the day by describing it as the *destruction* of the two Holy Temples, as if the catastrophe is the loss of a building. Do the American people mourn on 9/11 because of the destruction of the Twin Towers themselves or because of the thousands of lives lost in the conflagration? Contrast a person who mourns the absence of the majestic towers to the New York skyline with a person who mourns the loss of his father, caught on the 98th floor. Tishah B'Av is more like a death than a destruction, because on that day, the world changed irrevocably.

The world without the *Beis HaMikdash* is not the same world minus one magnificent structure. The world without the *Beis HaMikdash* is a totally different world. The *Beis HaMikdash* was the mystical vortex between the higher, spiritual worlds and this gross, physical world. The Temple service was an elaborate mystical procedure that kept the aperture between the worlds open and functioning. The Divine Presence manifested itself in the *Beis HaMikdash* and through the *Beis HaMikdash*. When the Temple was destroyed, that palpable Divine Presence removed Itself from our world. It was a loss as real and as searing as death.

My son was born into a world without my father. He will never know how the room lit up when my father entered, how secure and supported dozens of people felt because of the bedrock that was my father.

In the same way, we who were born into a world without the Divine Presence have never experienced the spiritual luminosity that radiated through the aperture of the *Beis HaMikdash*. We live in a dimmer, coarser world, where physical reality seems like ultimate truth while spiritual reality seems like a vague phantasm. We navigate in the nightmare without even knowing we're in it.

Divine Immanence

In the first *Beis HaMikdash*, ten miracles were evident for all to see. Among them were that no matter how the wind was blowing, the smoke from the Altar always went straight up, and that no matter how packed the crowds of people were, at the point of the service that required everyone to prostrate, there was always sufficient room. Any Jew who visited the Temple (and Jews were required to make pilgrimage three times a year) could see these miracles, these deviations in the laws of physics, simply by entering the Temple precincts.

While the first *Beis HaMikdash* (and the Tabernacle that preceded it) stood, prophecy was commonplace. The Talmud (*Megillah* 14a) testifies that in ancient Israel, 1,000,000 Jews were privy to the highest spiritual level possible. Disciples of the prophets abounded. So widespread was Divine revelation to the common people — the prophet Amos, for example was "a dresser of sycamore trees" — that the Talmud (*Pesachim* 66a) could assert that all Jews were either "prophets or the children of prophets."

The immanence of the Divine Presence during Temple times did not mean that everyone chose spiritual elevation. Even when Hashem is present, humans can — and did — choose against Him. The Talmud recounts the story of Yeravam ben Navat, who, after the death of King Solomon, split the Kingdom, usurped the throne of the northern half, and set up two golden calves for worship. Hashem appeared to Yeravam and said, "Repent, and I and you and Ben Yishai [King David] will walk together in Paradise." Yeravam had the gall to respond: "Who will go first?" When he heard that David would precede him, Yeravam rejected the Divine offer. The most remarkable aspect of this conversation is that Hashem appeared even to someone as wicked as Yeravam. The Divine Presence during the Temple era was so pervasive and apparent that anyone who bothered to open his eyes could perceive It.

How different is the world we live in! On the day of the Temple's destruction, the dogged illusion of Divine absence settled over our world like a perpetual fog. In this world where Divine hiddenness has replaced Divine revelation, we grope for proofs of Hashem's existence, like fish debating the existence of water. We are relegated to "believing" when once we simply knew. We struggle, through prayer and meditation, to experience a momentary inkling of the Divine Presence when once we simply basked in it. We are like amnesiacs who experience vague and fleeting memories of a different life, a truer identity, but the actual grasping of it eludes us.

Tishah B'Av made orphans of us all.

Achieving the Impossible

*I*n one essential way Tishah B'Av differs from death: the catastrophe is reversible. As Rabbi Avraham Isaac Kook declared: "The Temple was destroyed because of baseless hatred [among Jews]; it can be rebuilt only by baseless love."

"Baseless love" means loving every single Jew, no matter how much he/she differs in political or religious persuasion. It means loving Jews at the other end of the ideological spectrum. It means left-wing activists loving Chassidic Jews and vice versa. It means Gush Katif settlers loving the security forces who evicted them from their homes and vice versa. Given that the Talmud characterizes the Jews as "the most fractious of peoples" and the daily news corroborates that description, baseless love seems like an impossible achievement.

But if someone had told me on March 9, 1990, or any day thereafter, that I could bring my father back to life by doing X, is there anything, *anything*, I would not have done?

If we yearn enough to bring the Divine Presence back into our world, is there anything beyond our capacity to achieve it?

A few years ago I learned how to harness the seemingly impossible to the power of yearning, and fly. It was during the peak of the Arab war of terror against Israel. I had undertaken to visit terror victims in the hospital and to distribute teddy bears on behalf of Kids for Kids. Several days after a lethal bus bombing in Haifa, my 14-year-old daughter and I visited the Mount Carmel hospital where most of the injured — teenagers on their way home from school — were hospitalized.

I had never been to that hospital before. Clutching my list of terror victims in one hand and my bulging bag of teddy bears in the other, I accidentally stumbled into the intensive care unit. I asked a nurse, "Where is Daniel K.?" She pointed to the bed beside me. Lying prone on the bed was a thin, unmoving figure. I grabbed my daughter's hand and quickly exited, but the specter of that boy, the only patient I had ever seen lying face-down, haunted me.

Tishah B'Av: Waking Up to a World Without Hashem's Presence

In the waiting room, I sat with Daniel's desperate parents. They had made *aliyah* from Uzbekistan a few years earlier. They explained that 17-year-old Daniel's lungs had been punctured in the terror attack. The doctors were not hopeful.

I promised them I would pray for "Daniel Chai," but it was clear to all of us that nothing less than a miracle would save the boy. There is a spiritual law in Judaism called, *"Middah k'neged middah."* This means that whatever humans do, Hashem responds to them in kind. When we want Hashem to go beyond the laws of nature, we must go beyond our own nature. Therefore, tapping into this spiritual law, I suggested to Daniel's mother that she take on a mitzvah she had not previously done in order to save her son's life, and I left the hospital planning to do similarly.

When my children started to bicker in the car on the long ride home, I told them that they could contribute to saving Daniel's life by overcoming their urge to fight. To my amazement, they behaved like angels all the way home.

The next day, I had an argument with my husband. I walked away from him feeling hurt and rejected. I fled to my room, wanting only to distance myself from him. As I sat on the edge of my bed, I rehearsed to myself everything I had learned about life's essential choice: choosing between estrangement and connection. I knew that the higher road would be to reconcile with my husband, or at least be open to whatever conciliatory steps he took, but my whole nature wanted to run away from him. I sat there for some 10 minutes warring with myself. I knew exactly what I should do, but was as incapable of doing it as a paraplegic trying to pole-vault. Suddenly I was startled to hear myself say out loud: "I can't do it."

I answered my own voice, "Can you do it for Daniel Chai? Can you do it to save that boy's life?"

"Yes!" came my resounding reply. "To save Daniel's life, I can overcome my own nature."

When my husband came in a few minutes later, I battled my instinct to turn away, accepted his apology, and made peace. I felt like a heroine. I knew that I couldn't do it, but for Daniel's life, I did it.

[Postscript: Daniel's mother took on lighting Shabbos candles. Despite a dangerous infection that beset him that week, Daniel had a miraculous recovery.]

When I consider the prospect of all Jews truly loving each other, I hear the voice of realism saying, "We can't do it." Then I ask: Can we do it to bring the Divine Presence back into the world? Can we do it to dispel the choking fog of Divine absence? Can we do it to end all the national and personal catastrophes that ensue in a world where Hashem is not evident?

To reverse the cataclysm of Tishah B'Av, is there anything we can't do?

Days of Awe: Submitting Your Annual Report

A recent issue of my Brandeis University alumnae magazine devoted two-thirds of a page to the success of one graduate of the Class of '87. Her stunning achievement? She is Hollywood's only female sword-master and has become director of theatrical combat at the Beverly Hills Fencers' Club.

How does the magazine editor decide which graduate's career is worthy of highlighting? What criteria of success qualify to make one's alma mater proud? Wealth? Fame? Contribution to society? Uniqueness of profession?

The alumnae themselves are invited to write in to describe their own recent accomplishments. This latest issue, for example, lists these noteworthy and hard-won accomplishments:

- *A.L., class of '91, received her doctor of veterinary medicine degree from Washington State University*
- *J.H., class of '76, was named 2005 Psychologist of the Year by the Florida Psychological Association.*

- K.P., class of '73, was appointed executive vice president for development for the Birmingham Health Corporation.
- A.S., class of '82, published a book, "Mac Design Out of the Box."

Reading of my fellow alumnae's various achievements, I wondered what a spiritual version of the magazine would look like. After all, a person can be justly proud of getting a degree, a promotion, or an award, but are spiritual achievements any less important? If B.G. is feted because he got a promotion up the corporate ladder, shouldn't he be feted for becoming a kinder person this year? If N.H. is congratulated for getting a post-doc degree, shouldn't she be congratulated that she stopped yelling at her kids?

According to Judaism, the measuring rod of significance in life is a spiritual barometer. Thus, when N.H. gets that post-doc degree, from a Jewish standpoint she deserves congratulations because she exhibited the qualities of industriousness and perseverance to earn the degree. And if these qualities did not come naturally to her, she deserves even more accolades.

Contrary to popular perception, wealth, fame, and success are gifts from Hashem, Who endows people with talent, intelligence, and specific aptitudes.

My book *Holy Woman,* which was published in May, 2006, has gone into its 7th printing. Yesterday someone asked me, "You must be really proud to have written a bestselling book."

I replied, "Not really. All the ingredients of the bestseller — my writing talent, my becoming acquainted with such an amazing woman to write about, my access to the right people to interview [three of whom passed away within a few months after the interview] — all that came from

Hashem. I feel more gratitude than pride. But when I exercise enough self-discipline to get to bed on time, then I feel really proud."

The Yearly Issue

*M*y alumnae magazine comes out four times a year. Its spiritual counterpart, which really does exist, has only one issue per year: the Rosh Hashanah/Yom Kippur issue. This is the time for all of us to reflect upon and assess our spiritual accomplishments and failures. This is the time for our annual report.

While my alumnae magazine prints only those reports submitted by proud alumnae, its spiritual counterpart features a report by every one of us without exception. As the High Holy Day liturgy puts it: "The signature of every person's hand is in it."

And if, as Rosh Hashanah draws near, we realize to our chagrin that we have few spiritual achievements to report, it's still not too late. The ten days between Rosh Hashanah and Yom Kippur, called "The Ten Days of Repentance," are an ideal time to score some spiritual goals. The deadline for submissions to our spiritual alum magazine is Yom Kippur.

Progress Report

From an alumnae magazine, we can learn two important spiritual lessons. The first is: **Idealize upward movement.**

Alumnae generally report new jobs, promotions, recently awarded distinctions, etc. Similarly, in our spiritual lives we should strive to constantly reach new levels. V.N. would be embarrassed to report: "I'm working at the same mid-level job I've had for the last fifteen years." So why shouldn't V.N. be embarrassed to admit, "The same things that ticked me off fifteen years ago still make me go ballistic"?

J.H. would be loathe to submit for the 2006 issue, "I was named the 1995 Psychologist of the Year by the Florida Psychological Association." Yet how often when we search for our spiritual accomplishments do we revert to, "I became a *baal teshuvah* sixteen years ago." When we stand before Hashem on the High Holy Days, He wants to hear about how we grew, changed, and progressed *this* year.

The key word here is "progressed." As the Vilna Gaon writes in his commentary to *Mishlei* [2:4], spiritual achievement means that you're *better* in a particular character trait or mitzvah than you were last year.

So, if you are by nature and habit generous, reporting, "I gave $10,000 to Yad Eliezer for food distribution in Northern Israeli bomb shelters during the recent war," may not be at all impressive, because Hashem is primarily concerned with *progress* reports.

Let's say, on the other hand, you are by nature tight-fisted, rarely give to charity, and always throw out all your junk mail charity solicitations without even opening them. One day this August on your way between your mailbox and the trash basket, you noticed that one envelope was from Yad Eliezer and emblazoned on it were the words, "HELP ISRAEL'S

NORTHERN RESIDENTS." You opened the envelope, read the appeal, and battled with yourself about whether to donate money. Finally, you decided to help, and wrote a check for $25. THAT'S A SPIRITUAL VICTORY!

Here's where the spiritual sword-master comes in. All spiritual progress is a victory of one's higher inclinations (the soul) over one's lower inclinations (the *yetzer hara*). Where there's no duel between these two rivals, there's no victory. Doing what comes naturally or what you do habitually or what you've already done scores of times in the past is not a spiritual achievement. It doesn't qualify for the spiritual alum magazine.

That's why I feel prouder about getting to bed on time (in order not to be cranky the next day) than about writing a bestselling book. Writing comes easily to me. There's no battle involved, and therefore no victory. Getting to bed early enough to get a good night's sleep (a key to spiritual success), however, is a nightly fencing match with my *yetzer hara*. The *yetzer*, in collusion with my addiction to "getting just one more thing done," seduces me with temptations such as, "Just unload the dishwasher, so you can wake up to a clean kitchen." When I exercise enough self discipline to overcome its blandishments, I achieve a hard-won victory. I have to keep my sword to the *yetzer*'s throat until the moment I turn out the light.

Validating Victory

The second profound lesson we can learn from an alumnae magazine is: **Validate every accomplishment.**

One of the greatest detriments to spiritual growth is our minimizing of our spiritual victories. K.W. is proud to report that she got her M.D. from Middlesex School of Medicine. So what that it wasn't Harvard Med! Yet most of us downplay our spiritual accomplishments: "So, I said *Bircas HaMazon* with *kavannah* this afternoon, but I said it without *kavannah* this morning." "So I got up early to *daven* with a *minyan* even though I was exhausted. What's the big deal?"

We know that the best way to educate our children is with positive reinforcement. If we want a child to sit still when eating, we have to reinforce every 3 minutes she sits still, heaping on her attention and praise. Why, then, are we so remiss with reinforcing our own desirable behaviors?

When we face off with our *yetzer hara*, we have to be the home team. When a home team football player scores 5 yards, the fans cheer wildly. They don't pooh-pooh it, saying, "It was only 5 yards. It wasn't a touchdown." The more we cheer for our spiritual victories, the more victories we'll score.

Your mother pushed your button and you didn't snap back at her? Hurray! Bring out the band! Your neighbor started to gossip, and you changed the subject? Bravo! Give yourself a mental bouquet of roses!

When people tell me that reading *Holy Woman* inspired them to change, I ask them for concrete examples. After a few moments thinking (or hesitating), they tell me. As a result, I've accumulated a list of real people's spiritual achievements that, to my mind, vies with any alumnae magazine in sheer impressiveness of accomplishment. Here are but a few examples:

- L.W., *when her friends dropped by, used to tell them to help themselves to whatever they wanted from the frig. Now, she takes the time to serve them drinks and snacks.*

- *A.R. has stopped taking her emotional pulse every 15 minutes. "Life is not about how I feel," she says, "but about what I can give." This reorientation has changed her relationship with her children and her husband.*

- *L.P. has become more generous with giving charity. He now sees himself as a steward for the money he earns.*

- *E.S. relates that a woman comes to her apartment every month seeking alms. The woman, who is obviously not mentally well, knocks on her door, walks in, opens the refrigerator, and starts rummaging for food. In the past, E.S. has been offended by this violation of her personal space. This time, however, E.S. decided to act more compassionately toward this disturbed woman. Rather than treating her like an intruder, she treated her like an honored guest.*

- *V.B. has become more open to sharing her home. She used to hesitate to invite guests for Shabbos because she didn't want to have to share her bathroom. Now she's excited to perform the mitzvah of hospitality.*

Each of these exploits surely deserves at least as much recognition as becoming the first female sword-master in Hollywood.

As Rosh Hashanah approaches, sit down and make a list of all the ways you've grown and improved this year. Don't consider any accomplishment too small. Then resolve to make new strides in the new year — not giant leaps, but small, consistent steps.

THERE IS NO SUCH THING AS AN INSIGNIFICANT SPIRITUAL VICTORY. Emblazon that motto on your desk and start cheering!

Days of Awe: Stalking True Atonement

*I*t's not that I mind giving charity to all and sundry, but I do mind being rooked. That's why my "don't think you can fool me" persona went on high alert when the girl approached our table at an outdoor café one evening this summer. My husband and I were having supper with another couple, distant relatives from America. The girl wore blue jeans, a halter-top, dangling pink earrings that must have been six inches long, and gobs of makeup. Her hair was streaked with purple. I guessed that she was probably 16 years old. She mumbled that she belonged to a religious youth group called Bnei Akiva and that she was collecting for disadvantaged children, and she limply displayed her receipt book.

As an American living in Israel, I often miss the cultural clues that would save me from being conned. This time, however, I was savvy. I knew plenty of Bnei Akiva girls, and they didn't dress like that. In fact, at their meetings and when on "official business," they wear a uniform consisting of a white top, blue skirt, and blue neckerchief. Because we were speaking English, this girl must have thought that we were tourists and thus easy marks. "Where's your uniform?" I quizzed her in Hebrew.

The girl shrugged.

"What chapter of Bnei Akiva are you in?" I prodded.

"Musrara," she answered, surly.

Musrara? This is a low-income neighborhood to the north of the Old City walls, a neighborhood, I had heard, rife with drug addicts.

I took the receipt book and examined it. "Bnei Akiva" and something about disadvantaged children were printed in Hebrew beside the figure "5 shekels" (about $1.25). I turned to my husband and dinner companions. "Should we believe that she's really from Bnei Akiva?" I asked in English.

I was the best Hebrew speaker in the group. "It's your call," they told me.

Torah admonishes us not to close our hand or our hearts to our needy fellow, and requires that we give a minimum amount (enough to buy *some* item of food) to every individual who asks us. However, if someone is collecting for an organization, we're permitted to refuse.

I surveyed the girl uncertainly, debating within myself. "So what if she pockets the money for herself? If she lives in Musrara, she herself is a disadvantaged child. But what if she uses the money for drugs or alcohol? Then I'll be guilty of contributing to her delinquency. Or what if she passes on the money to her drug-addict parent?" The thoughts raced through my mind as the girl, her expression blasé, stood beside our table.

Finally my distrust prevailed. I handed the receipt book back to her and said, "I'm sorry. I don't believe that you're from Bnei Akiva."

She shrugged and turned away. For the rest of the dinner, I was plagued by second thoughts. What if her family needed the money for food or rent?

After parting from our relatives, my husband and I decided to walk home. On the way, we encountered two girls dressed in Bnei Akiva uniforms. One of them approached us and announced that she was collecting for disadvantaged children. She showed us her receipt book — the same book the other girl had sported.

I paled. So, Bnei Akiva girls really were out collecting tonight. "What chapter are you from?" I asked.

"Musrara," they replied.

"A girl claiming to be from your chapter approached us downtown," I told them urgently, "but she wasn't wearing a uniform."

The two girls nodded their heads knowingly. "We're supposed to wear our uniforms to meetings and whenever we're doing Bnei Akiva stuff. But most of the kids don't bother to. In fact, most of the kids in our chapter don't even come from religious families. Bnei Akiva started in our neighborhood as a kind of ... I guess you'd call it ... rehabilitation."

My heart sank. "Oh, no!" I thought. "I really blew it. Not only was she telling the truth, but she was trying to do a good deed, and I distrusted her." I felt like I had knocked a fragile crystal vase off a table, and now I stood there, disconcerted, staring at the broken pieces.

My husband reached into his pocket and gave the girls 5 shekels. As soon as they moved on, I asked him plaintively, "What do I do now?"

"*Teshuvah*," he replied.

Teshuvah, which can be understood as "turning around," is Hashem's great, supernatural gift to humanity. Through it Hashem gives us, who are the proud masters of our present and future, the keys to our past. By properly enacting the steps of *teshuvah*, human beings can actually undo the damage they have done. They can repair the crystal vase to be as good, or better, than its original state.

For sins between us and Hashem, *teshuvah* entails three steps: admitting we did wrong, feeling regret, and resolving not to repeat the sin. For sins between us and another person, there are two additional steps: asking forgiveness and making restitution.

Standing there on that Jerusalem street, I realized instantly that these last two steps would pose formidable difficulties. To ask the girl's forgiveness, I would have to find her — and I didn't even know her name. And to make restitution, to correct the wrong, I would have to personally hand her the 5-shekel donation, which meant descending into the depths of Musrara.

All the way home, I mulled over the mechanics of asking forgiveness and making restitution. As it turned out, the mechanics, though problematical, were the easiest part of my *teshuvah* process.

Elusive Teshuvah

As soon as I got home, I went to my neighbor's daughter Netta, a counselor in Bnei Akiva. She knew the counselor of the Musrara chapter and was willing to call her and explain my predicament.

As soon as Netta described the dangling pink earrings, Miri, the Musrara counselor, identified the girl. Her name was Daphna, and I could find her at next Tuesday night's Bnei Akiva meeting. Miri gave Netta the address where the youth group met, a bomb shelter on a street I had never heard of.

I spent all that week dreading having to roam around Musrara in the dark searching for the bomb shelter. When I finally got there, my efforts were for naught. Daphna didn't show up for the meeting.

The next Tuesday evening, I had a wedding to attend. The following Tuesday, Miri's cell phone was disconnected.

I was getting desperate. "Restitution" required making a donation to the cause Daphna was collecting for, but the fundraising campaign would not extend indefinitely. I had to get to Daphna before it was too late.

Delving Deeper

Since *teshuvah* was eluding me, I sat down and considered what I was doing wrong. Perhaps I was being too facile in my approach. What precisely did I have to do *teshuvah* on? Stinginess? Distrust? Skepticism?

I called my teacher, Rebbetzin Tziporah Heller, to discuss the matter. She explained that my sin was not my refusal to make a donation, but rather my telling the girl that I didn't believe her. In so doing, I had insulted her. Restitution would require building up her self-esteem to the extent I had damaged it. We decided that I should go to her home to ask forgiveness. Such a gesture on the part of an adult would be an ego boost to a teenager.

Everyday I tried calling Miri to get Daphna's address, but Miri's cell phone was out of commission. Finally, the following Tuesday, I got through.

Miri informed me that that very day was the final day of the fundraising campaign. The kids who had collected 200 shekels would get to go to Superland, Israel's biggest amusement park. No, Daphna had not collected enough. She was 70 shekels short and she had lost her receipt book, so there was no way for her to collect more money. Strangers would not give her donations without receipts, and apparently her own family did not have 70 shekels ($16) to contribute.

I was amazed. What Providence! I could give her the 70-shekel donation! Perhaps this whole, long, drawn-out drama was just so Daphna would not be left out of the trip to Superland. What better way to bolster her self-esteem than to give her the satisfaction of having raised her quota and of being included in the prize?

Miri gave me Daphna's cell phone number. I called Daphna right away. Yes, she remembered me, the American woman at the café who didn't believe she was from Bnei Akiva. I told her I wanted to come to Musrara that very afternoon to ask her forgiveness and to make a donation of 70 shekels. There was silence on the other end of the line. Finally, she said that that would be fine.

I told her that I didn't think I could find her house. We agreed to meet instead on the main thoroughfare that borders Musrara. I breathed a sigh of relief. My *teshuvah* was almost complete. And Daphna had fared better than if I had given her the 5 shekels at the café. The fixed vase was better than the original. Real *teshuvah*!

Or so I thought.

Even Deeper

As I drove to our rendezvous, my cell phone rang. It was Daphna. She had told her mother the story, and her mother wanted to see me. Her mother wanted me to come to their home. Her mother had a thing or two to tell me. Doing *teshuvah* on this one, I realized like a school kid about to be thrashed, would be *much* harder than I thought.

I picked Daphna up on the main thoroughfare, and she guided me through the narrow back streets of Musrara to her home. Her mother was sitting on the couch watching TV when we arrived. She did not get up to greet me.

She told me that she cleans houses for a living and her husband is a porter in a produce store and that they make an honest living and that I am not one wit better than they are.

Then she gestured toward Daphna, who was sitting on the second couch. Wearing neither make-up nor jewelry, she looked her real age, which, it turns out, was 14. "My kids aren't angels," her mother lectured me, "but they don't lie."

Instead of getting defensive at Daphna's mother's rebuke, I listened, truly listened. Then I realized that my *teshuvah* had to go much deeper than I had imagined. Behind every failure of action is a failure of character. Daphna's mother was accusing me of feeling superior. The truth, I realized, mortified, was that I did.

It was my vaunted pride that had made me judge Daphna negatively. I thought back to my own youth in the 60's in New Jersey. I was the top student in my public school class, and I looked down on the non-Jewish girls with teased, bleached blonde hair who barely got passing grades, girls who thought — when they thought at all — that the purpose of life was to be pretty. As I had dismissed those girls as intellectually and morally inferior, so I had dismissed Daphna.

Daphna's mother, who cleans other people's houses, had seen right through me. When she finished admonishing me (it took 15 minutes), I admitted she was right, and apologized for my affront to her family. In the process of fixing the vase, I was being compelled to fix myself.

Doing a Life Review

The period leading up to Yom Kippur is the time for doing *teshuvah*. Every Jew is supposed to reflect on the past year, identify wrongs committed against Hashem or one's fellow, and go through the steps of *teshuvah*.

Too often, however, a sincere personal accounting reveals that, despite the most ardent resolutions to change, this year's sins doggedly resemble last year's. The Slonimer Rebbe, *zt"l*, wrote that if one's *teshuvah* process addresses only *deeds* but not *motivations*, it's like cutting weeds rather than uprooting them.

While engaged in fixing the vase, I must ask myself: What character trait caused me to knock it over? Clumsiness? Boisterousness? Heedlessness of others' property? If I don't identify and fix the character trait, sooner or later other shards will be littering the floor of my life.

Rebbetzin Heller, based on classical Jewish sources, recommends a method that delves to the deepest levels of character and traces wrong actions to their source. This method, which she calls "A Life Review," is the first step toward permanent change.

Divide your life into its major periods, such as "childhood," "high school," "college," etc. For each period, write answers to the following questions:

1. *Which events were central to this time period in my life?*

2. *How did I respond to those events?*

3. *From my current perspective, which choices brought me closer to where I want to be today?*

4. *Which character traits motivated me to make the good choices?*

> 5. Which character traits motivated me to make the
> bad choices?

As you review the various periods of your life, a pattern of positive and negative traits will emerge. Because you want to work on what needs improving, when you are done, review all your answers to the final question. There will be many duplications and different aspects of the same trait. For example, you may have listed:

- *Pride*
- *A sense that I was always right and anyone who didn't agree with me was wrong*
- *Intellectual superiority*
- *Not legitimizing others' needs or point of view*
- *Arrogance*

Condense all such duplications into one character trait, such as "arrogance." When you are done, you will have no more than five core traits that are the culprits behind all your wrong, hurtful, and self-destructive actions. Pick one of these traits to do *teshuvah* on before Yom Kippur.

For any method of working on yourself to be successful, keep in mind:

- *Make a concrete plan of action based on taking very small steps.*
- *Chart your progress.*
- *Reward yourself for progress.*
- *Commit yourself to working on the trait for at least three months.*

According to the Vilna Gaon, we have come into this world for no other purpose than to fix our character traits. As he writes in his commentary to *Mishlei:* "For a person is alive only in order to repair a *middah* that he has not yet repaired; and if he does not do so, why should he bother remaining alive?"

We don't do real *teshuvah* with superglue, but with a very deep spade.

Days of Awe: The Gates of Forgiveness

It was not a demonstration. The posters billed it as a *Melaveh Malkah* — a Saturday night music fest to escort out the Shabbos Queen, accompanied by my husband's klezmer band and circle dancing. True, the location chosen was an abandoned cul-de-sac a block away from Orient House, the infamous P.L.O. headquarters in East Jerusalem. True, the point was to assert Jewish sovereignty in all of Jerusalem. True, the unveiling of the secret Oslo Accords eight months before had been followed by a series of massive demonstrations, which often deteriorated into hair-raising scenes of police brutality, complete with water hoses aimed at protesters' eyes. But this was not a demonstration. No placards, no speeches. Rather, an air of family festivity, with children and elderly people aplenty. I was glad I had come to hear my husband play.

While the band waited on the makeshift stage for the generator to be delivered, the organizers set up loudspeakers on high poles around the perimeter of the crowd. People conversed easily with a squad of border policemen, the paramilitary force known as the heavies of the defense establishment, whom we assumed were there to keep the Jews and nearby Arabs peacefully separate.

Finally, the music started, a lilting klezmer tune. In the center of the crowd, a large circle of men joined hands and began to dance.

Suddenly, out of nowhere, the border policemen charged into the crowd, swinging billy clubs and beating everyone in their path. Amid horrified screams and cries, they reached the generator and unplugged it. The music stopped mid-note.

Several policemen jumped onto the stage, grabbing clarinets and guitars out of the hands of the musicians. Other troops started to pull down the loudspeakers. Standing near the stage, in shock and horror, I noticed an old man positioned directly under one of the loudspeakers. I shouted to warn him, but could not be heard over the din of shrieks and wails. I ran toward him, but was cut off by the charge of a giant horse, twice the size of any horse I had ever seen. Terrified, I retreated toward the stage, which by now was encircled by border policemen to prevent the musicians from escaping.

I was a veteran of anti-Vietnam War demonstrations in America in the 60's, but I had never in my life experienced such ruthless police tactics — and without any justification! Unnerved and agitated, I started yelling at the police in my American-accented Hebrew: "What are you doing? How can Jews act this way? You are Jews, but you're worse than the American police!"

One tall, fortyish policeman with short, cropped hair hollered back at me: "You don't belong here. You're an American! Go back to America!"

He had pushed my button. Irate, I slapped him across the face.

He gestured to the policeman next to him. Each grabbed one of my forearms and pulled me away. The one I had slapped dug his fingers into my arm so forcefully that even a month later five bruises on my right forearm would testify to his brutality. They dragged me some 20 meters to a paddy wagon, then threw me into it so roughly that they cut a three-inch gash into my knee.

At the police station, a police officer asked me what had happened. I told him the whole story: how without warning the police had attacked the crowd, how they had endangered an elderly man, how I had been prevented from saving him by giant horses, how a border policeman had insulted me, how I had reacted, and how, instead of a civil, "You're under arrest," they had brutally manhandled me. After signing my deposition, I was sent home.

That was the last I heard of the matter for over two years. Then, after the assassination of Yitzchak Rabin, all the files against right-wing protesters were pulled out and dusted off. One day, a registered letter arrived for me. I had been charged with striking a policeman, and was summoned to appear in court.

I hired a lawyer, a middle-aged religious man. "In Israel," he quietly informed me, "there is a mandatory prison sentence for striking a policeman."

"What?" I answered, appalled. "I'm the one who was hurt. I still have the scar on my knee. Besides, he provoked me. He insulted me, told me to go back to America."

"Nonetheless," the lawyer answered calmly, "you confessed to striking a policeman. Why did you incriminate yourself?"

"What did you expect me to do?" I countered with righteous indignation. "Lie?"

"You could have kept silent."

Silence? It never occurred to me (and rarely does)!

"The only way to keep you out of jail is for you to throw yourself on the mercy of the court. It's a first offense. You have a pretty good chance of getting off, if you humbly admit you made a mistake and promise the court you won't repeat it."

It was a few weeks before Rosh Hashanah, and I had been studying the steps of *teshuvah*:

> 1. *Admit the sin to Hashem*
> 2. *Regret*
> 3. *Resolve not to repeat it*

The lawyer's prescription sounded eerily similar.

But why should I do *teshuvah*? I hadn't done anything wrong! I was the aggrieved party! I mulled over the matter for a couple of minutes. Then, protesting my innocence (after all, I had been sorely provoked), I told the lawyer I would do whatever he said. I didn't want to go to jail.

When our meeting was over, I gathered up my things to leave. "You know," the lawyer said parenthetically, more like a brother than a lawyer, "you were wrong."

"But he insulted me!" I defended myself.

"If you're walking down the street and someone comes up to you and insults you," the lawyer said quietly, "do you have the right to slap him?"

I stared across the desk at the lawyer's penetrating expression. It was the first time it occurred to me that perhaps I *had* done something wrong.

All the way home I weighed the matter. In three weeks it would be Rosh Hashanah, when every soul stands before Hashem in judgment. I was accountable for my actions. If I *had* done something wrong, then I would have to do *teshuvah*. But the three steps of confession, regret, and resolution for the future suffice only in sins against Hashem. Sins against another person require two additional steps: asking forgiveness and (when applicable) making restitution. With horror it dawned on me: If it really was wrong to slap the border policeman, I would have to *ask his forgiveness*.

As soon as I got home, I telephoned my rebbetzin. "Of course," she confirmed in a plain-as-the-nose-on-your-face tone, "hitting someone, except in self-defense, is prohibited by the Torah. Even if he did something wrong, it doesn't give you license to do something wrong. Of course, you have to do *teshuvah* for striking him."

"Including asking his forgiveness?" I asked, aghast.

"Of course," she replied. "You know Hashem doesn't grant forgiveness until the person you've wronged forgives you."

Long after hanging up, I sat there holding the telephone. How was I even supposed to find the border policeman? I didn't know his name. And if I did manage to find him and ask him for forgiveness, now, with the trial pending, he would certainly suspect that I was trying some extra-judicial trick to get him to reduce the charges against me. He would certainly hang up on me.

The next day, I called the lawyer. "Is there any way to find out the name of the border policeman I slapped?"

"Sure," came the immediate response. "It's right here on your charge sheet ... Ronny Tuito."

I gulped. That was too easy. "Well, how can I talk to him?"

"Just look up his number in the phone book," was his sanguine reply.

It took me a week, but, with Rosh Hashanah swiftly approaching, one day I summoned my resolve and looked up "Tuito, Ronny" in the Jerusalem phone book. There were two listings under that name. Apprehensively, I dialed the first number. A man answered the phone.

"I ... I'm looking for Ronny Tuito, the border policeman," I stammered.

"That's my cousin. 561-2393."

Great, I thought. Now I have no excuse not to call. I dialed the number. To my great relief, an answering machine picked up. I hung up. What time of day would a border policeman be home anyway?

The next evening, I tried again. A man's voice answered. "Is this Ronny Tuito?" I asked, nervously.

"Yes," came the crisp Hebrew reply.

I took a deep breath and blurted out the speech I had rehearsed thirty times. "Two years ago at a *Melaveh Malkah* near Orient House, I slapped you. What I did was wrong, and I'm sorry. Since Rosh Hashanah is approaching, and I'm more afraid of the Heavenly Court than the earthly court, I'm calling to ask you for forgiveness."

Only a moment elapsed before I heard his cursory response: "I forgive you."

Relief hit me like an avalanche. Of course! This is a Jewish country. Even a non-religious border policeman understands the dynamics of asking and granting forgiveness before the High Holidays. I felt cleansed, as if a piece of gum that had stuck to my skirt was suddenly gone.

"Thank you," I breathed. "And may you and your family be inscribed for a year of life, good health, and blessings."

"Thank you. You and your family, too," he said politely, and hung up.

Postscript: A month later I was sentenced to two months suspended sentence on condition that I didn't hit any more policemen for a three-year probation period. And I didn't.

Asking Forgiveness

*I*t's hard to ask for forgiveness. Sometimes the mechanics are sticky: locating a person from our past, initiating the conversation in privacy, getting the offended person to listen to us.

Harder still are the inner dynamics: examining actions we would rather forget; cutting through the rationalizations to admit that what we did was wrong, despite the provocations and extenuating circumstances; and humbling ourselves to ask for a gift (forgiveness is always a gift) from someone to whom we may have felt morally superior.

Hashem promises us atonement on Yom Kippur. Atonement is a wondrous, miraculous reality that bleaches out even the most stubborn stains on our soul. Atonement reconciles us with Hashem and our own highest selves. To procure atonement, all we have to do is *teshuvah*, the sincere changing direction of our heart and actions. Asking forgiveness, one of the five steps of *teshuvah* for a sin against another human being, is a relatively small price to pay for the soul-cleansing available to us on Yom Kippur.

And if the person we have hurt refuses to grant us forgiveness? The Torah requires that we humbly, sincerely ask for forgiveness three separate times. After that, the onus is on the one who refuses to forgive.

Granting Forgiveness

*W*hen asked for forgiveness, a Jew is enjoined to forgive. This can be the hardest act of all. After all, we may have been grievously hurt, in body, mind, or heart. To forgive is tantamount to executing a Divine function. It leaves the offender off the hook (presuming he or she has done the other required steps of *teshuvah* that would exonerate him or her before Hashem).

A Jew is not required to forgive an offender who has not undertaken the steps of *teshuvah,* such as regret and concrete change. A recent article in the *L.A. Times* about the aunt of an abducted child unilaterally forgiving the man who hurt her young niece is anathema from the Jewish viewpoint. Forgiving unrepentant evil only encourages its continuance.

On the other hand, nothing more quickly procures Divine forgiveness for our sins, both those we remember and those we don't, than forgiving those who have sinned against us. The principle of *middah k'neged middah* means that we get what we give. When we stand before Hashem on Rosh Hashanah and Yom Kippur our most compelling defense is: "I have forgiven those who sinned against me. Please forgive me in turn."

Every time we forgive, we open up the gates of forgiveness in the world. And we are the first ones to walk through.

Yom Kippur: Other People's Tears

"I don't care how you view the Disengagement politically," I thundered into the phone at my American friend, "but how can you not be devastated by 9,000 Jews losing their homes, their jobs, their whole way of life?"

It was three weeks since the images of weeping Gush Katif residents being led — or carried — away from their homes had sent me into paroxysms of grief, but, like most of my Israeli friends, I was still smarting. Every day my email carried pleas — for diapers, snacks, or sweaters against the Jerusalem chill — for the refugees, many of whom had left with only the clothes on their backs. I hung up the phone indignant at my American friend's apathy to their plight.

Then, I sat down at my computer, clicked on my internet news, and read the horrifying reports about flooding in New Orleans in the wake of Hurricane Katrina. I read about families stranded on their roofs, the chaos in the Superdome, and the anxiety of evacuated New Orleans residents who had no idea if their homes still stood. "This is terrible!" I muttered to my husband, shaking my head. Then I got up, made myself a late-night snack, and went to bed.

Where was my empathy? Why was I devastated by 1600 families losing their homes and jobs in Gush Katif, but not by the tens of thousands of families rendered homeless and jobless in faraway New Orleans? Physical distance had conspired with an existential difference between me and the residents of New Orleans — even the Jewish residents — to leave me feeling concerned, but not disconsolate.

Other People's Suffering

*E*ven the most sympathetic people fall into the trap of callousness toward other people's suffering.

A few weeks before the Disengagement, I noticed a small item in the newspaper. Some 15,000 Israeli families who had failed to keep up with their mortgage payments during the desperate downturn in the Israeli economy faced foreclosure by their banks. Of course, everyone knew that Israel's two biggest industries — hi-tech and tourism — had been devastated between 2000-2004, leaving tens of thousands of hapless people jobless. In 2004, the newspaper continued, nearly 3,000 families had actually received eviction notices — almost twice the number of families who, at that juncture, stood to be evicted from Gush Katif.

Where was the outcry for those families? Their plight was similar to the residents of Gush Katif, but the people themselves were so different — politically, religiously, and socially. While many of my friends were vociferously doing everything they could to stop the eviction of 1600 Gush Katif families, nobody I knew mentioned nor cared about these 3,000 destitute families who similarly stood to lose their homes, without the benefit of a supportive community and an entire sympathetic camp who would rally to their aid.

It's human nature to empathize with others only to the extent that we identify with them. Had I had an elderly parent in a nursing home anywhere, the reports of bloated corpses in New Orleans nursing homes would have driven me to tears. Lacking such an identification, I read the news, shook my head, and went about my business.

Even Jewish residents of Houston, who extended a generous helping hand to Jewish refugees from New Orleans, remained on the other side of the empathy divide until the approach of Hurricane Rita flung them into the same position.

As Barbara Raynor, a staff member of the Jewish Federation of Greater Houston, speaking on her cell phone during the pre-Rita exodus, told *The Jerusalem Post:* "It's very emotional, packing up your home for the unknown and deciding what to take with you … Now I get what happened to them [the Jews of New Orleans]. They talked about what happened to them, but you don't really understand it until you go through it yourself."

The three years of terror during Israel's Oslo War proved to me how much empathy is tied to identification. When a bus blew up in Tel Aviv, I felt the pain like a giant paper cut on my finger. When a bus blew up in Jerusalem, where I live, I felt the pain like a sliced finger that needs a dozen stitches. When the victims of a homicide bombing were English-speakers, I felt the pain like a severed finger. And when the victims of a homicide bombing were children the same age as my children, I felt the pain like a knife in my heart; I cried all day.

Plural Prayer

How is it possible to break the empathy barrier? To feel the pain of people we don't identify with? To weep for other people's tears?

One of the antidotes that Judaism offers is: plural prayer. Most of the Jewish liturgy is phrased in the first-person plural. In the most important Jewish prayer, the *Shemoneh Esrei*, we pray that God will grant *us* healing, livelihood, forgiveness, redemption, etc.

This is not just a literary convention. According to Kabbalah, all Jews constitute one collective soul. The spiritual reality of the Jewish people is that we are all cells in the same spiritual body.

To make collective prayer real, it helps to visualize a cross-section of the Jews whom one is praying for. For example, when praying for Divine wisdom, I visualize the doctors whose judgment can make the difference between life and death for their patients, the teachers whose approach can educate or destroy their students, the social workers, the engineers, the parents, the students, the writers, the lawyers, the musicians, etc., all of whom need that influx of Divine wisdom to properly fulfill their tasks.

The Arizal, the great 16th-century Kabbalist, recommended that when one prays for the world's complete redemption in the *Shemoneh Esrei*, upon reciting the words, "for Your salvation we hope all day," one should visualize oneself praying together with all Jews everywhere. This includes: Jews who are much older/much younger than you; Jews in Australia, Alaska, Hawaii, and Hungary; Jews politically to the left and to the right of you; Jews at every point in the religious spectrum from Chassidim to agnostics; and Jews who are despicably poor and brazenly rich.

The more one prays for all types of other Jews, the more one will empathize with them. Plural prayer breaks the empathy barrier.

Other People's Sins

Plural prayer is particularly conspicuous in the Yom Kippur liturgy. In the *Shemoneh Esrei* of Yom Kippur, the worshiper finds himself confessing to forty-four sins: devaluing parents and teachers, speaking *lashon hara*, insulting others, breaking promises, acting arrogantly, etc. As the worshiper mentions each sin, he beats his heart in regret. In fact, confessing sins without truly regretting them is one of the forty-four sins.

Now, I can feel remorse for forty-one of these sins, but there are always three that I don't relate to at all: "stalking a fellow Jew," "taking a vain oath," and "joining a lewd gathering." When, years ago, I asked how I could sincerely confess to sins that I have not committed, Rebbetzin Tziporah Heller explained that we confess in the plural, "For the sin that *we* have sinned before You ..." Undoubtedly some Jew somewhere in the world has committed that sin.

This explanation left me in an untenable position. Some Jew somewhere in the world is participating in lewd gatherings, and *I* have to regret the sins of that lowlife? The liturgy was forcing on me an identification that I didn't feel and didn't want.

Perhaps the greatest obstacle to empathy is our critical nature. The sentiment, "*I* would never do such a thing," builds a high wall between us and our relatives, neighbors, co-workers, and friends who do indeed manifest weaknesses that we do not share.

If, for example, you are such a paragon of honesty that you never even conduct private phone conversations on your boss' time, then how can you identify with co-workers who pilfer pens and envelopes from the office or executives who embezzle funds from the corporation? During the Yom Kippur service, how can you possibly pronounce the words, "We have stolen," and allow the plural pronoun to lump you together with pilferers and embezzlers?

Rebbetzin Heller explains our commonality with all Jews as follows:

> *Visualize the thief. What are his battles? He's possibly battling against his upbringing, his education (or lack thereof), his environment, and his own passion for acquisitions. And he's losing! Make no mistake: he's losing his battles! The Torah condemns his dishonesty.*
>
> *Now think of your own inner battles. Have you ever lost a battle? Your battles are <u>not</u> the same as his battles, but if you have ever lost one of your battles, that's what you have in common with him.*

One of the sins we confess to on Yom Kippur is judging others harshly. This Yom Kippur, perhaps on your way to synagogue, take time to think of a Jewish individual or group that you judge harshly. Then tear the wall down. Think of your own lost battles, and of theirs, and open your heart to a "we" that includes them.

This Yom Kippur, let's pray for all Jews everywhere. Let's cry for our own lost battles and for the lost battles of all other Jews. Let's weep for the suffering of all of us. As we plead in the final blessing of *Shemoneh Esrei*: "Bless us, our Father, all of us as one ..." Because we are one.

Yom Kippur: Becoming the Person You Could Have Been

When I was 11 years old, my parents, bucking generations of athletic ineptitude, sent me for tennis lessons. The instructor fired instructions at me: "Stand like this! Position your head like this! Hold the racket like this! Swing the racket like this!"

I tried as hard as I could (I really did!), but whenever the ball flew toward me, I could remember only one or two of the instructions. This was not sufficient to get the ball over the net and into the opposite court. I never became a tennis player.

A couple of decades later, a book, *The Inner Game of Tennis*, became popular in the New Age world I inhabited. The author's premise was that a person doesn't learn tennis — or any skill — by heeding a battery of rules and instructions, but rather by watching an expert tennis player play. The more one watches an expert, the more some subconscious mechanism in the brain internalizes all the correct movements. Later, on the court, without even thinking, one simply duplicates those expert movements.

"Inner game theory" enjoyed great popularity for a while, then went the way of all other New Age systems. When I subsequently started learning Torah, however, I discovered that the same approach is a mainstay of Judaism. A Chassidic aphorism encapsulates the concept: "I didn't go to my Rebbe to learn exalted wisdom from him, but rather to watch the way he laces and unlaces his shoes."

Identifying holy people, observing them, and emulating them was a Jewish method of spiritual growth two millennia before *The Inner Game of Tennis*. Much of the Talmud is devoted to recounting anecdotes from the lives of the sages so that later generations could model their behavior after them. The idea is not to mimic holy people, since Hashem is not into carbon copies, but rather to recognize a clear ideal and to strive toward it. Following in the footsteps of the great does not require wearing the same size shoe but only walking in the same direction.

For example, Rabbi Yochanan ben Zakkai, the greatest sage of his era, was so humble that the Talmud informs us that he always greeted everyone he passed without waiting to be greeted first. Two thousand years later, whether we're taking a Shabbos walk around our neighborhood or circulating during a Bar Mitzvah, we're supposed to remember Rabbi Yochanan's example and emulate it (men greeting men and women greeting women, of course).

We may not become a world tennis champion, but we can at least get the ball over the net.

The Person You Could Have Been

*T*he Jewish concept of Gehinnom is that after the soul leaves the body and ascends to the spiritual worlds, it encounters a fearsome being: the person it could have been. This person looks a lot like him, but is kinder, less judgmental, more patient, less self-centered, more generous, less lazy, and more truthful. Burning regrets over unrealized potential are the real fires of Gehinnom.

The good news is that as long as you're breathing, it's not too late to become the person you could have been. That's what the period from Rosh Hashanah to Yom Kippur is all about. The imperative to do *teshuvah* means: Become the person you could have been.

This is the method of *teshuvah* endorsed by the Rambam. He says to visualize your ideal self, and then formulate specific steps for how to get from here to there.

The same concept is embodied in the Talmudic recommendation to adopt a higher level of religious observance during the "Ten Days of *Teshuvah*" between Rosh Hashanah and Yom Kippur *even if you know that you can't maintain that level all year.* While some would regard such observance as hypocritical, the sages understood that even temporarily living on a higher level shows a person what he/she is capable of achieving. The ideal lingers even after the behavior has sagged. And the memory of the ideal percolating in one's subconscious can have a transformative effect.

Imitating Hashem

On a much higher level, the Torah commands us to emulate the most exalted ideal: Hashem. "… and you shall go in His ways." [*Deuteronomy* 28:9]

How can human beings possibly know the ways of the infinite God? The Torah tells us that after the sin of the golden calf, Moses ascended Mount Sinai a second time and pleaded for Divine forgiveness. Hashem revealed to Moses His "Thirteen Attributes of Mercy." [*Exodus* 34:6-7] These include compassion, kindness, patience, and truthfulness.

The "Thirteen Attributes of Mercy" are recited whenever Jews seek to bring down Divine forgiveness. They form the crux of the penitential prayers (*Selichos*) recited by Sephardic Jews every night starting a month before Rosh Hashanah and by Ashkenazic Jews starting the Motza'ei Shabbos before Rosh Hashanah and continuing until Yom Kippur.

While the Thirteen Attributes of Hashem can be recited out loud only in the presence of a *minyan*, a Jew can and should meditate on these Divine qualities when alone, especially during this time of year. They provide the ultimate role model that Jews should strive to emulate.

In fact, the great 16th-century Kabbalist, Rabbi Moshe Cordovero, in his seminal work, *Tomer Devorah,* takes the prophet Micah's rendition of the Thirteen Attributes and explains how human beings can emulate them in their own lives. Many Jews follow the custom of studying this *sefer* during the High Holy Day period.

Heroes and Friends

Is it possible that the decline of morality in secular Western society — from corporate stealing to post-hurricane New Orleans looting — is due to the dearth of positive role models? John F. Kennedy was popularly considered the last of the great American heroes. When negative reports surfaced posthumously, pundits mourned that there are no more heroes. Now, instead of exemplars, America has only rock stars; instead of role models, America has only mega models.

Judaism has always had, and still has, heroes. These are the *tzaddikim*, the holy men and women whose deeds can have a transforming effect on anyone who bothers to observe them and emulate them. Tales of the *tzaddikim* have been a staple of Jewish literature from time immemorial.

Here's a two-step Jewish process for self-improvement:

> **1. Read biographies of *tzaddikim*.** *A search through Jewish bookstores or websites will yield dozens of such biographies.*

Emulating an ideal includes two possibilities: Emulate the ordinary actions of great people or the great actions of ordinary people. Thus, step number two is:

> **2. Associate with people who are spiritually one notch higher than you.** *Make friends with them. Live near them. Hang out with them. Watch them and emulate them. Pirkei Avos teaches: "Who is wise? One who learns from all people." Friends do not have to be famous tzaddikim for you to learn from their best traits.*
>
> • *From my friend Pamela I learned that it's possible to love complete strangers.*

- *From my friend Chasya Batya I learned that it's possible to consistently put others first.*
- *From my friend Penny I learned that it's possible to give without looking for payback.*
- *From my friend Uriela I learned that it's possible to respond to situations with forethought and deliberation.*
- *From my mother-in-law I learned that calling people, "dear," even El Al operators on the phone, makes them feel beloved.*
- *From my husband I'm still learning that it's possible to think before reacting, and that the longer I think, the better the reaction will be.*

The point of both the above steps is to allow these examples to affect us on the level of motivation, not just inspiration. Observing the great deeds and character traits of others should expand our own vistas of what we, too, can become. *Teshuvah* is the art of the possible.

This method is undermined by the raspy voice that whispers in our ear: "Who do you think you are? How pretentious to attempt to be like _____!"

The difference between pretension and aspiration is the difference between pretending to have reached the goal and striving to get there. Failure to recognize one's infinite Divine potential is not humility but blindness.

An acorn is not an oak tree, but it's not a stone either.

Yom Kippur: Whom We Hurt

A doctor at Tel Aviv's Ichilov Hospital had just told 18-year-old Polina Vallis, one of the teenagers injured three months before in the terrorist bombing at the Dolphinarium Discotheque that killed 21 people, that her legs would be deformed for life. Polina had spent a half hour crying on a bench outside the hospital.

Now we were on our way to Jerusalem, where Israel's foremost plastic surgeon had just agreed to give Polina a second opinion, that very day — at no cost.

Unfamiliar with Tel Aviv, I had managed to get us lost en route to the Ayalon Expressway. We were stalled in bumper-to-bumper traffic, approaching a huge intersection where I had no idea in which direction to drive. I lowered my window and asked the driver of the white Renault to my left how to get on the Ayalon.

"Turn left at this light, I'll let you into my lane. Then right at the next light, then right again," he was telling me.

Meanwhile the car behind me, a crimson Subaru, honked to let me know that traffic was moving again. But I had not finished getting the directions. By the time I moved forward, into the left lane ahead of the Renault, the light had turned red.

The Subaru, now on our right, drove up beside us. Its driver started to shout imprecations at us, directly into Polina's passenger seat window, for making him miss the light. I lifted both my palms upwards in a helpless gesture meant to convey that I had no choice; I didn't know which way to go. The driver, a man with graying hair, continued to berate us with agitated gestures.

Polina, suppressing tears, sat gazing at him in silence. I thought to myself, "If this man knew that the girl he is venting his anger on is one of the wounded from the Dolphinarium, he would be mortified."

Just then there was a tapping at my window. The middle-aged driver of the Renault had gotten out of his car to give us more explicit directions. As I thanked him, I thought to myself: "If this man knew that his kindness was benefiting one of the wounded from the Dolphinarium, he would be gratified."

The light turned green, and we each drove off in our separate ways.

Who Suffers?

The Torah prohibits verbally oppressing a widow or an orphan. [*Exodus* 22:24] Rashi comments that the prohibition extends to hurting anyone with words; the Torah specifies widows and orphans only because they are the most commonly recognized sufferers. In fact, the commentators explain, all persons suffer, therefore we must be careful in how we speak to everyone.

This insight, that we must refrain from speaking harshly to all because we do not know their inner anguish, is even more relevant today, in our anonymous urban lives, than to the inhabitants of close-knit Biblical villages.

The salesclerk who acted impatiently with us may be having *shalom bayis* problems. The upstairs neighbor who turned on his CD player at midnight may have just returned from visiting his terminally ill mother in the hospital. The employee who made a stupid mistake may have just received bad news about downsizing in his firm. The friend who is inconsiderate may be preoccupied with financial problems of which we have no inkling.

This is not to exonerate anyone for his or her misbehavior. All human beings are accountable for their actions — even under duress. But knowing that our upstairs neighbor just came from his mother's deathbed should affect the tone we use when we ask him to lower the volume.

The Day of Truth

Most of our interactions are with people whose private pain is hidden from us. Several months ago Aish.com carried an article by Mara Frei Goldblatt. Mara had made *aliyah* from America and was living with her husband Danny and 2-year-old daughter Rachel in a small town on the edge of the Judean desert. One night an Arab terrorist entered their house through the sliding glass door, slit Danny's throat, and stabbed Mara, who was expecting, numerous times, killing her unborn child. Mara survived, a 20-something widow with physical and emotional scars to last a lifetime.

In the article, Mara, now remarried with twins, relates an incident that took place in an indoor playground in Israel. A quarrelsome 6-year-old boy had jumped on her babies. Perhaps over-reacting from a place of understandable vulnerability, Mara picked up the boy and roughly removed him from her crying toddlers. The boy's grandfather, a veteran Israeli, upbraided her, and an argument ensued. The grandfather let Mara know that she was a spoiled American, who had contributed little to Israel compared to his self-sacrificing generation, who had drained the swamps and fought the wars.

As a reader, I was horrified at the image of this man publicly berating Mara, who, as a maimed widow with an orphaned daughter, had probably suffered much more than he had in pursuit of the Zionist dream.

"If only he could see my scars, I thought to myself," wrote Mara. "If only we had the ability to see into other people's background and thus be able to appreciate their position. That's what I really wanted to say to this gentleman and to all the onlookers."

Mara chose to say nothing. In the five years since her husband was murdered, she has struggled to free herself from the self-definition of a victim. So, some time later, she approached the man and apologized for being rough with his grandson. He accepted the apology and walked away, oblivious to who the object of his calumny really was.

Our sages teach us that our oblivion, our unawareness of the full ramifications of every harsh word and action, lasts only until the day of death. Then every soul stands in judgment and is made to witness, nay experience, the unedited video of his or her own life.

The grandfather of Mara's story will see the scene again, but this time without the space-and-time blinders of this physical world. He will see Mara and the wounds of her body and her heart with perfect clarity, and he will see how his imperious words flung salt onto those wounds.

How will he feel? That is precisely what Gehinnom is: the inner inferno of remorse when we realize the full scope of the injury we have wrought. No external fire can compare in burning intensity to the regret we will each feel when we perceive the suffering we ourselves have caused.

Yom Kippur

We do not have to wait until the day of death to face and deal with all our harsh words, all our abusive actions. Hashem has given us the gift of Yom Kippur, a day that has the potential to wipe clean our slates.

During the days before Yom Kippur, we are bidden to examine our interactions of the previous year: to remember the times we spoke in anger, the insults that seemed so justified, the scathing criticisms we leveled, the sarcastic jibes we uttered against victims whose inner topography was hidden behind the opaque wall of our cognitive limitations.

Logically, there should be no way to eradicate the hurtful mistakes of our past. But *teshuvah*, repentance, is a miracle. If we go through all the steps of the *teshuvah* process, then on Yom Kippur Hashem grants us the unbelievable gift of atonement. It is as if Hashem presses the "delete" button, and all the murky mess on our soul's screen disappears.

But the miraculous process of *teshuvah*, of fixing the past as well as the future, can come only when we admit the harm we have done and feel regret for the enormity of the damage. All sin, by definition, damages our relationship with Hashem. All sin, by definition, distances us from realizing our true potential. Interpersonal sins, in addition, hurt other people, usually much more than we had intended to hurt them.

Without the Ash Coating

On the morning of 9/11, my friend Amita was walking from her Greenwich Village home to her office on Wall Street. She passed people who had fled from the World Trade Center.

At the moment that the first tower collapsed, to the horror and anguish of everyone who witnessed it, one ash-covered woman cried out loudly. Her husband worked in that building. Amita immediately held her hands and spoke to her in soothing tones: "We don't know anything yet. You work in the other tower, and you were evacuated immediately. You are here safe. God-willing, your husband is safe somewhere else." Compassion was Amita's immediate and instinctual response.

The massive tragedy has left in its wake tens of thousands of mourners across America and the world: bereaved parents, spouses, children, siblings, and friends. In the coming months, they will not be recognizable by a coating of ash when they sit across a desk from you or stand on the other side of a sales counter. How will you make sure that you do not add to their pain with a harsh word? Only by resolving to observe the Torah's commandment to entirely refrain from harsh speech — no matter how justified.

Had the driver of the red Subaru known how vulnerable and distressed the girl in the passenger seat was, his heart would no doubt clench in remorse for his diatribe. The Torah instructs us that all human beings are vulnerable. For this new year, let's earnestly strive to hurt no one with our words.

Yom Kippur: Through the Gate of Tears

After crying intermittently for 36 hours, ever since the eerie wail of ambulance sirens carrying the dead and wounded from the terror attack at the Hillel Café woke me up last Tuesday night, I thought I had no more tears to shed. Then I saw the picture of the wedding dress.

It appeared in an Israeli newspaper — a photo of a long, white, taffeta and chiffon gown, hanging forlornly on a hanger on the door of the bride's bedroom closet, because the 20-year-old bride, Nava Appelbaum, is clothed in a shroud instead. Nava was buried together with her father, Rabbi Dr. David Appelbaum, on the day that was supposed to be her wedding day.

The photo next to it shows Nava's fiancé Chanan Sand beside Nava's open grave, holding the wedding ring he had intended to place on her finger. He placed it instead on her lifeless corpse as it was lowered into the grave.

There are other pictures in that day's newspaper: a picture of the handsome, smiling 39-year-old Yaakov Ben Shabbat, who was killed in Tuesday's terrorist attack outside the Tzirfin army base. He had left work early in order to purchase a cake for his 8-year-old daughter's birthday.

There's a photo of a bereft, crying 12-year-old, Moshe Sapir, being supported by relatives at the funeral of his mother, killed while sipping coffee with her friend at the Hillel Café.

There's a picture of the weeping, anguished parents of 22-year-old Alon Mizrachi, the guard at the Hillel Café, who fell on the terrorist, struggled with him, and was blown up with him.

In my newspaper, however, the page with the most tear stains is the one with the photo of the wedding dress. The tragedy of Nava Appelbaum is the most wrenching of all of Tuesday's fifteen victims because it represents all that could have been — that came so close to being — but was not: the joy of the two sets of parents, the jubilation of the young couple, the union they had planned and waited for, and the rejoicing of the 500 guests who were invited to the wedding and attended the bride's funeral instead.

I look around me and see on the tear-stained faces of everyone I meet that we, the broken and bleeding Jews of Israel, who have sustained over 800 losses during the three years of the Oslo War, are decimated by the pain of holy Nava's aborted wedding.

Tears on the Days of Awe

*J*ews are supposed to cry on Rosh Hashanah and Yom Kippur. Rabbi Avigdor Nebanzahl wrote that if the Jewish people would cry tears of repentance on Rosh Hashanah, when all the occurrences of the subsequent year are determined, we would not have to cry tears of grief throughout the year.

It's hard to summon tears of repentance. What we did throughout the year — in terms of others and Hashem and ourselves — may not have been exemplary, but was it really so bad? I feel a twinge of guilt when I remember speaking harshly to someone, but should I shed tears over that little misdemeanor? I regret my impatience with my husband and children, but, after all, I'm only human.

The sages say that ever since the destruction of the Second *Beis HaMikdash*, the "gate of prayer" is closed, but the "gate of tears" is always open. What is the secret to accessing the well of tears?

Starting at the onset of Elul, the month before Rosh Hashanah, and culminating in Yom Kippur, Jews are bidden to examine their deeds and "do *teshuvah*." The word *teshuvah*, usually translated as repentance, means "returning." We are supposed to return to Hashem and to some improved version of ourselves. The term is fraught with irony; most of us have never even visited the spiritual level we aspire to "return" to.

Teshuvah means not a sudden change of lifestyle, but a determined change of direction. If I was proceeding southward, now I turn around and take my first sure steps eastward. *Teshuvah* entails making a concrete plan to actualize change in small but steady increments.

The Gap

The prospect of *teshuvah* frightens many of us, because we consider it a calumny against who we already are. The English term "repentance" implies that I am a despicable sinner, loathsome in my own eyes and in the eyes of Hashem, sullied by my actions, like a filthy, smelly vagrant in need of a bath.

Rebbetzin Tziporah Heller points out the true Jewish attitude toward *teshuvah:* Not, "How wicked I am because I did that," but rather, "How could someone like *me* have done something like *that?*" *Teshuvah* is an affirmation, not a rejection, of our highest self. Rather than being characterized by our lowly actions, we repudiate our lowly actions as being unworthy of the holy souls we inherently are.

We cry on Rosh Hashanah and Yom Kippur when we reflect on what we could have been, when we compare our majestic potential to our shabby reality. Every one of us has the potential to be spiritually great, to perfectly accomplish our unique task in this world, to valiantly meet our challenges, and to dexterously fix our shortcomings. On the High Holy Days, we reflect on the perfected vision of ourselves, and cry over the mediocrity we permitted in its place.

- *We could have been magnanimous. Instead we were petty.*
- *We could have been generous. Instead we were stingy.*
- *We could have been honest. Instead we told self-serving lies.*
- *We could have buoyed up others with kind words. Instead we wounded them with deprecations.*
- *We could have esteemed our parents for their ongoing contribution to our lives. Instead we made them feel useless and behind the times.*

- We could have made our homes sanctuaries of love and peace. Instead we degenerated into bickering and blaming.
- We could have spent our spare time studying the profundities of the Torah. Instead we opted for schmoozing and wasting time.
- We could have dressed with the dignity of a "daughter of the King." Instead we dressed with an eye to fashion and peer pressure.
- We could have become the person Hashem created us to be. Instead we settled for a mediocre imitation.

My friend Sarah Friedman taught me to visualize what she calls "my full potential self." This is the perfected image of myself in all its details. I see the way my full potential self walks, the gentle, soothing tone with which she speaks, the warm smile she gives to everyone she encounters, the delicate touch with which she caresses the world.

While each of us has a unique "full potential self," the Torah delineates the general form of every Jew's full potential self: it does not speak ill of others, nor embarrass others, nor afflict others with words or actions; it respects the property of others; it controls untoward passions; it honors parents; it is scrupulously honest in business; etc.

The "sins" we do *teshuvah* for on Rosh Hashanah and Yom Kippur are the instances we fell short of our full potential self. One word for "sin" in Hebrew is *cheit,* which means "missing the mark." The disparity between our full potential and our present reality fuels our heartfelt *teshuvah.*

Too Late

The culprit that keeps us from crying over our failures is the sense that we have all the time in the world to fix them. Twenty years ago I had a plaque on my desk that proclaimed: "Be patient. God isn't finished with me yet." Unfortunately, patience — a sterling trait when applied to others — can degenerate into complacency when applied to ourselves. Such an attitude depletes our spiritual quest of energy and urgency. Instead of hastening to actualize our inner goals, we amble.

Personally, I find that I never finish any project that doesn't have a deadline. The Jewish calendar gives us a deadline for *teshuvah:* Rosh Hashanah. Then Hashem in His mercy grants us a ten-day extension. Yom Kippur is the final deadline.

The *U'Nesaneh Tokef* prayer of the High Holy Day liturgy declares: "On Rosh Hashanah it is inscribed and on Yom Kippur it is sealed … who will live and who will die, who will die at his predestined time and who not at his predestined time, who by water and who by fire, who by sword, who by beast, who by famine, who by storm …"

Rosh Hashanah forces us to confront the truth that we do not have all the time in the world, for two reasons: The other people in our lives will not always be here; and we will not always be here.

The relationships we need to mend can be mended only as long as the other person is alive. The place in the Yom Kippur service where I shed the most profuse tears is the line in the *Vidui,* "For the sin I have committed before You in devaluing parents and teachers." Both my parents have gone to the Next World. Now there is no way to fix the words uttered with an exasperated tone, the conversations with them curtly curtailed for "more important" obligations. My ability to do complete *teshuvah* on this relationship was buried with my parents.

The other illusion that makes us procrastinate in doing *teshuvah* is our failure to face our own mortality. One searing lesson we Jews in Israel have learned from this war of terror is the fragility of life. I venture to say that not one of us is sure he or she will be here next Rosh Hashanah — or tomorrow.

Our friends Reuven and Gila live in the town of Efrat. During the first year of the Oslo War, the "tunnels road" to Efrat was an intermittent target of terrorist gunfire. Several people were killed on that road. One evening Reuven was driving home while talking to Gila on his cell phone. They started to argue about something. Suddenly Reuven realized he was on the "tunnels road." He abruptly ended the argument, saying, "I'm driving on the 'tunnels road' now. How would we feel if the last conversation we ever had was an argument?"

Ultimately, we are all driving on the "tunnels road." For all we know — given the exigencies of accidents, heart attacks, and terror attacks — every conversation could be our last. What a tragedy it would be if our last encounter in this world ends up being an argument, a nasty complaint, a sarcastic joke, a petty criticism …

Two millennia ago the sage Hillel taught: "If not now, when?" If I don't actualize my potential now, who knows if I will have another chance? If I don't fix my bad traits now, in this world, which the Kabbalists called, "the world of fixing," I might very well be buried with my shortcomings.

Death is the final, unbridgeable chasm between what could have been and what is. The ultimate agony is the remorse each of us will feel when we find ourselves in the "other world," totally unable to fix any of our flaws or failures. This is the Jewish definition of Gehinnom.

The Kittel

*Y*om Kippur is a miraculous gift Hashem gives us every year. Hashem's offer is too good to refuse: If we do *teshuvah,* He will give us *kapparah,* atonement. This means that He will press the "delete" button on the actions and patterns that entrap us. When the shofar blows at the end of Yom Kippur, we are, for that moment, our full potential self.

Of course, we are able post-Yom Kippur to lapse into old patterns of behavior, to pick up where we left off, to change directions back again. But on Yom Kippur itself, if we have done *teshuvah,* Hashem lifts us up and moves us over the chasm between who we are and who we truly want to be.

According to Jewish tradition, one's wedding day is like Yom Kippur. The bride and groom fast, *daven* the prayers of Yom Kippur, and are forgiven all their sins. When they stand under the wedding canopy, they are in a state of pristine perfection.

Orthodox grooms wear a long-sleeved, knee-length white garment called a *kittel.* The *kittel* is worn for the first time at the wedding, then on Yom Kippur and Pesach, and finally as a burial shroud.

It is possible to be spiritually great. It is possible to be as pure and exalted on the day of death as on Yom Kippur or the wedding day. Rabbi Dr. David Appelbaum, who, with selfless dedication, single-handedly changed the face of emergency medicine in Jerusalem, did it. Nava Appelbaum, who lovingly, joyfully cared for juvenile cancer patients, did it. For such individuals, the shroud and the wedding garment are one.

Chanukah: The Capture of Saddam

The headline of the *International Herald Tribune* screamed: **DEVIL IN THE DETAILS: A FIBER BETRAYS SADDAM.** The article went on to report how the most wanted man of the year had been found when an American soldier, combing the area for a second time, noticed a tiny tuft of fiber protruding from the dirt. "Only a sliver of a mat was evident under the dirt where he was standing. But the soldier thought it was strange." When he yanked at the mat, he uncovered the hole in the ground where Saddam Hussein was hiding.

Reading the account, I was intrigued. Had the soldier not paid attention to that tiny detail, the dramatic capture would never have happened. Yet details generally get bad press in modern Western culture. Focusing on picayune details, nit-picking, and fastidiousness are all considered symptomatic of small minds. Big minds, according to secular culture, see the big picture.

In fact, the most oft-repeated charge against Torah Judaism is that it is too concerned with the details. Why not observe

Shabbos, goes the argument, by simply resting? Don't go to work and don't clean the garage, have dinner with the family and relax on the deck. Why have so many detailed *halachos* — no writing, no cooking, no completing an electrical circuit, no washing out a stain in your best white blouse, etc.? Isn't Judaism missing the forest for the trees?

Perhaps this scorn for detail-consciousness is reserved only for religion. No one ever blames a nuclear physicist for focusing on itsy-bitsy particles. No one ever tells a painter of the school of Super Realism to discard his tiny brush and just paint wide swatches of color. No one ever castigates the builders of jet planes for paying too much attention to details. Where religion is concerned, however, only grand, sweeping ideas are appreciated.

The truth is that everyone living in the age of microbes and sub-atomic particles knows that something invisible to the naked eye can make the difference between life and death. The issue is not size, but whether the object in question can be observed at all. The ancient Greek method of discovering truth, on which all secular people were raised, is: observation, understanding, conclusions. Therefore, as long as something can be observed, even if only by a high-power electron microscope or by inference from the movement of other observable bodies, it is real.

Spiritual entities such as Hashem and the soul, on the other hand, are not observable by any physical means. From the Greek point of view, therefore, they are illusory. The war between the Greeks and the Jews that forms the backdrop of Chanukah was really a *Kulturkampf* that only toward the end turned into a military battle. The Greeks believed that reality is primarily physical. The Jews believed that reality is essentially spiritual, with a veneer of physicality.

These competing concepts of reality determine which details are worthy of concern. The Greek worldview recognizes that a microscopic virus is a real danger to the body; the Jewish worldview recognizes that a violation of a fine point of Torah law is a real danger to the soul.

Dark Energy

*C*hanukah is an appropriate time to appreciate that there's more to reality than what we can observe with our eyes — or our high-powered instruments. In fact, the latest scientific discoveries, the culmination of the Greek method, seem to bear this out.

A recent *Newsweek* science article deals with "mysterious, theoretical stuff called dark matter." Dark matter has never been observed, and *cannot be observed*, because it doesn't reflect light and barely interacts with anything else. Why then are many physicists convinced that it exists? Because in 1998, astrophysicists discovered that the universe's expansion, which should be gradually slowing down since the Big Bang, instead is accelerating. This phenomenon can be explained only by positing that a "mystery force, called dark energy, may work against gravity, driving the galaxies faster and faster apart."

The truly startling discovery, which deals a knockout blow to the observation-based Greek worldview, is: "Recent data from WMAP [the Wilkinson Microwave Anisotrophy Probe] suggests that dark matter in fact accounts for 90 percent of creation."

What? Ninety percent of the universe is made up of something that cannot be observed by physical means? I checked to make sure I was reading *Newsweek*, and not the Torah.

The Second Lesson

The second lesson I learned from the capture of Saddam Hussein is also a Chanukah allegory. Saddam thought of himself — and built monuments to himself — as the reincarnation of Nebuchadnezzar, the ancient Babylonian emperor who destroyed the First *Beis HaMikdash* in Jerusalem and drove the Jews into exile. Certainly Saddam's compulsion to again destroy the Jewish state made him a worthy successor to the malevolent Nebuchadnezzar.

The image of Saddam, disheveled, dusty, and disguised, climbing out of his hole and obsequiously surrendering to American forces rather than heroically fighting to the death, provides a stark metaphor for the true nature of evil. The Gemara describes evil as a giant standing at the crossroads, fiercely swinging his machete, filling all onlookers with fear. A closer look, however, reveals that the giant has no feet.

Evil has the power to destroy, but it does not have the power to endure. For all its bluster, it always eventually meets an inglorious end. Nothing has proven this as graphically as the downfall of Saddam Hussein.

When people rise up to fight evil, rather than cowering before it, they must somehow believe in the possibility of victory. They must intuit that, despite all appearances, evil ultimately has no feet.

When the aged High Priest Mattisyahu, with the help of his sons and his friends, launched his rebellion against the mighty Greek empire, no objective observer would have credited him with any chance of success. Who could have imagined that one day this meager Jewish fighting force would drive the invincible Greek army out of Jerusalem, out of the *Beis HaMikdash*, and eventually out of the land? Somehow Mattisyahu must have believed that the great Greek army had no feet.

The Chanukah liturgy extols Hashem: "You delivered the strong into the hands of the weak, the many into the hands of the few ..." Chanukah is the triumph of the small over the great, of the unperceivable over the apparent.

Which brings us back to details. The miracle of the oil, which we commemorate by lighting the Chanukah candles, is a celebration of focusing on the details. In the vast recesses of the Temple storerooms, amid the chaos following the battle, amid countless cruses of profaned olive oil, one person — perhaps one soldier — noticed a single cruse of oil with the seal of the High Priest still intact. The sages assert that finding that one unsullied cruse was in itself a miracle.

The *Herald Tribune* got it wrong. It's not the devil, but rather Hashem, Who is in the details.

Purim: Unmasking the Divine

Nineteen years ago, during my first month living in Israel, I was riding a bus up Jerusalem's main thoroughfare, Jaffa Road. The bus stopped for a red light, and I gazed out the window. I saw an elderly, overweight woman trudging up the hill, shlepping many large bags. A beggar was sitting on the pavement, his hand outstretched. The old woman stopped, set her bags down, one at a time, on the sidewalk, rummaged through her purse, took out her wallet, and handed a coin to the beggar. At that point, the light changed and my bus drove off.

Last week, I left my house late for an appointment. Loaded down with bags of empty bottles to recycle at the supermarket after my appointment, I walked as fast as I could toward my car, parked in the Jewish Quarter parking lot, a 5-minute walk from my house. Nearing the parking lot, I passed a beggar woman, her hand outstretched. I had given to this particular woman the week before, but now I was in a hurry and my arms ached from the weight of the bottles. As I raced by her, I called out, "This time I can't. I'm sorry."

I was 5 or 6 meters down the street when I remembered the old woman on Jaffa Road nineteen years before. She was older, heavier, and more overburdened than I, yet she had stopped in her tracks in order to give a beggar a coin. If she could do it, so could I. I turned around, walked back the several meters to the beggar, put all my bags down with a clank, rummaged through my purse for my wallet, and gave the woman a shekel coin. She smiled and heaped blessings upon me.

Three-Dimensional Actions

*E*very action a human being does has three dimensions of effect. It affects the performer of the action, like a point on a page. It affects the other person or persons involved, as when a point extends to a line or a square. And it affects those who witness the action, indeed the whole society, as when a square swells into a cube.

For example, if A steals money from B, A affects himself; his own level of honesty and integrity is diminished. He also affects B, who is not only out that amount of money, but whose level of trust is now diminished. In addition, he affects whoever witnesses or hears of the theft, for stealing is now added to their concept of possible human behavior. The more thefts they witness or hear about, the more the "possible" becomes the "normal."

This third effect actually encompasses not only those individuals who witness or hear about the theft, but the whole society. Growing up in the 1950's and 1960's in America, I never saw a store with anti-shoplifting detectors at the exit. The plastic tags attached to every garment in every clothing store today did not exist. People could pay for their purchases by check without having to provide three different proofs of identity. What happened?

Individuals started to steal. Each and every theft chipped away at the standard of honesty in American society. What was once idiosyncratic became the norm. In this same way, every action performed by every individual, subtly but tangibly, affects the whole.

Judaism has two words that embody this concept. *Kiddush Hashem* means those actions that reveal Hashem's presence in the world. *Chillul Hashem* means those actions that hide Hashem's presence.

Whenever a human being performs an act of integrity, honesty, kindness, compassion, or self-sacrifice, he/she is revealing Godliness in the world. *Kiddush Hashem* literally means "sanctifying the Divine Name." Although the term is most often used to describe grand, heroic deeds, such as when Jews have chosen death rather than forsaking their religion, it applies as well to any action that reveals Hashem in the world.

The old woman on Jaffa Road stopping to give the beggar a coin performed a *kiddush Hashem.* By revealing her capacity for kindness despite the hassle involved, she made me aware of my own capacity to choose kindness over convenience. She raised my standard of "How much am I willing to trouble myself to help someone?" Since kindness is an attribute of Hashem, more kindness in society means a greater revelation of Hashem in the world.

Conversely, whenever a human being performs an act of meanness, cruelty, avarice, dishonesty, or selfishness, he/she is hiding Hashem's presence in this world. *Chillul* comes from the Hebrew word for "empty space"; a *chillul Hashem* makes the world seem empty of Hashem.

Every action is a stone thrown into an infinite pond; the ripples it causes go out in ever greater circles, endlessly.

Nineteen years ago, an elderly woman on Jaffa Road put down her bundles to give a beggar a coin. She had no idea she was being observed. Nineteen years later, inspired by that old woman, I walked back 5 meters and set down my bags in order to give a beggar a coin. I have no idea whether I was being observed ...

The King's Feast

Revealing and hiding the Divine is the essence of Purim. We usually view the Purim story in terms of its mega-heroes: Esther, Mordechai, Achashverosh, and Haman. Yet the sages attribute the catalyst for the decree of doom to the common Jews, who were guilty of *chillul Hashem*.

The Book of Esther begins by describing a lavish feast thrown by King Achashverosh for his subjects. Like everyone else, the Jewish citizens of the realm attended. The sages assert that the genocidal decree against the Jews that Haman later enacted (with the approval of the king) was the result of ordinary Jews attending the feast.

According to the Gemara, King Achashverosh was celebrating the conclusion of seventy years since the beginning of the exile from Judea. Since the prophet Jeremiah had prophesied that the Babylonian exile would last for seventy years (counting from the destruction of the First Temple, not from the initial stage of the exile), Achashverosh concluded (wrongly) that the victory over the Jews could now be deemed complete and final. For his celebratory feast, he used the sacred vessels from the *Beis HaMikdash*, and came dressed in the garments of the High Priest.

The sages are quick to point out that kosher food was served to the Jewish citizens. No laws of the Torah were transgressed at the feast. Yet, the sages maintain, the punishment for attending was a decree of extermination from which the Jews only narrowly escaped. Why?

Attendance at King Achashverosh's banquet was a *chillul Hashem*. While the *Beis HaMikdash* and its vessels were intended to sanctify the mundane components of the physical world, Achashverosh's feast did precisely the opposite: By using the sacred vessels for mundane purposes, the festivities degraded that which was holy. The Jews should have responded to this sacrilege by mourning and distancing themselves. Instead, the temptation to attend a party at the palace overcame them. Their attendance was an implicit endorsement of Achashverosh's worldview, a world in which Hashem was conspicuously absent.

According to the Mishnah, *chillul Hashem* is the hardest sin for which to atone, because, by its very nature, its effect is so widespread that it is virtually impossible to undo the damage. Once the stone has been thrown into the pond, who could possibly stop the ripples?

Unmasking the Divine

The Book of Esther is the only book in the Bible where Hashem is never mentioned. The sages explain that that epoch, immediately after the destruction of the First Temple, signaled a monumental change in the way Hashem relates to His world. The *Beis HaMikdash* itself (and before that the

Tabernacle) was a medium of Divine revelation. When the Temple was destroyed (because of rampant sin), Hashem entered a mode of hiddenness. In fact, the Divine Hand shapes the entire Purim story, but it is concealed in the guise of "coincidence," "luck," and the natural unfolding of events.

"Hiddenness" is an essential characteristic of Hashem in this world. Even the Hebrew word for "world" — *"olam"* — comes from the root word meaning "hidden." From the time of the Purim story until today, our challenge in this world is to uncover the Divine hiding behind the appearances of our everyday world.

The term for that is *kiddush Hashem.* Every time we choose generosity, kindness, truth, or integrity we are revealing Hashem in this world. We are unmasking the Divine.

Every time we choose meanness, pettiness, harshness, or dishonesty, we camouflage Hashem and add another layer to the Divine camouflage. This generates a *chillul Hashem.* We create a world where, for ourselves and everyone around us, Hashem is missing.

The climax of the Purim story takes place when Queen Esther, risking her life to do so, invites King Achashverosh and his viceroy, the debonair and courtly Haman, to a private dinner in her quarters. There Queen Esther reveals the plot of genocide against her and her people. The king, outraged, demands to know who is the culprit behind the plot. In one of the most dramatic flourishes in Scripture, Queen Esther points to Haman and exposes his true identity: "A vile man! An enemy! This evil Haman!"

Purim is about hiddenness, shrouded identities, and beguiling appearances. It challenges us to reveal the truth, like Queen Esther did. Unlike Queen Esther, however, we point not at the villain, but at the Divine. "Here He is ... behind what happened to me today." "Here He is ... behind the beauty of nature." "Here He is ... behind the newspaper headlines."

At every moment, we can reveal Hashem either by identifying Him or emulating Him. Our models are Queen Esther pointing her finger and the elderly woman setting down her bundles. We don't have to be an illustrious personage to reveal Hashem in this world.

Purim: Hidden Miracles

The Book of Esther is the only book in the Bible that does not mention Hashem. After 3,000 years of Biblical history where Hashem speaks to a cast of characters from Adam to Job, appears in dreams, works sensational miracles, reveals Himself at Sinai, and sends His prophets with explicit messages for the people and the kings of Israel, suddenly . . . a story without Hashem.

Or is it?

The Book of Esther takes place six decades after the destruction of the First Temple. This cataclysmic event changed the way that Hashem relates to human beings. While the *Beis HaMikdash* brought the Divine Presence into explicit manifestation (witness the ten open miracles everyone could see there), with its destruction, the Divine Presence receded into a state of hiddenness. The sages called this new (and still prevailing) *modus operandi* "hester panim," meaning "hidden face," from the same root word as the name *Esther*. *Megillas Esther*, the scroll of Esther, can as well be translated: the scroll of hiddenness.

If someone is hiding, it means he is there, but you can't see him. Nevertheless, certain signs, such as a bulge in the curtain, may hint at his whereabouts. The Book of Esther is full of coincidences, the right person "happening" to be in the right place at the right time, and dramatic, unexpected reversals of fortune. These are the bulges in the curtain that hint at the Divine orchestration of events. A witness can choose to attribute such serendipitous happenings to "luck" or to Hashem.

Our challenge since the destruction of the First Temple is to find Hashem hiding behind the curtain of history, to identify the Divine hand behind current events, and to recognize Hashem's direction in the seemingly fortuitous occurrences of our own lives.

Coincidence?

To give an example of a hidden miracle in my own family's life: My cousin Larry and his wife Ruth were married for several years when they realized that they could not have children. Longing for a family, they adopted a baby. Randi was a beautiful child, with blond hair and big blue eyes, but soon it became apparent that she suffered from a chronic breathing problem that required constant medical care, tests, and periodic chest X-rays, all of which posed a burden and strain on the whole family.

Years passed. Meanwhile Larry and Ruth had adopted a second child. Then, much to their surprise and delight, Ruth found out that she was expecting. This precious news resulted in the birth of Amy, a healthy and robust baby.

Ruth naturally took Amy with her wherever she went. When the baby was about one year old, Ruth took Randi for one of her regular chest X-rays. While they waited for Randi's turn, Ruth decided that, since Amy was coughing and they were going through this whole rigmarole anyway, she might as well also have the baby's chest X-rayed.

Amy's X-ray revealed that she had a rare and fatal cancer.

Because they caught it so early, before the baby was even symptomatic, they were able to effect a total cure. Almost three decades later, Amy is married and has her own baby.

The Six-Day War

*S*uch camouflaged sequences of Divine action also take place on the national level.

In May 1967, Egyptian and Syrian troops massed on Israel's borders, Egypt closed the Straits of Tiran to Israeli shipping, and Egyptian president Gamel Abdal Nasser filled the airwaves with calls to drive the Jews into the sea. The mood in the nineteen-year-old country of Israel was bleak. Facing five well-equipped, Soviet-trained Arab armies, Israel's defeat was virtually a foregone conclusion. The black humor on everyone's lips that spring was: "The last one out, don't forget to turn off the lights."

Everyone knows that instead of defeat, Israel achieved a stunning victory. On June 5 at 7:46 a.m., Israeli planes destroyed the entire Egyptian air force on the ground. In six days, Israel tripled its territory, gaining the Sinai Peninsula, the Golan Heights, the West Bank, and — most precious of all — the Old City and the Temple Mount.

The crucial strategy of destroying the Egyptian air force while their planes were still on the ground opened the way for the Israeli victory. The success of the maneuver is generally attributed to the Israeli planes flying below the tracking altitude of Egyptian radar. Many other factors, however, contributed to the success of the air strike and the subsequent battles. In fact, the coincidences and unlikely happenings at precisely the right time were so plentiful that, as we learn the details of the victory, the bulge in the curtain almost knocks us over.

For example, a few days before the war, the commander of Egyptian forces in the Sinai was ordered to change commanders in most of his brigades, putting in charge officers who did not know the terrain or their forces.

On the very morning of June 5, three hours before the Israeli air strike, Egyptian intelligence did in fact issue a warning that an Israeli air attack would begin "within minutes." At that point, Egypt still had time to get its aircraft off the ground and save them. The message reached the command bunker in Cairo. An aide-de-camp signed a copy, but no one bothered to look for the commander-in-chief.

On the same morning of the attack, Egyptian officers stationed at the radar station in northern Jordan picked up the scrambling Israeli aircraft, and sent a red alert message to Cairo. The sergeant in the decoding room of the supreme command attempted to decipher the message using the previous day's code and failed.

And where was Egypt's commander-in-chief? The night before, he and most of his top officers had attended a party at an air force base in the northern delta area, at which a renowned dancer performed. Early the next morning, he took off for the Sinai, where he had ordered all his top commanders to assemble in order to meet a high-level Iraqi delegation. When the Israeli strike happened, not one senior officer was at his post.

Today's Miracles

The daily news in Israel is replete with miracles. The latest took place on February 8, when a car bomb packed with a whopping 15 kilos of explosives blew up in a narrow street in the densely populated religious neighborhood of Meah Shearim. According to eyewitnesses, debris from the explosion soared 150 meters into the air. Yet no one was killed, and only one person was lightly injured.

A few minutes before the car bomb went off, a truck filled with propane gas drove past the parked car. Ten minutes before the explosion, which took place at the height of the local shopping period, a vegetable store directly adjacent to the car closed briefly so its owner could *daven Minchah*. Normally, the wife of the store owner fills in for him during that time, but, when he telephoned his wife to come, she was at a critical point in her Shabbos cooking. By the time she turned off the stove and ran around the corner to open the store, it was a gutted out hole, without even a floor. Only 20 minutes after the bomb went off, dozens of indigent people were scheduled to line up on the adjacent sidewalk for their weekly charity food allocations.

The magnitude of the miracle was so obvious to the local residents that they broke forth in spontaneous singing and dancing and praises of Hashem, which lasted for 2 hours.

The next day, signs went up on every tree and telephone pole enjoining people to recite Psalm 21 in gratitude for the miracle. And a "thanksgiving feast," required by Jewish law when one's life has been saved, was held on the very place in the street where the bomb that had been devised to kill and maim had exploded in its futile blast.

Responding

Some years ago, I read an article about a woman parachutist. On one of her jumps, her parachute failed to open. She pulled the cord for her back-up parachute, but that, too, was defective. As she free-fell thousands of feet toward the solid ground, she was sure she was going to die. Then she landed in a large pool of water, unhurt.

The reporter asked her to what she attributed her improbable survival. She answered with conviction: "Luck."

Hidden miracles operate by the same economics as lactation. The more a baby nurses, the more milk is produced. Similarly, the more we respond appropriately to Hashem's hidden miracles, the more miracles He bestows on us. The converse is also true.

The appropriate response to a miracle is not to say, "Wow! That's amazing!" but rather, "Wow! Hashem's amazing!"

The victory of the Six Day War was so dramatic and unexpected — especially the regaining of the Temple Mount after 2,000 years — that virtually everyone in Israel considered it a Divine miracle. Even the avowedly secular chief of staff Moshe Dayan acknowledged Hashem's hand in the triumph. Coming to the Western Wall the day after its liberation, Dayan, following the prevailing custom, wrote a message and stuffed it into a crevice between the ancient stones of the Wall. As soon as he left, of course, newspaper reporters extricated the note and read it. It contained a line from the Psalms: "From Hashem this emanated. It is wondrous in our eyes."

But finding Hashem in this long, dim era of hiddenness requires both recognizing His hand and remembering what you have seen. Only months after the war, people were already crediting the military prowess of the Israeli Army for the astonishing victory. Banners throughout the country proclaimed a parody of the Biblical verse: *"Yisrael! Yisrael! Betach b'Tzahal!* Israel! Israel! Trust in the I.D.F. [Israel Defense Forces]!"

This attitude, that the might and brilliance of the Israeli Army had saved the day, prevailed until the army's near-defeat during the Yom Kippur war, with its 2,000 casualties and Syrian tanks trampling the Galilee on their way to Haifa. Miracles have to be not only acknowledged, but also responded to in ways that change the beneficiary of the miracle.

Judaism, a religion that abhors the nebulous, instructs us how to respond to miracles in concrete ways. These consist of both praising Hashem publicly and thanking Him in kind: Just as He has been magnanimous to us, so we should be magnanimous to His children.

Thus, a person whose life has been saved should recite *"Bircas HaGomel,"* a blessing of thanksgiving in the presence of a *minyan*. When a car bomb exploded recently in downtown Natanya during the height of the evening shopping hour, and no one was killed, the secular Mayor of Natanya enthused: "We should all say the blessing *Bircat HaGomel.*"

Notice that *Bircas HaGomel* must be recited in public. The point is to publicize what you have experienced. The veil of hiddenness thins every time you reveal Hashem's revelation to you.

That's why the Chanukah menorah must be lit where others can see it, either outside, as we do in Jerusalem, or in a window, or in a public room in front of others. The whole point of that mitzvah is "to publicize the miracle."

If you have experienced a miraculous salvation, such as recovery from a life-threatening illness, you are also enjoined to make a "feast of thanksgiving." This provides an occasion both to relate the miracle to others and to express your gratitude to Hashem, as well as an opportunity to feed other people, just as you have been fed from the largesse of Hashem's kindness.

Other appropriate responses to a miracle are to give charity or to upgrade one's service of Hashem.

Now we can understand the four mitzvos of Purim. We read the Book of Esther not to remember a tale of palace intrigue and Shakespearean-like reversals in ancient Persia, but to publicly acknowledge how Hashem orchestrates events in this post-Temple era. We also make a feast, give charity to the poor, and send two foodstuffs to a friend. Since King Achashverosh's kingdom encompassed virtually the entire Jewish population of that era, every Jew living today (other than converts) is descended from someone who was saved by the hidden miracles of Purim. The appropriate response is these four mitzvos.

Hashem hides in order that we will look for Him — and find Him. Once, as a child playing hide-and-seek, I came upon a great hiding place. I waited and waited for my friends to find me, as my titillation turned to impatience and finally to despair. When, after what seemed like an eternity, I emerged from my hiding place, I found that my friends had given up and gone on to a different game.

Hashem does not despair of human beings. He stands behind the curtain waiting … and waiting … and waiting …

GREAT PEOPLE

More Holy Woman

Eli and Shaya, two yeshivah *bachurim* from England, decided to launch a hi-tech company. Since they had neither financial backing nor experience, they understood how important it was to engage an expert business consultant. The consultant they turned to was a septuagenarian Chassidic woman who lived in Jerusalem. She always wore two housecoats, one atop the other, and a babushka. Her own business experience had consisted of running a dairy farm of eight cows, a venture that had never been particularly profitable. Her name was Rebbetzin Chaya Sara Kramer.

Eli and Shaya called the rebbetzin every week and consulted her about everything. Every month on Rosh Chodesh, Shaya, who had moved to Jerusalem, brought her money. They informed her that she was a partner in their business.

A year and a half after founding their company, Eli and Shaya were sued by a famous American blue-chip corporation. The young entrepreneurs hired lawyers. After reviewing the case, their lawyers informed them that they didn't have a chance of winning against such a large, powerful conglomerate. Disconsolate, Eli and Shaya went to Rebbetzin Chaya Sara and told her their lawyers' prognosis.

Her response was: "Fire your lawyers and fight!"

However doubtful of their prospects of winning, they obeyed. The conglomerate's lawyers were callous and intimidating. When they phoned Eli from New York to discuss the case on September 11, 2001, just after the collapse of the Twin Towers, Eli told them: "Maybe we shouldn't discuss business today so that we can be together in bereavement for what happened in the United States." The sharks replied: "Business is business."

Finally Eli and Shaya were to meet with the American conglomerate's lawyers at their London office. It was raining. The two young *frum* men were standing in front of the imposing high-rise office building. On their cell phone, they called Rebbetzin Chaya Sara in Meah Shearim. She told them in Yiddish, "Be strong, fight it! Don't let them intimidate you. You are right, and you will win completely."

Tremulous, Eli and Shaya got into the elevator and pressed the button for the top floor, where the meeting was to be held. As they stood there flicking through the thick files in their hands, they suddenly saw a document they hadn't noticed before. With a start they realized, "This is the winner."

After two torturous hours of intimidation, Shaya took out that document, laid it on the table, and told the sharks, "Read this. It's either everything or nothing. You have until tomorrow to give in, or we'll counter sue you and make a big noise on Wall Street."

The next day, Eli and Shaya received an email saying, "You won." They received a settlement of over $200,000.

Different Case, Different Advice

The next time Eli and Shaya got involved in litigation, they were sure they were right and were determined to fight. The opposing company's lawyers wanted to make an out-of-court settlement, but Eli and Shaya refused. Six months into the dispute, they went to Rebbetzin Chaya Sara for a blessing to win. She told them, "Don't fight. Negotiate."

"We didn't want to negotiate," Eli recalls. "We were in the right and we wanted to win the dispute." They tried to convince Rebbetzin Chaya Sara, but she was adamant that they should compromise. She even told them the exact amount for which they should settle.

Reluctantly, they contacted the other company and offered to negotiate. It was too late. The other company was now determined to take it to court.

They told Rebbetzin Chaya Sara the latest developments. She replied, "Let it go to court. After the hearing, they'll be willing to negotiate. But don't waste money on lawyers."

The litigation dragged on for another two-and-a-half years. During that period, most dot.com companies went broke because of protracted litigation and legal fees. Eli and Shaya, heeding the Rebbetzin's advice not to spend money on lawyers, managed to stay afloat.

After the case went to court, the two companies negotiated a settlement for the exact amount that the Rebbetzin had stipulated two-and-a-half years earlier.

No Operation

Rebbetzin Chaya Sara's prescience was not limited to business matters. When Eli married Chani, he was learning in *kollel* in Jerusalem. They went regularly to Rebbetzin Chaya Sara for a *berachah* to have children. One Sunday, thirteen months after their wedding, the young couple went to visit the rebbetzin. She looked through the peephole in her door and told them to come back in a few days. "It was the only time she ever sent us away," remembers Eli.

He took his wife to Netanya for five days. The following Sunday, they again visited the rebbetzin. She turned to Chani and told her in Yiddish, "You're expecting." A blood test the next day verified the rebbetzin's words.

Three years later, Eli and Chani had moved to Antwerp. On Succos they visited Jerusalem together with Eli's parents. Chani was expecting their third child, but it was too soon to tell their parents or the rebbetzin. On Chol HaMoed, Eli, Chani, and his parents visited rebbetzin Chaya Sara. Chani walked in carrying a heavy bag. The rebbetzin immediately turned to Eli and told him, "Take the bag, because your wife is expecting." His parents were totally surprised.

In Antwerp, one Shabbos in 2001, Chani, in terrible pain, had to be rushed to the hospital in an ambulance. Her breathing was so labored that the medics had to put her on oxygen. At the hospital, the doctors diagnosed a kidney stone. Whereas most kidney stones are small and pass out of the body naturally, this kidney stone was large and lodged in a place from which it would not budge. The doctors asserted that there was no way to get rid of the kidney stone except through emergency surgery. They scheduled the surgery for the first thing Monday morning.

Early Sunday morning, with his wife still in excruciating pain, Eli phoned Rebbetzin Chaya Sara in Jerusalem. She declared: "There will be no operation." Eli explained that the surgeons had said there was no alternative to surgery, but the Rebbetzin only repeated, "There will be no operation."

That evening, the nurses prepped Chani, still suffering intense pain, for surgery the next morning. Eli stayed with her until late in the evening and then left to go home. A half hour later Eli was still en route when his cell phone rang. It was Chani. "I have no pain," she declared in wonderment.

Eli turned the car around and rushed back to the hospital. He told the doctors on duty that he wanted another scan. They performed the scan, and, to their amazement, the kidney stone had disappeared. Chani was discharged that very night.

Yossi's Story

When Eli and Chani's son Yossi was 10 months old, they noticed that he was very pale and weak. On a Thursday afternoon, they took him to a pediatrician, who ordered a blood test. At 11 p.m. that night, the phone rang. Their pediatrician, sounding grave, informed them that the blood test revealed that Yossi had no iron at all in his blood. He needed an emergency transfusion, scheduled for 6 a.m. the next morning.

At the hospital at dawn, two specialists sat down with Eli and Chani and told them that they believed that Yossi was suffering from leukemia. His hands trembling, Eli left the room and phoned Rebbetzin Chaya Sara. She told him: "Everything will be all right. Do the transfusion, but it's not what the doctors say."

After the transfusion, Yossi's blood was taken for tests. Eli and Chani were informed that it would take 4 hours for the results to reveal whether Yossi was indeed suffering from the lethal disease. During those 4 hours, the young parents felt like they were in shark-infested waters; their only life raft was Rebbetzin Chaya Sara's reassuring words.

At the end of the interminable 4 hours, the doctors, not masking their surprise, announced that Yossi did not have leukemia after all. That one transfusion was sufficient to restore his health.

Still Looking After Them

During the period from 2000 to 2002, most hi-tech companies crashed. Nervous, Eli and Shaya considered liquidating their company. Rebbetzin Chaya Sara told them not to, to stay in there and weather the storm. They emerged from that disastrous period not only intact, but prosperous.

On the last Purim of Rebbetzin Chaya Sara's life, Shaya visited to give her their monthly cash donation. The rebbetzin's small room was full of women waiting to hear the reading of the Megillah. As soon as Shaya peeked into the room, Rebbetzin Chaya Sara called him over and said, "You're coming to bring money. How much are you giving me?"

Shaya told her the figure. She said, "No, you have to give X amount more."

Shaya responded, "Rebbetzin, how do you know I have X amount more in my pocket?"

She replied, "I know."

Shaya reached into his pocket, took out all his remaining money, and counted it. It was almost the exact amount Rebbetzin Chaya Sara had asked for.

Whenever Shaya went to visit Rebbetzin Chaya Sara, he always had Eli in Antwerp on the line on his cell phone. Every Erev Yom Kippur, Shaya went to Rebbetzin Chaya Sara for a *berachah*. She would write their names and the names of their wives in her *machzor*. On the last Yom Kippur of her life, the Rebbetzin took Shaya's cell phone from his hand and said to Eli: "I asked R' Yaakov Moshe before he was *niftar*, 'Who will support me?' He turned around to me and said, 'Don't worry. Whoever will support you will have big *yeshuos* [salvations].'"

Eli and Shaya felt that this was her way of thanking them for their years of support.

The *yeshuos*, however, did not end with Rebbetzin Chaya Sara's demise. As Eli declared two years after her passing, "We still believe that our success these days is because of her. She always said she would look after us."

A Taste of Heaven

One Shabbos a young American student from the Hebrew University was among the 100 guests who crowded into the modest Jerusalem apartment of Rabbi Mordechai and Henny Machlis. This student, wearing a nose ring and an eyebrow ring, was determined to undermine every word of Torah Rabbi Machlis tried to share with his guests. Every time Rabbi Machlis spoke, the student would yell out, "That's stupid!" or "That's archaic!" or he would laugh out loud.

Finally Rabbi Machlis gave up. He sat down and said to his wife, "That's it. He's just too disruptive."

Henny encouraged her husband. "Ignore what he says. Don't speak to him; speak to his *neshamah* [soul]."

Rabbi Machlis somehow continued. At the end of the meal, the obnoxious student left. As he walked out the door, 7-year-old Moshe, one of the Machlises' fourteen children, asked him, "Why do you have that dumb thing in your nose?"

The student retorted, "Why do you have that dumb thing on your head?"

Moshe answered: "Because I always have to know that there's Someone above me and higher than me and better than me. Now why do you have that dumb thing in your nose?"

The student returned to his dorm room and wrote in his diary: "Just imagine — that little kid knows why he's wearing a *kippah,* but I have no idea why I'm wearing a nose ring."

Three days later he returned to the Machlises' apartment, and announced, "I want to learn more about what it means to be a Jew. And I want to learn how to put on *tefillin.*"

The Light and the Warmth

For more than two decades Rabbi Mordechai and Henny Machlis have opened their home to an amazing assortment of Shabbos guests. Every week 60-100 guests show up for Friday night dinner, and an equal number for Shabbos lunch. Who comes? Travelers, yeshivah students, university students, the homeless, the mentally ill, Hadassah ladies, tourists, lost souls, U.J.A. mission visitors, new immigrants, drunkards, widows, orphans, Sar El volunteers for Israel, Birthright participants, and truth seekers.

While most of their guests are from English-speaking countries, the Machlis family has hosted people from every continent, and from countries as far away as Japan, China, and the Philippines.

Some people come hungry for food — the ample helpings of home-cooked gefilte fish, chicken soup, chicken with barbeque sauce, at least three kinds of kugel, an array of salads, vegetarian alternatives, and four kinds of cake. Of course, destitute souls could pick up food at a public soup kitchen, but what is Shabbos without Shabbos songs and words of Torah, which Rabbi Machlis provides as abundantly as his wife's cooking?

Some people come hungry for love and warmth. Two orphaned young women in their early 20's have an apartment and good jobs, but on Shabbos they miss the family atmosphere they once knew. A refined 67-year-old widow ate alone every Shabbos for five years after her husband died; her independent persona dissuaded her friends from inviting her. Now all three enjoy the palpable warmth of the Machlis table.

Some people come for the spiritual inspiration and unconditional acceptance Rabbi Machlis radiates. Religious and secular guests sit side by side, most wearing *kipot*, some opting not to. Most people say the appropriate blessings, often for the first time; some opt not to. Everyone is encouraged to say a few words, of introduction or wisdom or personal reflection. Everyone is lovingly received.

A smattering of non-Jews, curious to experience a Jewish Sabbath, manage to find their way to the Machlis house on Shabbos. Once a group of ten Mormons came. When it was their turn to speak, each one rose and politely thanked the Machlises for their hospitality. When the last Mormon — a young woman — rose to speak, she burst into tears. She finally managed to compose herself, and declared: "I'm Jewish. Both my parents are Jewish. This is the first time I'm in a real Jewish home. I had no idea how beautiful Judaism is."

Once an American man in his early 20's partook of all the Shabbos meals at the Machlis home. At the end of Shabbos, he approached Rabbi Machlis and admitted that he was confused. Although his mother was born Jewish, she had raised him completely secular. In fact, he had become a born-again Christian, and had come to Israel with an Evangelical group in order to missionize the Jews. But what he had seen over Shabbos revealed that, contrary to what he had thought,

Judaism was a vibrant, profound religion, full of love and compassion.

After a long conversation, he and Rabbi Machlis agreed that the young man would return with his whole Evangelical group the next day for lunch, and Rabbi Machlis would engage in a debate with the head of the group, who had a master's degree in theology. If Rabbi Machlis' arguments prevailed, the young man decided, he would enroll in a yeshivah to study Judaism; if his group leader won the debate, he would continue with his missionary activities.

Apparently Rabbi Machlis won, for the erstwhile missionary enrolled in yeshivah. The story did not end there, however. Several weeks later the fellow's mother flew to Israel. She stormed into the Machlis home and accused them of kidnaping her son into a cult. He had written that he would not eat in her home unless she made her kitchen kosher!

Rabbi Machlis calmed her down and brokered a deal between her and the heads of her son's yeshivah. Her son would return to America and study at a yeshivah close to home, on condition that she make her kitchen kosher.

Several years later, while attending a Torah class in New York, Henny ran into the young man, now sporting a beard. He told her that he was married, with two children, and that his mother had likewise become observant.

Sometimes Henny herself is surprised by the impact her home makes. One Rosh Hashanah, they had only thirty guests, including a young couple who had come to Israel for their honeymoon. The bride was an American reform Jew and the groom was a German gentile. The couple said very little, and seemed "pretty icy." Two years later, the Machlises received a letter beginning, "You probably don't remember us …" (Since there had been so few guests that Rosh Hashanah, Henny remembered them well.) The woman went on to write: "When we left your place, we said, 'This is the kind of home we want to have — the light and the warmth and the children.' I had never realized that there was anything more to being Jewish than what I grew up with. We started studying Torah. Then we started keeping Shabbos, then kashrus, then added other mitzvos. We just want you to know that next week my husband will be undergoing an Orthodox conversion."

※

Actualizing Their Ideals

*B*oth Mordechai and Henny are Brooklyn born and bred. Both of their fathers were Orthodox rabbis. Mordechai, born in 1952, has rabbinic ordination, an M.A. in Jewish history, and is close to finishing his Ph.D. in Talmud. Mordechai is a much-loved rebbe in a boy's yeshivah, and also teaches Jewish Studies at Bar Ilan.

Henny, born in 1958, has a B.S. in education plus a Hebrew teaching degree from Stern College and studied dietetics at Brooklyn College. She used to teach Jewish subjects in adult education classes. Since the birth of her sixth child, she is a full-time mother and homemaker.

The couple met in 1979 in New York. Shortly after they started seeing each other, it became clear that, as Henny says, "We both wanted to share the love and the joy and the beauty of Judaism, and to share Shabbos with everyone."

The young couple wasted no time in actualizing their ideals. For the first three months after their wedding, they rented a two-bedroom apartment in Brooklyn, so that they would have a room to accommodate homeless people. The very first Shabbos in their apartment, Mordechai brought home to his

21-year-old bride a mentally ill couple to sleep over and eat with them for Shabbos. This couple became regular guests for the whole period the newlyweds were in Brooklyn.

Three months later, Mordechai and Henny actualized another cherished ideal. They moved to the holy city of Jerusalem.

Within a year, the Shabbos scene began. Mordechai prayed the Shabbos morning service at the Kosel. Walking through the Arab *shuk* on his way home, the 27-year-old Mordechai encountered a middle-aged Jewish woman, an American tourist. He invited her to come home with him for Shabbos lunch. "I'd love to," she replied, "but I'm here with a few friends."

"Bring them along," Mordechai offered warmly. "There's enough food for everyone."

When Mordechai crossed his threshold a short while later, he had 40 Hadassah ladies in tow. Henny amiably cut up the gefilte fish into paper-thin portions. Impressed by the 22-year-old Henny's warmth and hospitality, the middle-aged women kept telling her, "You remind me of my grandmother."

Another Shabbos both Mordechai and Henny were walking home from the Kosel. In the *shuk,* they met a doctor from Holland who was in Israel for a laser convention. They invited him home for Shabbos lunch. After Mordechai made *Kiddush*, he passed small cups of grape juice around to his guests. The Dutch doctor's hands were shaking so much that he could not grasp his cup. Finally, in an impassioned voice, he declared: "This is my first Jewish experience. Both my parents are Jewish, and Holocaust survivors. They would not let any Judaism into our home at all. Even when my son was born, they insisted that we not circumcise him. When I get back to Holland, I'm going to start studying about my Jewish roots."

Within two or three years of their marriage, the Machlises were hosting 20-30 guests at each Shabbos meal. From there, "it just grew. We bought another table, and filled it. We just kept adding tables."

Ninety people fit tightly into the Machlises' book-lined living room. The two sofas and the imitation Oriental rug, the only furnishings in the room during the week, are moved out for Shabbos. The overflow of guests sits in the fiberglass-roofed courtyard. When the guests exceed even the courtyard — as they often do, depending on the season — they sit in the small kitchen or at the tables set up outside the front door of the garden apartment. Henny's dream is to have the money to expand the living room, so everyone can sit together comfortably.

Shoes in the Windshield

The Machlises' hospitality is not reserved for Shabbos. Rare are the days when needy persons are not sleeping in the Machlises' extra beds, or on their two couches, or on the rug in the living room. Every night one, two, or three men, too drunk or crazy to want to sleep inside the house, sleep in the Machlises' van. When Mordechai leaves for work in the morning, he can tell how many "van guests" he has by how many pairs of shoes he sees in the front windshield.

Once a drunk Russian immigrant in his early 50's came for Shabbos dinner. When everyone else had left, the Machlises discovered this man asleep on the floor. He woke up, vomited, and was invited to sleep on the couch. He stayed for a few months, during which time he gave up alcohol cold turkey. When he started to suffer withdrawal symptoms, Henny, alarmed, called up specialists to make sure he would be okay. Eventually, they found him a job and an apartment.

Mordechai and Henny's ingenuous, non-judgmental acceptance makes them a magnet for troubled people. One day an American man, disheveled and emotionally distraught, came to their house. He told them he had no money, no place to live, and no food. So, as usual, they invited him to stay with them. Then he told them a story that was hard to believe. He claimed that he was a prominent attorney, a graduate of a prestigious law school, and that he was being pursued in the United States by certain people who had grievances against him related to his law practice. He said that he had fled to Israel a few days before with nothing but the shirt on his back, but that he owned a large house in New Jersey filled with his valuable possessions.

Since the man was an emotional wreck, anyone else would have dismissed his claims as wild ravings. Henny and Mordechai gave him the benefit of the doubt. They asked friends in America to check out his story.

It turned out that it was all true — including the house in New Jersey. These friends, granted power of attorney, managed, over a period of months, to sell the house, pack up all of its contents, and send them to him in Israel. Today the attorney is successfully practicing law in Israel. He is happily married and owns a large apartment in Jerusalem.

Often during the week destitute people pop into the Machlis home and ask if they can help themselves to staples from the kitchen shelves. The answer is always, "Yes." A fortune of tuna fish and canned vegetables disappears this way.

In addition to the Machlises' fourteen children, Mordechai and Henny have scores of spiritual progeny — couples who have found each other at the Machlis home or people who have been inspired to become observant by the Machlises' example. When these people have no money to pay the rent or buy food, to whom do they turn? Their spiritual parents, Rabbi and Rebbetzin Machlis, of course!

Who Pays?

The massive Shabbos meals cost the Machlises at least $2,000 a week. Where do they get the money?

The Machlises live frugally, and support their Shabbos project with personal and bank loans. They have mortgaged their apartment as much as the bank will allow.

In recent years, "special friends" have helped them with the enormous expenses. One friend even set up a charity fund, American Friends of Chesed L'Orchim.

Do they ever consider abandoning their Shabbos project for lack of funds? Henny answers with a story. During the last year of the Holocaust, the Nazis needed funds, so they were willing to accept ransom money for Jewish lives. At the very end, the desperate Nazis were selling Jewish lives for $1 a piece. A Jew in England sold his house, his business, and all his possessions for $150,000, enough to rescue 150,000 Jews. Whether or not the Germans actually delivered the Jews, would anyone question this man's choice to give up all that he owned? "We are living in the midst of a spiritual holocaust," Henny asserts. "Most Jews today have no idea of the beauty and depth of Judaism. How can we not do everything in our power, including going into debt, to reach out to our fellow Jews?"

Henny's Secret

Henny's kitchen is an apt metaphor for her heart. A glimpse into the kitchen, less than a third the size of a normal American kitchen, leaves one wondering how 200 Shabbos meals a week can issue from such a room. Similarly, one wonders how so much love and compassion for literally thousands of individuals can issue from one human heart.

The 44-year-old Henny looks a decade younger. Although she wears no make-up, her lineless complexion appears like the face of a woman of leisure, rather than the busy mother of fourteen children.

Many mysteries intrigue me about this open, ingenuous woman: How can the mother of so many children always appear relaxed and cheerful? How can she shop for, cook for, serve, and clean up from 60-100 guests every Friday night and every Shabbos afternoon, 51 weeks a year, without burning out? How, contrary to all the child-rearing literature, can she devote so much time and attention to helping strangers and still raise children who turn out to be sweet, modest, kind, and — why not just say it? — angelic? What supernatural ingredient does she put into her food so that scores of people, upon eating one of her Shabbos meals, are forever changed? And — this is the question I really want to answer — how can a woman who never goes out to dinner maintain such a high level of joy?

Eager to solve these mysteries, I ask to interview Henny. Rushing to make my appointment with her, I have forgotten my tape recorder. Henny offers me the use of theirs, and asks her 4-year-old son Eliyahu to go downstairs to one of the basement bedrooms and bring it up. Henny and I sit on one of the two slip-covered red couches — the only furniture in the living room except for two dining tables.

Minutes later Eliyahu stumbles into the living room and *throws* the tape recorder onto the rug. I emit a gasp, and manage — after all, he's not my child — to suppress a storm of expletives: "What are you doing! You'll break it! What's wrong with you!" Henny, unruffled as if she had a supply of new tape recorders in the back room or the money to buy them (she has neither), says softly to the 4-year-old: "You have to treat machines more gently. Otherwise, they can break."

Sara Rigler: I would have blasted my kid for doing that!

Henny Machlis: Of course, we all lose it sometimes, and we all have our struggles. We *try* not to yell or hit. Rabbi Shamshon Raphael Hirsch wrote that if you have a choice between being rigid and educating your children in all the values and behaviors that you cherish, or being loving and educating them without anger and not getting everything you want, it's preferable to educate without anger. I always had a dream that I would have a peaceful home. Then it was just a matter of attaining it, with God's help and *tefillah* [prayer].

SR: And a lot of effort and self-control, I imagine. How do you have time to raise your children well when you're devoting so much attention to other people?

HM: The success that we have in bringing up our children is up to Hashem. It has to do with Divine Providence and lots of prayer. We definitely have to put in our maximum — psychologically, physically, emotionally — but our success depends on Divine blessing.

Although we devote most of our Shabbos to guests, there is plenty of opportunity for private, quality time between Saturday night and Friday afternoon. Every day during the week we try to have either lunch or dinner with the children. Also, we schedule the Friday night meal late, to give people time to walk in from different parts of Jerusalem. So immediately after *Maariv*, we have a dinner alone with the children, before the guests arrive. Then the children have a chance to give their *divrei Torah* and sing their songs.

I have been a full-time mother since the birth of my sixth child. When a mother is around and available to her children on a constant basis, then she's there for crucial educational lessons to be given over and many, many heart-to-heart talks about things that are troubling her children.

The Satmar Rebbe commented on the verse: "All day he gives and lends, and his children will be blessed." [*Psalms* 37:26] He said that you would think that someone who is busy helping other people won't have enough time for his children, but there's a special Divine blessing that protects them.

One can also postulate that much of a child's inability to deal with himself and the world comes from egocentricity. When a child learns to care, think, love, and give to the other, he or she actually matures quicker and builds his or her character to be a more efficient, responsible, and effective human being in society.

This is also an argument for having a large family, because the more siblings there are, the more types of personalities children learn to deal with, and the more social skills they develop in terms of tolerance, patience, sensitivity, and love.

Elisheva, Henny's married 21-year-old daughter, is sitting on the rug listening to our interview. I turn and ask her:

As a young child, did you ever resent your parents dedicating so much time and energy to strangers?

Elisheva: When I was very little, I wouldn't talk to the guests or even smile at them. My mother used to say to me: "What if, God forbid, someday you were in their shoes and you had no place to stay and no place to eat on Shabbos, and you came to a family, and the children didn't smile at you or talk to you? How would you feel?" She kept encouraging me to empathize. So I started smiling and talking to the guests.

SR (to Henny): By letting homeless, mentally ill, and drunk people stay in your house, aren't you endangering your children's safety?

HM: Unquestionably our children's welfare is our primary concern. Every dedicated parent must use discretion. In the more than two decades we have been doing this, we have not, *baruch Hashem*, had a single bad incident. Of course, if there is someone who is emotionally or psychologically disturbed to the point that it could threaten the children, we relegate them to sleeping in our van, or deal with them in some other way.

SR: When you were growing up, who was the greatest influence on your life?

HM: My parents, Murray and Edith Lustig, were very hospitable, very warm, good, and loving. I always valued my mother's *chesed* [deeds of kindness] and compassion — the way she treated the cleaning woman, the fix-it man, the carpenter, with such kindness and respect. As you get older, you realize how much of what you are is from your parents.

My father was so generous and kind. One time, the daughter of my parents' friends got hurt. She was 16-years-old, and was riding her bike, and somehow hit a tree. She went into a coma. As soon as my father heard about it, he rushed to the hospital. He went over to his friend, handed him a blank, signed check, and said, "Don't spare any medical expense to help your daughter." We heard about this story only years later, after my father passed away, when his friend told us.

Two of my rabbis in school, Rabbi Teichtel and Rabbi Reuven Fink, also had a major impact on my worldview.

SR: How often a year do you take a break?

HM: We used to take off a few weeks a year, and we would inform the people in advance. A couple of years ago, my married daughter had a baby boy on a Shabbos, so the *bris* was the following Shabbos, in a different city. Whoever called during the week, we told them not to come, but there was no way to announce it to our "regulars." Just in case, we arranged for a rabbi to be here to conduct the meal and I cooked a little, and we left challah, salads, drinks, and provisions. I thought, "Maybe 20 people will come." Well, 80 people showed up that Friday night, and 65 people the next day for lunch.

So now, if we want to go away for Shabbos, we inform people that Rabbi Machlis won't be here to give *divrei Torah*, but that there will be someone else to run the meal. And I cook the food anyway. Fifty-one weeks a year.

Only on Pesach we don't have guests, and we go away, because of the special Biblical mitzvah to teach your children on Seder night. So we concentrate exclusively on the children and attempt to celebrate the holiday in a private family setting.

SR: Do you ever feel a need for a break more often than that?

HM: Not really. This is our raison d'etre. This is holiness. This is happiness. In my former years, maybe I would have wanted more time off, but as time goes on, and I get into a system, and I get more dedicated to the idea, I think Hashem has withdrawn some of the pitfalls, and it runs more smoothly.

They say that in Jerusalem of old, when people would eat, they would hang a tablecloth outside their door. If anyone would see the tablecloth, they would know they could come in and eat. So I'm hoping for the day when everyone will hang out a tablecloth so that people can just come in. If all people would just open their doors, it would really be a brilliantly shining Jerusalem.

SR: Do you ever feel like you need time alone without your husband and children?

HM: In recent years, I have felt that way. I go to the Kosel, or I'm alone with Hashem in my room and read or say *Tehillim*.

I think one of the most important things in life is to pray for success. We have no independent success. It's all Hashem's blessing.

I enjoy brisk walks, and try to use the time for creative introspection and meditation.

SR: What makes you so happy?

HM: To be living in the holy city of Jerusalem, the holiest place in the world, and to be able to pray under the Throne of Glory. It makes me happy to be married to a wonderful person, who is wise and learned. It makes me happy to have my beautiful children, and to see them growing up to be holy, healthy, happy, giving, loving, sensitive human beings. It makes me happy to be very connected to Hashem and to be able to share that connection with all humanity. Shabbos makes me very happy. I love Shabbos. And I love to share the joy of Shabbos and the thrill of the holiness of Shabbos.

SR: I have to say that I think something supernatural is going on here. Many Jews who are committed secularists or who are even practicing a different religion have been turned on to Orthodox Judaism after just one Shabbos meal in your house. What's your secret?

HM: I read a long time ago that the wife of Rabbi Levi Yitzchak of Berditchev, before she cooked, would pray that the people who eat her food would imbibe *yiras Shamayim* [awe of Hashem] and do *teshuvah*. Rebbe Nachman of Breslav says that when you cook, the energy that you cook with goes into the food. So if you cook with a lot of anger, you can give people food poisoning. But if you cook with joy, you can give them good health.

So, we pray before and while we cook: "May the food have the taste of *Gan Eden* [paradise]." And we say *Tehillim* while we're cooking. And we pray that the people who eat this food should love Shabbos and love Hashem and do *chesed* and love Torah and be in touch with themselves and that they should have the joy of Shabbos, and that the food should be for the honor of Hashem and for the honor of the holy Shabbos.

SR: What would you say to women who hate to cook and to do domestic work?

HM: All giving is a little bit of imitating Hashem. Giving builds one's character, and makes one more God-like. One should view domestic responsibilities as a means to grow as an individual, to become more giving and loving and sharing, to get out of oneself and into the other, and to become more God-like. Of course, there's nothing wrong with hiring help for domestic duties, as long as one knows that it's important to overcome a certain level of this discomfort in order to be as giving as can be.

SR: What would you say to women who are conflicted between career and staying home with their children?

HM: I used to go out to teach Jewish subjects to adults. Even now I sometimes go out to lecture. For a few years, I ran a series of lectures in the neighborhood, where I taught Jewish philosophy to women. I really think that everyone should be an emissary of Hashem and teach whatever they know. Every woman is blessed with *her* particular qualities and interests. Everyone should be encouraged to maximize her singular form of expression.

But it's very important that every woman should know that there is no one else in the whole world who can be a mother to her children except for her, nor a wife to her husband except for her. Women's priority should always be first and foremost to give to their families. This is their most unique and important contribution to the world, that no one else can do. No one else can give over my particular psychological, emotional, spiritual self to my children, except for me. I encourage women to use all their potentials and talents and education to give to society as much as they possibly can, but always remember that their first priority is their home, to build a Jewish home.

Let's not forget that all spirituality in the world comes from the Jewish woman. It is her strength and her values that will build her children and the world around her, and will pave the way for the Ultimate Redemption.

Note: Henny Machlis personally invites every reader to come for a Shabbos meal. Their address is: 137 Maalah Dafneh, Apt. 26, Jerusalem. For exact mealtimes, feel free to call the Machlises. Their telephone number in Jerusalem is (02)581-0786 or 581-3910.

Jewish Nobelity

The picture on the bulletin board of his Hebrew University office says it all. Taken shortly after the announcement that the 2005 Nobel Prize in Economics was being awarded to Prof. Yisrael [Robert] Aumann, the photo shows three generations of the prizewinner's grinning descendants, 32 people in all. In the middle, with his long white beard and *kippah*, sits the 75-year-old Prof. Aumann, propping up a meter-high portrait of his beloved late wife Esther.

A few weeks later, Prof. Aumann took the entire clan to Stockholm for the prestigious awards ceremony. In addition to his five children and their spouses, his nineteen grandchildren, his grandson-in-law, his two infant great-grandchildren, and his brother, the Aumann entourage included his second wife Batya, who is Esther's widowed older sister and whom he had married just a week earlier. Putting them all up at the exclusive Grand Hotel for ten days at $300 a night certainly ate a chunk out of Prof. Aumann's $650,000 prize (his half of the $1.3 million prize shared with Prof. Thomas C. Schelling of the University of Maryland), but obviously in Prof. Aumann's system of inner economics, family togetherness is worth the cost.

How does a person attain the pinnacle of his career without neglecting his family? "Nobody gets the Nobel Prize just because he's smart. You have to work hard," asserts

Miriam Aumann Baris, the professor's daughter. Her father certainly worked hard, putting in 13-hour days and traveling extensively.

"Academic life forces you to travel," explains Miriam. "You get paid for a sabbatical only if you're out of the country. They do this as an incentive, to encourage communication between colleagues." For the year-long sabbaticals, Prof. Aumann's family accompanied him. For shorter periods, Esther preferred to keep the children at home, because she believed that children need stability. During those times, Prof. Aumann always came home for Jewish holidays, and while in Europe, he flew home every other Shabbat. While putting in long days and nights at the Hebrew University, Prof. Aumann came home every evening at 7 p.m. for dinner with the family, even if he had to go back to work afterwards.

With such long absences, what kind of a father was he?

"He was much absent *and* he was a wonderful father," she avows. "When he was here, we had a lot of concentrated father time. He took us skiing, scuba diving, hiking. Every Friday afternoon when my mother was cooking for Shabbat, he took us out so that we wouldn't bother her. And he was a great husband. They had an arrangement between themselves. She did the housework and raised the children. He made the money and made the fun."

The arrangement lasted only as long as Esther wanted it that way. When Miriam was in the 8th grade, her mother decided to go to work. Yisrael, ever the devoted husband, supported her choice. A decade later, Esther decided to go back to school and pursue Jewish studies. Again, her husband supported her choice.

"My father and mother had a very special relationship of love and respect and joint effort," Miriam recalls. He always complimented her cooking and bought her dresses and jewelry. On Shabbat afternoons, they learned together: the Torah portion of the week with the commentary of Rashi.

"My mother always believed in him," states Miriam. When their father was lying on the couch with his eyes closed, their mother would hush the children: "Don't bother Abba. He's working." When the eminent mathematician and economist would monopolize the bathtub and the children would complain, "What's Abba doing in there for so long?" their mother would tell them: "He's working."

Their great loving union of forty-five years ended when Esther died of cancer. Once she became sick, her husband, at the peak of his career, canceled all his travel plans. "Life stopped," Miriam remembers. "He was constantly there for her."

Dr. David Rosen, the Aumanns' son-in-law, remembers his father-in-law waiting for hours outside a doctor's office to ask a question about Esther's treatment. "He was willing to mortgage everything he owned to get her well."

Alas, Esther died six years ago. "He was devastated when she died," David recalls. "He thought that he would die of sorrow, that he couldn't live without her."

Resilience, however, is one of Prof. Aumann's cardinal traits. An avid mountain climber, thrice he's fallen and broken his leg. The first time, thirty years ago in the Yosemite Valley, the rescue team looked at the stricken climber and said, "We hope this doesn't stop you from climbing mountains." Yisrael, in agony, answered through his clenched teeth, "Don't worry. It's not going to."

After another mishap, his son Shlomo told him: "There are many more mountains left in you." Indeed, there were.

A Man of Many Loves

Prof. Aumann officially retired five years ago, but, at 75, he continues to fling himself into his quadruple loves: Torah, game theory, family, and nature. He still learns Torah regularly with the same *chavrusah* [study partner] he's had for thirty years; teaches three classes at the Hebrew University; picks up his grandchildren from kindergarten and takes them home with him when their parents are occupied; and skis, treks, and climbs some of the world's most beautiful mountains.

He takes every grandchild, upon reaching 14, on an extended trip to the High Sierras or to the South American jungles or to India, in order to share with them his own appreciation of Hashem's wonders. Together, they ride on horseback into the wilderness, camp out in tents, and climb mountains. Five years ago, the 70-year-old Prof. Aumann scaled his highest peak: the 18,192-ft. Mt. Kala Patthar in the Himalayas.

At the age of 72, Prof. Aumann took his 18-year-old granddaughter Shanni to New Zealand. After attending a one-week professional conference, they spent three weeks in the New Zealand wilderness. "We trekked, kayaked, and swam in freezing-cold lakes," Shanni reminisces. They took along kosher soup-mixes from Israel and ate hard-boiled eggs and salmon the rest of the time. Every night, when they came back to their encampment, her grandfather would learn Torah with her by kerosene lamplight.

When they returned to Israel, the shared Torah studies didn't stop. Shanni visits her grandfather every Friday, and they learn together until Shabbos approaches. In the long days of summer, that means five hours of joint study.

For the Bar Mitzvah of every grandchild, Prof. Aumann presents a set of the Talmud. He tells them: "I give you this if you promise that in a few years it won't look like it looks now." Once, a grandson was reprimanded by his father for eating over his book. His scholarly grandfather demurred: "Eat over your book, drink over your book, live over your book."

The professor's excursions into nature are also an expedition into the words and wonders of Hashem. Shanni describes how they'll be out in the wilderness, far from everything, and her grandfather will stop at a point overlooking a meandering river and will explain, from a mathematical and natural standpoint, why the river turns and why it divides. Then he'll tie it all into a lesson from that week's Torah portion.

Prof. Aumann, a connoisseur of everything, connects everything to its Divine source. When he hears thunder or sees lightning or smells a flower, he immediately pronounces the appropriate blessing. A wine connoisseur, whenever he puts a superior bottle of wine on the table, he recites the blessing, "He is good and does good." This was the blessing he recited publicly in front of 1400 guests while delivering his toast at the royal banquet following the Nobel awards ceremony.

Once, Prof. Aumann sponsored an expedition to climb Mt. Kilimanjaro for his daughter Tamar and her husband David. He told them, "If I'm going to pay for it, you have to be at the summit for sunrise, in order to see Hashem's beauty — the sun coming up over Madagascar."

The Land of His Dreams

*Y*israel Aumann was born to an Orthodox Jewish family in 1930 in Germany. In 1938, the Aumanns escaped to the United States, where Yisrael studied in Yeshivah Rabbi Jacob Joseph [R.J.J.]. He credits his math teacher there, Joseph Gansler, with first sparking his interest in mathematics.

"On the Jewish side," declared Prof. Aumann in an interview,* "the high school teacher who influenced me most was Rabbi Shmuel Warshavchik. ... He attracted me to the beauty of Talmudic study and the beauty of religious observance. ... Rabbi Warshavchik's enthusiasm and intensity — the fire in his eyes — lit a fire in me also."

For a while the young Aumann debated between becoming a Talmudic scholar or a mathematician. For one semester, he raced back and forth between the yeshivah and City College. "Then it became too much for me, and I made the hard decision to quit the yeshivah and to study mathematics."

After receiving his Ph.D. at M.I.T., he did a post-doctoral program at Princeton. In 1956, it was time to launch his career. Dr. Aumann applied for several positions in the United States and a position in Israel at the Hebrew University. As he related the story to me in a recent interview in his Hebrew University office:

> *I was offered the job here and also several jobs in the U.S. In fact, I accepted one of them, at the Bell Tel Laboratory in Murray Hill, New Jersey. I was really hesitating and debating in my mind whether to accept the job in Israel or the job in Bell Tel Laboratories, but I took the job at Bell Tel. That very evening, I knew it was a mistake. If I'm going to go to Israel at all, I should go now, I realized. I shouldn't delay it. So, the next morning, I called them and said, "Look, I accepted the job and I'm a man of my word, so I'm coming. But they abolished slavery with the 13th amendment. So I'll come to work for you for one year, and then my obligation to you will be fulfilled, and I'm moving to Israel." They told me, "Aumann, you're off the hook. You don't have to work for us if you don't want to."*

Why did the promising young mathematician choose to come to Israel, an embattled country that was at that time all of eight years old?

"I made *aliyah* because this is a dream that the Jewish people have dreamt for thousands of years, and I wanted to be part of that dream."

It has not been easy. In 1982, the Aumann's firstborn son Shlomo was killed while serving in the Israeli Army, during a battle with Syrian tanks.

"Was this a crisis of faith for you and your wife?" I ask.

"It wasn't a crisis of faith for one moment," Prof. Aumann replies. "We were extremely proud of him. We realized that we had brought him up to this. Israel is not an easy place to live. People are getting killed here all the time. When it happens to you, it's not any different than when it happens to somebody else. ... This is part of the price you pay for living in Israel."

The Roots of Integrity

*I*n the world of business, people steal money. In the world of academia, people steal ideas. One of Prof. Aumann's outstanding traits is his punctiliousness to give credit to others, whether they be his teachers, colleagues, or even students. At a press conference held the day the Nobel Prize was announced, Prof. Aumann surprised his audience by declaring that the Prize should have been awarded to someone else: "Lloyd Shapley of U.C.L.A. was worthy, and should have won. I see him as the high priest of game theory."

Prof. Aumann learned the concept of "intellectual property" from the Torah. As he tells the story:

> *There was a period fifteen, twenty years ago, when stealing software was considered okay by many people, including many academics. There was an item of software that I needed, and I was wondering whether to "steal" it — make a copy of which the developers of the software disapprove. Then I said to myself, why do you have to wonder about this? You are a religious person. Go to your rabbi and ask him. I don't have to worry about these questions because I have a religion that tells me what to do. So I went to my rabbi — a Holocaust survivor, a very renowned, pious person [Rav Gustman]. I figured he won't even know what software is — I'll have to explain it to him. Maybe there is a Talmudic rule about this kind of intellectual property not really being property. Whatever he'll say, I'll do. I went to him ... He said, "Okay, if you really want to know, it's absolutely forbidden to do this, absolutely forbidden." So I ordered the software.**

A self-declared believer that Hashem gave the Torah to the Jewish people at Sinai, Prof. Aumann has made his hardest decisions based on the directives of the Torah as interpreted by the rabbis. He related to me this story:

> *I was so close to my rabbi, Rabbi Munk, that when he died, his widow called me first. I made all the funeral arrangements. But the funeral was going to be held that afternoon, at the same time that I had a lecture scheduled at the Hebrew University. I asked Rav Gustman what I should do. Was I permitted to miss my lecture in order to attend the funeral of my Rav? Rav Gustman said, "No," that since I draw a salary from the Hebrew University, missing a lecture for personal reasons would be stealing from the University. So I missed my Rav's funeral.*

Prof. Aumann sums up the connection between Torah and integrity: "In short, you can be a moral person, but morals are often equivocal. ... The point I am making is that religion — at least my religion — is a sort of force, a way of making a commitment to conduct yourself in a certain way, which is good for the individual and good for society."*

ನ

Religion and Rationality

At a press conference at the Hebrew University given before he left for Stockholm to receive the Nobel Prize, Prof. Aumann sat in front of a large blue banner proclaiming, "THE CENTER FOR RATIONALITY," and told a startlingly irrational story: Every male present at the Awards Ceremony, including his 7-year-old grandson, is required to wear tails and a white bowtie, provided by the Nobel Foundation. Since the Torah forbids wearing *shaatnez* [a forbidden mixture of linen and wool], Prof. Aumann realized that he would have to have these garments checked for *shaatnez*. This required having the Chief Rabbi of Sweden pick up one such outfit and bring it to Israel, where it could be checked with a microscope in one of Jerusalem's many *shaatnez* labs. This examination revealed that the tuxedos were indeed *shaatnez*, so then a team of tailors had to remove the linen threads from all the suits the Aumann men and boys would wear.

Later I asked Prof. Aumann: "*Shaatnez* is the antithesis of rationality. How do you reconcile these opposites?"

"I don't see any contradiction between *shaatnez* and rationality," the venerable Nobel Prize winner replied. "Not everything in the world has to do with rationality. You do all kinds of things that are orthogonal."

Jewish Nobelity / 365

To illustrate the meaning of "orthogonal," Prof. Aumann got up and strode to the whiteboard on the opposite wall of his office. "If you have a line," he explained, drawing a green line pointing to the right, "then you can go in the opposite direction," and he drew a brown line pointing to the left. "But you can also go off in a totally different direction," he added, drawing a purple line going straight up. "That's called orthogonal."

Returning to his seat, Prof. Aumann continued:

> *Shaatnez is not irrational. It has nothing to do with rationality. When you sit down and play the piano, are you doing something rational? No! Are you doing something irrational? Also, no! It's orthogonal to rationality. The same goes for climbing a mountain or going skiing. The whole lifestyle of a religious Jew is not rational or irrational. It's a beautiful way of living.*
>
> *Shaatnez is part of a big whole. It's something that you can't understand by itself. If you said, "Just don't wear a mixture of linen and wool," it wouldn't make any sense. But it's part of a lifestyle. As part of this lifestyle, it makes sense. ... To understand the Torah, you have to understand it as one whole, not separate pieces ...*
>
> *I was talking about playing the piano. Let's say you say, "Let's take one bar of the music," and you play just that. You don't play the whole sonata. Of course, it doesn't make any sense. It's part of the whole sonata, that's what speaks to you.*

The world got a rare glimpse of that "beautiful way of living" by observing Prof. Aumann in Stockholm. Although the Awards Ceremony was scheduled for late Saturday afternoon, the shortness of the Swedish winter day enabled the Aumann family to attend after the close of Shabbos. They — all 35 of them — had moved before Shabbos to a hotel located just 200 meters from Stockholm's Concert Hall, where the Awards Ceremony would take place. As soon as they made *Havdalah*, the Aumanns dashed to the Concert Hall, arriving just 90 seconds before King Karl XVI Gustaf's arrival and the closing of the doors.

At the royal banquet afterwards, the menu of snow-grouse breast covered in reindeer meat was not served to the members of Prof. Aumann's entourage. Instead, they were served a special kosher dinner featuring goose covered in fillet of beef, as well as fine kosher wines and special kosher liquors.

Since the laws of *kashrus* prohibit eating from china and cutlery previously used for unkosher food, while the rules of royal etiquette prohibit serving guests on anything other than royal china, new china plates with the royal pattern were specially kilned for Prof. Aumann and his family. Their place settings were completed with newly-forged gilded silver cutlery and recently blown gold-stemmed crystal.

In a world where Jews have so often sacrificed their religious principles to fit in, we can be proud at how this noblest of Nobel Prize winners stands out.

---

* From "An Interview with Robert Aumann" by Sergiu Hart, March 2005, Discussion Paper #386 of the Hebrew University Center for the Study of Rationality.

Who Will Save the Baby?

*I*f anyone in the Cracow ghetto stood a chance of surviving the Holocaust, it was Avraham Shapiro.* At 22 years of age, he was a smart and resourceful young man whose mind had been honed during years of yeshivah study. He understood that the Germans were out to annihilate every Jew, and he took the precautions necessary to save himself and his middle-aged parents. He obtained expertly counterfeited papers identifying the three members of his family as foreign nationals. He built and stocked a bunker in a remote location underneath the ghetto. And he procured a map of the sewers and plotted an escape route for the day the ghetto would be liquidated. His master scheme was to escape to the safety of Hungary.

But then one day ... an 18-year-old neighbor named Chaya Rivka knocked on the Shapiros' door holding a baby. The baby, who was 20 months old and who could neither stand nor sit up by himself, was her nephew Chaim. His parents had been shipped to Treblinka. Chaya Rivka knew that the Shapiros had foreign citizenship papers. She calculated that, of all the doomed Jews in the ghetto, the Shapiros had the best

---

*"Shapiro" is a pseudonym. The protagonist prefers to remain anonymous.

chance to escape. Therefore, she had approached the Shapiro family several times, asking them to take the baby with them to safety, but they had refused. A baby would be a liability that would endanger their own chances of survival.

This day — March 8, 1943 — was different, however. Chaya Rivka had received notice that she was being deported to a labor camp. She simply couldn't take the baby along. With heart-breaking cries, she begged Avraham, who was the only one home at the time, to take the baby.

Avraham, the logical thinker, the careful planner, was prepared to overcome the Nazis, but that day he overcame his own character. As he would later declare, "My compassion overwhelmed my intellect, and I decided to accept the child."

When his parents came home and saw Avraham holding the baby, they were aghast. How could he have risked their three lives for such an act of reckless compassion? Avraham replied that the baby was now his, and either the baby escaped with them, or they would all remain in the doomed ghetto.

Avraham's immediate need was to forge a birth certificate proving that the baby was his. He knew a rabbi who had an official stamp, but where to get a form? Somehow Avraham managed to locate a typewriter. He had never in his life typed, but that night he stayed up all night, and by dawn he had produced a credible birth certificate. He ran to the rabbi to stamp it. "At that moment," Avraham later wrote, "a son was born to Avraham Shapiro."

All of Us Together!

Two days later the Germans liquidated the Cracow ghetto. They assembled the Jews in a large square and divided them into groups for deportation: the young for work, the elderly for old age homes, and the children for children's residences. Avraham knew it was all a sham. "I never believed the Germans and I always tried to do the opposite of what they said." When someone tried to take the baby from him, Avraham refused to surrender him, shouting, "All of us together!"

It was impossible that day to reach the bunker he had prepared because it was in the other half of the ghetto, separated by a barbed-wire fence. Avraham handed the baby to his mother and told his parents not to budge. He would find a temporary hiding place and be back to fetch them.

After a desperate search, he found an empty building with steps leading down from the entrance hall into a cellar. Amid the peril, he managed to bring his parents and the baby there. Avraham knew that the Germans would search every building and cellar, but Divine Providence had provided an unlikely protection for them. Someone in the building had had sewage problems, and in the desperate circumstances of the ghetto, could not find a plumber. So they had filled a large barrel with the waste from their toilet and put the barrel in the stairwell. With great effort, Avraham managed to overturn the barrel, pouring excrement all over the steps leading down to the cellar. He calculated that the fastidious Germans would not be willing to soil their boots to look for Jews.

That evening they heard the Germans enter the building. To keep the baby from crying and giving them away, they had planned to give him food, but they had with them only dry challah with no water to soften it to make it edible. So Avraham and his parents hurriedly chewed the challah, spit it out, and fed the baby the softened morsels. They heard the Nazis complaining about the stink. Avraham was right; they did not deign to descend into the cellar.

This was the night, following the liquidation of the ghetto, that Avraham had planned to escape through the sewers to the "Aryan side" of Cracow. Looking at the baby, however, he was faced with a dilemma. He had heard of Jews who had fled through the sewers with their children, and the children had suffocated on the way. No, he decided, he would not risk the baby's life by escaping through the sewers. He would have to devise a different plan.

Avraham knew that they could not stay in the cellar for long. They would have to make their way to the bunker he had prepared, but a barbed wire fence blocked the way. Avraham, using a pocketknife and superhuman strength, succeeded in cutting a hole in the barbed wire. Stealthily running through the streets, emptied of the living but scattered with Jewish corpses, the Shapiro family reached the bunker.

Avraham had previously set up a light in the bunker by cutting electric wires out of the wall of their apartment and connecting them in the bunker. However, there was no way to pipe in water. Each day Avraham had to go up and draw water from a faucet. One day he was caught. Despite their protestations that they were foreign nationals with the papers to prove it, the three of them and baby Chaim were sent to the Gestapo prison.

The Fire of Love

*E*ventually, using a gold cigarette case weighing 250 grams, they bribed their way out of the prison. They immediately fled Cracow for a nearby village, where they rented a room and hid. It was autumn, 1943. Hungary was practically the last country in Europe where the "Final Solution" had not been implemented. They hired a guide to smuggle them across the border to Slovakia and from there to Hungary.

Throughout the journey, they subsisted by eating raw potatoes, which Avraham and his parents would chew, spit out, and feed to baby Chaim. Friday night, October 28, found them deep in the forest on the Polish side of the border. The family was tired, cold, and frightened of being caught. Abruptly the guide announced that they would have to spend the night there, because they could not cross the border that night. Then, without another word, the guide disappeared.

The Shapiros began to organize themselves to sleep. Avraham, who had been carrying Chaim the whole time, suddenly realized that the baby was damp, silent, and not moving. He quickly removed his wrappings and saw that the baby was blue.

Avraham, trembling with fear, quickly gathered wood and branches and lit a fire to warm the baby back to life. It was an act of exquisite irrationality. The fire was a bold announcement of their whereabouts, but Avraham's compassion yet again conquered his intellect. He held the baby as close to the fire as was safe, turning him from side to side, while Mrs. Shapiro stood on the other side of the bonfire drying and warming the baby's clothes.

Chaim revived. He regained his color and started to move. And Avraham, who had and would face repeated danger to his own life throughout the Holocaust, would remember those minutes of fear for the baby's life as the most traumatic of the war.

All of Shabbos they waited, wondering if the guide would return. As darkness fell on Saturday night, the guide appeared. When he saw the ashes of the fire, he became enraged at their recklessness.

It was time to proceed toward the border. To prevent a repetition of the calamity, Avraham took a sheet and tied the baby to his chest, facing toward him. This gave him a constant awareness of Chaim's condition, but totally blocked his field of vision of the ground. Treading over rocks and rough terrain, all invisible to him, Avraham at one point tripped, tearing off the sole of his shoe. He tied some rags around his foot and kept going. Hours later they crossed the border into Slovakia.

For the Good of the Child

Eventually the fugitives made it to Budapest. They were put up in refugee quarters. A Jewish aid worker, hearing that they had with them an orphan baby who was not their own, suggested that they give the baby to the Schonbruns, a well-to-do, childless, religious Jewish couple.

This time Avraham's intellect and compassion converged. Little Chaim, now 2 years old, was malnourished and sickly, and still could not even sit up by himself. Avraham knew that his baby's welfare required a stable, normal home, where he would be fed three meals a day and be safe from the danger that still hung over the Shapiro family. Over the virulent protests of his mother, who had grown attached to the baby, Avraham took Chaim to the Schonbruns' house. There he was impressed not by the lavish furnishings but by the ample bookcases full of holy books. Confident that he was doing what was best for Chaim, Avraham handed his son over to the Schonbruns.

When Avraham occasionally met Mr. Schonbrun in synagogue and inquired about Chaim, he received only cursory answers. Avraham inferred that the Schonbruns did not want Chaim to know anything about his past. "I distanced myself from the family," wrote Avraham, "for the good of the child."

On March 19, 1944, the Germans occupied Hungary. On a Shabbos night two months later, Avraham and his father were apprehended in synagogue. They were transferred from place to place until ultimately they were loaded onto a boxcar heading to Auschwitz. With a knife he had procured from an old cobbler, Avraham was able to enlarge a tiny window in the boxcar. As the train sped through Slovakia on its way to the death camp, Avraham and his father jumped out.

They spent the rest of the war in Slovakia, masquerading as gentiles. As soon as the Russians liberated Slovakia, Avraham and his father made their way back to Budapest, back to the dwelling where they had left Mrs. Shapiro almost a year before. When they opened the door, they found Mrs. Shapiro sitting by the table eating a piece of matzah. It was the first day of Passover, the holiday of freedom.

The Box

Only once in postwar Budapest did Avraham spot little Chaim. The child was walking (yes, walking!) on the street with his nanny. "Tears welled up in my eyes," wrote Avraham in his memoirs, "but I never approached the child."

Communist Hungary was no place for religious Jews. Shortly after the war, the Schonbruns left for Belgium, then Montreal, Canada, where Chaim grew up and eventually married. In 1950, Avraham Shapiro married and moved to Israel.

But the thread of their lives, knotted together by a compassion stronger than logic or even love of life, was not severed. Avraham continually kept tabs on Chaim, and Divine Providence conspired that Chaim's wife's aunt, who lived in Haifa, was a close friend of Mrs. Avraham Shapiro.

Several years after his marriage, Chaim was told by his uncle in Belgium, "There's a Jew in Israel who carried you from Poland to Hungary, and saved your life." Chaim, however, had no idea as to the identity of his benefactor, who continued to watch him from afar.

In 1980, at the age of 38, Chaim brought his family to Israel for his son's Bar Mitzvah. His wife's aunt sent him a message that the Jew who had saved his life was named Avraham Shapiro. Mr. Shapiro, now 57, lived in Haifa and was finally ready to meet Chaim.

That very day, Chaim took a taxi from Jerusalem to Haifa. "Our meeting was very emotional," Chaim recalls. "We both cried and cried, and we spoke for hours."

It was the beginning of a close bond between their two families. During the succeeding twenty-seven years, Avraham has attended the weddings of all of Chaim's children, and Chaim has attended the weddings of all of Avraham's grandchildren.

"We are very, very close," Chaim attests. "I consider him like a father, and he considers me like a son."

But why had Avraham not made contact with Chaim sooner? Why had it taken him thirty-five years to reconnect?

The answer was perhaps contained in a box. Before they parted that day in 1980, Avraham told Chaim, "I have something to give you." He handed him a box, saying, "I have waited thirty-five years to give you this."

Chaim opened the box and saw that it was packed with pieces of gold. Avraham explained that before Chaim's mother was shipped off to Treblinka, she had given this box full of gold to her younger sister Chaya Rivka, and charged her to use it to save the life of her only child. When Avraham agreed to take the baby, Chaya Rivka transferred the box to him.

During their flight from Poland, the Shapiro family used up their own supply of gold. Avraham was forced, reluctantly, to use little Chaim's gold. By the time they reached Budapest, there was nothing left. This greatly bothered Avraham. "I had done the mitzvah of saving a life," Avraham explained to Chaim, "and I didn't want to sell this mitzvah for any amount of gold."

In the wake of the war, as soon as Avraham started working, he set aside some of his wages every week to buy gold. It had taken him thirty-five years, but he finally had the exact amount of gold originally contained in Chaim's mother's box. He handed the box to Chaim, content that he had taken no profit from the enormous mitzvah of saving a life.

In the Cracow ghetto, compassion had overcome Avraham Shapiro's intellect. Nothing ever overcame his integrity.

Holy Woman: The Story Behind the Story

Many authors say that publishing a book is like bringing a child into the world. Certainly I experienced that. My book, *Holy Woman: The road to greatness of Rebbetzin Chaya Sara Kramer*, took on a life of its own, independent of its mother, I mean author. And, like any human life, it was guided by much *hashgachah pratis*.

Even before the book was "born," Divine Providence guided its conception. When the first four sample chapters arrived in the ArtScroll office in New York, as I sat in Jerusalem praying it would be accepted, the staff's response was mixed. Everyone liked the manuscript, but some were skeptical about its veracity. After all, they reasoned, if R' Yaakov Moshe and Chaya Sara Kramer were such big *tzaddikim*, why had nobody heard of them? Perhaps, they wondered, the book was more fiction than biography.

Then suddenly Mindy Stern, a member of the ArtScroll staff, spoke up. She "happens" to be related to Miriam Stern, who took over Rebbetzin Chaya Sara's care in the final years of her life. Indeed, Mindy testified, Miriam Stern had taken her to meet the *tzaddekes* Rebbetzin Chaya Sara Kramer and she had received her blessing. It was all true. Thus ArtScroll agreed to publish the book.

It became an overnight bestseller. *Holy Woman* is now ArtScroll's second bestselling biography (right behind *Reb Moshe*) of the sixty-two biographies it has published.

When the decision was taken to translate the book into Hebrew, Shmuel Blitz, the ArtScroll representative in Israel, chose a young woman named Nava Garman to be the translator. It "happens" that Nava's grandfather, Avraham Adler, was one of the twenty men on the boat that brought R' Yaakov Moshe Kramer from war-torn Europe to Palestine in 1945. Avraham Adler settled in Kibbutz Chafetz Chaim and remained a lifelong friend of R' Yaakov Moshe Kramer, often visiting him in Kfar Gidon.

Elisheva

*Y*et, the most moving evidence of *hashgachah pratis* attached to *Holy Woman* involved the very person who first introduced me to Rebbetzin Chaya Sara Kramer.

In the summer of 1985, I had been in Israel barely a month. Hearing that I was a writer, someone who was trying to put together a book called *A Spiritual Guide to Eretz Yisrael* (which was never published) asked me to write a chapter on "Holy Women." I was at a loss as to how to track down such women when a stranger told me, "You have to call Elisheva Buxbaum. She knows everyone worth knowing."

The person gave me Elisheva's phone number, and I called her. She told me that I must meet Rebbetzin Chaya Sara Kramer, who lived in a moshav named Kfar Gidon, north of Afula. Elisheva told me how to get there by two Egged buses, and she also gave me the phone number of an English-speaking family on the moshav who would be willing to host me for a Shabbos.

That was it. I never met Elisheva nor spoke to her again. I turned the key that she had given me and walked through the portal into the aura of the holy *tzaddekes* Chaya Sara Kramer, and my life was forever changed. But by the time I realized how much I owed Elisheva, I had lost the scrap of paper with her phone number.

Many years passed. I married and had children. By that time, the Kramers had moved to Meah Shearim, a 20-minute walk from my home, and R' Yaakov Moshe had passed on. I often visited Rebbetzin Chaya Sara and took friends to get her blessing.

When my younger child went to first grade, I started writing again, for the new educational website of Yeshivas Aish HaTorah, Aish.com. Of course, it occurred to me to write a book about Rebbetzin Chaya Sara. I asked her permission, and received a laughing but firm, "No!"

Knowing that hiddenness was her trademark, I was not surprised, but I was ready with a second offer: I would change her name and all identifying details. No one would ever find her from my book. She laughed again, but her "No" was adamant.

Several years passed. My friend Chasya Batya begged me to write a biography of Rebbetzin Kramer. "We *frum* women need role models," she implored. "There are enough biographies of great roshei yeshivot and Rebbeim. We need biographies of women."

I told her that I heartily agreed, but Rebbetzin Chaya Sara refused to let me write about her. Asking again would do no good. Chasya Batya, however, would not be deterred. Finally, just to placate her, I went and asked Rebbetzin Chaya Sara again.

She consented!

Like a child, a book descends into the world only at the designated time.

I started doing research. Often, at the end of an interview, the interviewee would ask me, "How did you meet Rebbetzin Kramer?"

I would answer lamely, "Someone named Elisheva told me about her." In all those years, my path had never again crossed Elisheva's. Or perhaps it had, and I simply didn't know what she looked like.

The more material I gathered, the more I realized that this book would be not only a good book, but a great book. As my debt to Elisheva grew, so did my frustration at having no way to find and thank her after almost twenty years.

Rebbetzin Chaya Sara went to Gan Eden on 3 Sivan, 5765 [2005]. Rav Yitzchak Berkowitz told me that I did not have to protect her anonymity any longer. The book could come out with her real name.

By Chanukah 2005 the book was almost completed. My husband and I were invited to a *Melaveh Malkah* for a yeshivah where he had once learned. Rav Asher Weiss spoke, and afterwards refreshments were served.

Alone on the women's side, I knew hardly anyone. I was relieved to spot my old friend Nechama Bergman. Nechama used to live in my neighborhood, but several years ago she moved to a moshav outside Jerusalem. I sat down beside her and asked her what was going on in her life. When she finished catching me up, she asked me what I was doing these days.

"I'm writing a book," I answered.

"Really? On what?"

My standard reply to that question, "It's a biography of Rebbetzin Chaya Sara Kramer," always drew a blank stare.

This time, however, Nechama answered, "Rebbetzin Chaya Sara Kramer! Elisheva and I used to go visit her all the time."

I was stunned.

"Y-y-you know Elisheva?" I finally managed to stutter.

"Of course, she's one of my best friends. She and I used to go up to Kfar Gidon and visit the Kramers all the time."

"Where does she live?" I asked eagerly.

Nechama's face changed to a sad, almost heartbroken, expression. "In Neve Yaakov," she replied quietly. "You don't know about her? She's very sick."

A light went on in my head. Just a month before, Rebbetzin Tziporah Heller, at the end of one of her weekly classes in my home, made an appeal. She said that there's a young woman who lives in Neve Yaakov who is alone, unmarried with no children, who is bedridden. She needs women to attend on her.

My heart sank. That was Elisheva!

Nechama gave me her phone number. The next morning I called. Elisheva remembered me. In fact, she used to read my articles on Aish.com when she was still well enough to sit up. We arranged that I would visit the next day.

I had known friends in the final stages of cancer, but I was totally unprepared for the sight that greeted me in Elisheva's room. The sheet covering her body barely rose from the mattress. Her shoulders and neck were skeletally thin, and the skin of her face was taut like photos of concentration camp survivors.

Yet, set into that emaciated face was a broad, radiant smile. As we talked, the smile never waned, except when it was replaced by a jubilant laugh.

Gazing at Elisheva, my cognitive dissonance was total. There was almost no body left except for that broad smile. I felt like I was conversing with a soul almost shorn of its body.

After an hour I left, promising to return again with the manuscript of the book that owed its existence to Elisheva.

Two days later I went for a final interview with Miriam Stern, Rebbetzin Chaya Sara's caregiver. I had asked her to lend me any photographs of the Rebbetzin that might have remained in her Meah Shearim apartment so that they could be used in the book.

For no particular reason, I took my friend Pamela along on the interview. In the car on the way, I told her about how I had miraculously found Elisheva after twenty years, just in the nick of time it seemed. Pamela, it turned out, had known Elisheva years before.

Miriam Stern handed me a pile a photographs. I eagerly went through them. Several were photos taken in recent years with various people who had visited the Rebbetzin. As I gazed at one picture of Rebbetzin Chaya Sara surrounded by visitors, Pamela pointed to a young woman standing behind the Rebbetzin and commented, "That's Elisheva."

I looked hard at the picture, but I could not identify the healthy young woman in the photo with the emaciated person I had met two days before. "It's definitely Elisheva," Pamela insisted.

I took the picture, copied it, framed it, and brought it as a gift to Elisheva, with the manuscript. She was thrilled to receive it.

A month later, she finished reading the manuscript. In a faint voice she told me, "I love it."

A few weeks later Elisheva Chana bas Avraham died at the age of 42, knowing that she had been the catalyst for a book that would exert a profound effect on thousands of readers.

I have often felt that, since Rebbetzin Chaya Sara was childless, everyone who reads *Holy Woman* and is inspired to grow becomes the Rebbetzin's spiritual child. Elisheva also died childless. The readers of *Holy Woman* are no less her spiritual children.

It's Not Too Late

Some readers of *Holy Woman* have expressed their frustration, "I was in Jerusalem while this great *tzaddekes* was alive, and I didn't meet her!" My response to this lament is: "It's not too late to form a relationship with Rebbetzin Chaya Sara Kramer."

As it says, "The *tzaddikim* are alive even after they're dead, and the wicked are dead even when they're alive." Rebbetzin Chaya Sara was never the type to sit back and do nothing. I am sure that even in Gan Eden she is busy helping people. I certainly feel her presence in my own life.

How to form a relationship with her now? *Daven* in the merit of Rebbetzin Chaya Sara bas Mendel Yosef. Visit her *kever* on Har HaMenuchos in Jerusalem (in the section *Derech Talpiot, Gush tet zayin, chelkah beis*). And light a candle on her *yahrzeit*, the 3rd of Sivan.

Countless times Rebbetzin Chaya Sara encouraged me to relate to her "*k'mo ima, k'mo ima* [like a mother]." If you regard yourself as her spiritual child, she will certainly become your spiritual mother.

Adi's Angel

Adi Huja, 16, observed the second anniversary of the terrorist bombing that almost took her life at Hadassah Hospital, preparing to undergo her 26th operation. On that fateful Saturday night two years ago, Adi and her cousins had gone to eat ice cream sundaes at a café on Jerusalem's Ben Yehuda pedestrian mall. Two Arab homicide bombers blew themselves up, killing 12 young people and injuring scores more.

The doctors told Adi's mother, Mollie, that they couldn't save her daughter. When, despite their dire predictions, Adi didn't die, the doctors told Mollie that they would have to amputate her right leg, which was partly torn off by the bomb. But, miraculously, they were able to reattach the leg. Two years later, however, it has still not healed, leaving Adi with constant infections and pain. The threat of amputation hangs relentlessly over her.

I am sitting beside Adi's bed in a drab room in Hadassah Hospital, a week after her 26th operation. "What did they do this time?" I ask Adi's mother.

"They put in a metal plate and a pin," Mollie answers.

"But she had a metal plate in her leg all last winter," I protest. "I remember her telling me how cold it made her feel. And the last operation was to take out the plate because the doctors thought it was the cause of her infections."

"Right," Mollie nods. "But her leg is broken, so they had to put the plate back in."

I look at this petite girl sitting in the bed, and ask, "So how do you feel, Adi?"

Adi answers with a single word: *"Mar* [bitter]."

What can I say to console her — for all the pain, for all the trauma, and for two years gouged out of her young life? I am struggling for something positive to say when my attention is drawn to a commotion at the door of Adi's ward. A man is trying to maneuver a wheelchair past chairs and beds. Sitting in the wheelchair is a young woman with a pretty face and two shriveled legs. The man pushes the wheelchair right up to Adi's bed.

"I came to say good-bye," the young woman says to Adi. "I'm being discharged."

The young woman's name is Leora. She and Adi converse for several minutes in Hebrew too fast for me to follow. Then they lovingly bid each other farewell. Leora's father backs the wheelchair out of the room.

"What's with Leora?" I ask Adi.

"She's totally crippled," replies Adi. "She's paralyzed from the waist down ... from birth."

Although I never philosophize with terror victims, my relationship with Adi is close enough that I venture: "You know, you can see your cup as half empty or half full. Compared to Leora, you're very fortunate. When you recover from this operation, you'll walk again."

"I'll hop with a crutch," Adi corrects me, resentfully.

I try another tack. "You've lost a lot, Adi, but you've gained even more. Most girls your age are shallow and self-centered. Because of all you've suffered, you've become deep, compassionate, and sensitive to other people's suffering. Before the terrorist attack, could you have related to Leora so warmly?"

Adi thinks about this. "No," she replies, shaking her head. "I wouldn't have related to her at all. I wouldn't want to look at a crippled girl. I wouldn't talk to her."

"See how much you've grown?"

Adi is not listening to me. She's gazing past me at the hospital corridor. Suddenly she shouts, "It's Malkiel!! *Ima*, go get him! Bring him in!"

Mollie runs out to the corridor and returns with a man in his mid-30's wearing a *kippah* and dressed in the blue uniform of a municipal sanitation worker. "Malkiel, I'm so glad to see you!" Adi effuses, smiling broadly.

I gaze at this man. I think I recognize him, but why is he dressed like a garbage collector? "You're Malkiel Lerner, aren't you?" I ask.

I had met Malkiel the previous May. At that time, he had given me his card that read: "Brother of the Wounded." He explained that he has made it his mission to visit every wounded person in Israel — whether from a terrorist attack or an army-related incident.

He had shown me and my husband a photo from his wedding two years earlier. In the photo, Malkiel, the heavy-set bridegroom, is sitting in a chair being hoisted into the air. "That's Ohaad," Malkiel had pointed proudly to one of the young men lifting his chair. "He lost his leg in the war in Lebanon in 1997. But there he is, dancing and lifting my chair."

The day before I met Malkiel, a terrorist attack had occurred in Afula, a two-and-a-half-hour drive north of Jerusalem. Although I usually visit terror victims in Jerusalem hospitals, I was not about to undertake the long drive to Afula, even though I own a car. Malkiel, by contrast, had risen at 5 that morning, and, for lack of a car, had taken a bus to Haifa and from there another bus to Afula to visit the victims. Fifteen hours later, he excused himself early from our meeting to work his night shift as a hotel clerk. I was in awe of Malkiel's dedication.

But now, in Adi's hospital room, I can make no sense of what I'm seeing. Why is he wearing a trash collector's uniform? I know that one of his brothers is a lawyer, another is a computer programmer. I ask him why he's dressed like this.

"I lost my job at the hotel," Malkiel answers, "so I'm working as a street cleaner. You can view it in two ways: You can say that it's dirty, disgusting work, or you can say that Jerusalem, the holy city, is the courtyard of the King, and that I'm privileged to make the King's courtyard cleaner and more beautiful."

Talk about seeing the cup as half full!

"Besides," Malkiel continues, "the hours are good. I get up at 4:30 a.m., *daven Shacharit*, catch the 5:30 bus, and start working at 6:00. I finish by 1:00, so I can spend two or three afternoons a week visiting the wounded."

Since Malkiel keeps up with all the terror victims in Israel, I ask him for an update on 20-year-old Ronit D. I had last seen Ronit 13 months ago, in Hadassah's Intensive Care Unit hours after a Jerusalem bus bombing. She had suffered massive injuries to her head and neck; her face was swollen to twice its normal size. A month later, I encountered her parents in the I.C.U. waiting room. Ronit was still unconscious.

"Two weeks ago," Malkiel announces, smiling, "she *bentched gomel* [recited the blessing for recovery from life-threatening illness]. Do you want to see her picture?"

Malkiel reaches into a plastic bag and pulls out a pile of photos. He hands me one of himself standing next to a sprightly young woman whose smiling face resembles a purple topographic map. I recoil in horror and wonder how any woman, vain as we are, could let her picture be taken like that. I wonder even more at her smile.

"Let me see!" Adi asks. I hand her the photo. Now Malkiel starts to pass around other photos. There's one of Malkiel flanked by two smiling young women. One is Ronit. The other woman's face has the same grotesque purple terrain as Ronit's. "This one," he explains, pointing, "was a waitress at that Tel Aviv café that was bombed."

Adi, appalled, asks, "Will their faces heal?"

"Ronit will eventually look better," Malkiel explains. "But the waitress will always be scarred."

Adi grimaces. I say to her, "*Baruch Hashem*, your pretty face wasn't damaged."

"*Baruch Hashem*," Adi responds, still staring at the picture.

"You have a lot to be grateful for," I add. "The truth is, your cup is three-quarters full."

Adi acquiesces with a nod. She looks up at Malkiel and tells him how bitter she has been feeling. Malkiel launches into a story.

"When I was 9 years old, I was run over by a car and badly hurt. I was unconscious for a week. I had a major concussion — and my leg was shattered. A lot like you," he adds, looking at Adi. "It took me many years to recover. I never finished school, and never got a high school diploma. I was bitter. For 19 years I would look up at heaven and ask, 'Why me? Why would You make a young boy suffer so much?'

"Then one day, when I was 28 years old, it suddenly came to me in a flash: I had to suffer such injuries so that I could help other people who are injured. I realized that my mission in life is to give strength and encouragement to the wounded. That's when I committed myself to visiting every single wounded person in Israel, no matter where they are."

I glance over at Adi. She is transfixed by Malkiel's story. Her cup is getting fuller by the minute.

Malkiel continues. "When I visit the wounded, I tell them what's written in *Pirkei Avot:* 'Who is rich? The one who is happy with his portion.' I tell them: 'If you have eyes, teeth, hands, and feet, rejoice!' To people like Ohaad, who don't have feet, I say, 'If you have eyes, teeth, hands, and a head, rejoice!'

"And you want to know something? It really works. They trust me because they know I've gone through something similar. They invite me to their weddings and to their babies' *brisses*. They feel like they have a friend who understands them."

I turn to Adi and ask, "Well, what do you think?"

"I think that Malkiel is great," she responds.

"You could be as great as Malkiel," I tell her earnestly. "Because you've suffered so much, you can also help people who are suffering."

Adi grins. Her cup is full.

Heroes: A True Story

Anne was an abused child. When she grew up, she did what many abused kids inexplicably do: she married a man who turned out to be an abuser. When she realized the scope of the damage her husband was inflicting on their three children, Anne took the children and fled.

Life has not been easy for Anne. Although she is a college graduate, because she is in hiding under an assumed name, she cannot use her diploma. She supports her children by cleaning houses and taking in ironing.

Money is scarce. Half her meager monthly income goes to pay psychotherapists for her children. The kids, especially the boys, are aggressive, belligerent, and rebellious. They feel they got a raw deal in life. Since their father is not around, they blame their mother. It doesn't help that she has no money to give them to buy the things the other kids have, not even treats. The oldest, 13-year-old Nate, was caught stealing candy at the local supermarket.

A strong, strapping boy, Nate often gets into fights with the neighborhood kids and with his younger siblings. Verbal sparring matches between Nate and his 10-year-old brother Donny are vicious and uncontrolled.

Like many people who were abused by their fathers, Anne has a hard time forging a relationship with Hashem. Since moving to Israel and living among religious people, whose lifestyle she admires, Anne has set new goals for her family. They now keep Shabbos and kashrus, and the children go to religious schools. As much as she appreciates the beauty of Judaism, however, Anne has a host of gripes against Hashem.

"I don't blame him for the marriage," she says. "I went into that with my eyes open. But why did Hashem have to give me such monsters for parents? And why, even now, does He have to make my life so difficult?"

Anne suffers from a battery of minor health problems. Frequently she must choose between buying a new pair of shoes for one of the kids or paying the electric bill. The telephone company recently disconnected her telephone. "It's easier to live without a telephone than without electricity," she explains to me. "My kids are afraid of the dark."

Last Friday, Anne called me. (Someone lent her money to pay her phone bill.) "I'm about to have a nervous breakdown," she told me grimly. "On top of everything else, my iron broke. How does Hashem expect me to earn money without my iron? And I can't afford a new one."

On Saturday night, after Shabbos, I telephoned Anne with the good news that a neighbor of mine had an extra iron that she was willing to give her. She informed me that over Shabbos the plumbing in the upstairs bathroom had broken down. She had no money to call a plumber.

"I just wish Hashem would lighten up on me," Anne complained.

I didn't know what to say. She certainly does have a difficult lot in life, I thought. I tried desperately to summon up a spiritual perspective that would lift her out of her depression.

"Hashem does give you a lot of challenges," I said finally. "But who knows? Even all the stuff you suffer — the broken iron, the broken plumbing — may be Hashem's mercy instead of giving you something worse like …" Here I faltered. What could be worse than all the hardships she has endured?

Nothing Changes; Everything Changes

The next morning, Sunday, Nate needed to go to Beersheva. He stood at the entrance of their small town in order to hitch a ride. A white Mitsubishi with two women stopped to pick him up. Nate got into the back seat and asked them where in Beersheva they were headed.

When they told him, Nate had second thoughts. Their destination was far from where he needed to go, and he didn't really have money for bus fare within the city. Maybe he could get a ride that would take him closer to his destination. On the other hand, maybe he couldn't. For a few seconds, he vacillated. Then Nate thanked the two women and got out of the car.

Five minutes later, the father of one of Nate's friends picked him up. They had traveled no more than a few minutes down the highway when the traffic stopped dead. Nate got out of the car to see what the trouble was.

He saw the road splattered with blood. Then he saw a hand lying on the road. Then a foot. Horrified, his eyes moved to the two vehicles that had crashed: a bus and the white Mitsubishi, now crushed like a discarded tin can.

Both women were dead.

As soon as Nate reached Beersheva, he called his mother. His voice was shaking. "I was in the car," he repeated over and over again. "Five minutes before the accident, I was in the car. I'm not even sure why I got out." Anne could not remember the last time she had heard Nate crying.

When Anne called me a few hours later, she was still trembling so hard I felt like the telephone wires were shaking. "Do you realize how close he came to being killed?" she asked me, trying desperately to convey her sense that her son had been miraculously plucked out of the doomed vehicle just in the nick of time.

She had one pressing question for me: "How do I thank Hashem?"

Nothing had changed. Anne still had no money, no good job prospects, poor health, broken plumbing, and three scarred kids. But suddenly, in the split second that it takes two vehicles to collide on the highway, everything had changed. Her eldest son was alive.

She felt like a woman blessed beyond words.

Giving It Back to Hashem

The accident was Sunday. On Monday evening, while Anne was washing dishes in the kitchen, her 8-year-old daughter came running in. "Mom, there's a flood."

Anne rushed upstairs to see two inches of water covering the whole upstairs floor, gushing out from under the bathroom door where Donny had gone to take a bath. All she could think of was the electronic game always sitting, plugged in, on the floor of her sons' bedroom. Yelling to her daughter to stay downstairs, she ran to the bedroom. Water covered the floor except for the corner where the game lay.

Next she ran to the bathroom. Flinging open the door, she saw Donny floating face down in the tub. Her heart stopped. She grabbed him and yanked him out of the tub. Donny burst into laughter. He had been playing dead. He had not noticed the bathtub overflowing.

Anne took a deep breath and surveyed the damage. They were in the process of moving to a smaller apartment; packed suitcases and boxes lay all over the floor of the hallway and bedrooms. Now everything was soaked. She would have to unpack everything, hang up every item of clothing, every sheet and blanket, and throw away what could not be salvaged.

She returned to the bathroom and motioned to Donny to come to her. Donny knew that look on his mother's face, that look of tension, of being so overwhelmed that she lost control. People parent the way they were parented. Donny put his hand over his face and flinched.

Then something miraculous happened. More miraculous than Nate getting out of the car. More miraculous than the water not reaching the electronic game. Instead of slapping her son, Anne cradled his face in her two hands and said, "I'm really upset about all the work you caused me, and all the ruined stuff. But you're my child, and I love you no matter what you do." And she bent down and kissed his forehead.

All she could think of was: "Thank Hashem my children are alive."

Momentous Actions

That very same night, Nate was rehearsing for a school play.

During the break, one of the teachers gave Nate money to go to the pizza parlor and buy pizza for all the performers.

Nate was chosen to go because he had a spiffy new bike. His aunt had sent him $250 for a super-duper bike, a belated Bar Mitzvah present, because it had taken her almost a year to save the money. Nate had purchased the bike, the only truly wonderful object he owned, two weeks before. Because there was no money left over to buy a lock, Nate never left the bike unattended.

That Monday night, Nate took the bike into the pizza parlor with him. A gang of kids, a year younger than Nate, was hanging out in there. Nate knew them. He had once helped these same kids drag a load of wood up a hill for a Lag B'Omer bonfire. He had seen them struggling, and because he was bigger, he had helped them.

When Nate turned to order the pizzas, the kids grabbed his bike, took it outside, and slammed it against a wall so hard they demolished the bike. Nate came running outside after them to find his precious bike a mangled carcass.

Nate's first thought was: "How could they do this to me? I helped them!"

His second thought was: "I want to kill them."

His third thought was: "I promised my mother I won't fight or swear anymore."

His fourth thought was: "Violence doesn't help. Even if I cream them, it won't bring my bike back."

Then Nate did something so momentous its effect will be felt for generations: Nate refrained from beating up the boys who had destroyed his bike. In so overcoming his own tendency, Nate picked up a machete made of his aspiration to become a better person and, with one mighty blow, severed a chain of violence that stretched back generations. *Pirkei Avos* says: "Who is a hero? He who overcomes his own self."

Nate left the pizza parlor dragging the remains of his new bike. If I were a film maker, I would shoot the scene in slow-motion. I would play a score of triumphant music in the background, with lots of trumpets. I would have fireworks going off in the night sky above Nate and his mangled bike.

And that's probably how it looked in the higher worlds. But in this physical world there was simply a tearful boy dragging home the mangled mess that had been his most prized possession.

One thing is certain: Few happenings that took place in the world that Monday night, including the events that grabbed the next morning's headlines, were as significant as Nate's and Anne's victories over violence. They are models of true heroism.

An Ordinary Woman

My friend Rivka was an ordinary woman — a Valley girl, an "A" student, the only daughter of an assimilated Jewish family. When she was 17, fresh out of high school, Bev (as she was known in those years) married her classmate Terry. It was 1956, the era of the somnambulant 50's, when most young women's heroines were Betty Crocker and Miss America, when most young wives' goals were to bake the perfect cake and have kitchen floors so clean they could see their own reflections.

Terry was drafted into the U.S. Army. In the unlikely setting of an army base in Millington, Tennessee, Bev, the most ordinary of young brides, made an extraordinary decision: She decided to learn what being a Jew was really all about. She decided she could learn this only from an Orthodox rabbi. Millington, Tennessee, however, boasted not a single Orthodox rabbi. The closest one was Rabbi Goodman, who lived in Memphis, an hour's ride away. Undaunted, Bev made a weekly pilgrimage on the Greyhound bus to study with Rabbi Goodman.

Eventually Terry was transferred to Biloxi, Mississippi. There, too, Bev felt driven to continue learning Torah. She found a rabbi to start a class (for one) in basic Judaism.

By the time, a few years later, they moved to El Cajon, California, the Rakovs had two children. "Rivka needed a Jewish pre-school," Terry recalls. "There was no Jewish pre-school in El Cajon, so she made one. Then she had to have an Orthodox synagogue, so she made one of those."

In 1964, the family moved to San Diego. Now the Rakov children, who numbered five, were older. They needed a Jewish day school, but San Diego had no such institution, so Rivka helped start the Soille San Diego Hebrew Day School. Forty years later, it's still thriving.

And, as always, Rivka longed to learn more Torah. She brought one of America's greatest rabbis, Rabbi Simcha Wasserman, to San Diego once a week to teach adult classes.

As Paul Vann, a young Jewish sailor stationed in San Diego during those years, later wrote: "Beverly's attitude was, 'If you want it, go get it.' This was not necessarily about material things. It was about life."

Despite her active involvement in Hadassah and in the Ladies' Auxiliary of the local Orthodox synagogue, Rivka's priority was always her family. Every day the family sat down to eat dinner together at 6 o'clock. This family time was sacrosanct. Anyone who showed up at 6:30 didn't get dinner. Rivka also insisted on the annual family vacation: one or two months of camping out all over North America and beyond — from California to Newfoundland to Hawaii.

Amid her manifold commitments, her husband came first. As Terry eulogized her at her funeral, "Her husband was #1. She made sure that he got everything he needed, including care, the respect of the children, everything." The true magical power of the truly great: they shine their total love and attention on family members, friends, and needy strangers, and no one ever feels that he's getting only a sliver of sunshine.

In San Diego, Terry opened a motorcycle store. As Paul Vann, who had become like a member of their family, recounts, "Terry sold me a motor scooter and then took me home to dinner. That was pretty common. Everyone always had dinner and a place to sleep at the Rakovs'. I used to worry that

Beverly would be personally responsible for the extinction of the chicken."

Learning and growing were Rivka's life-long passion ... but not her only one. She loved to eat, to cook, and to serve culinary masterpieces of her own creation. She loved ice cream. Her best friend Ethel Adatto recalls how, upon meeting Rivka and Terry in London one winter, Rivka immediately whisked her off to Baskin Robbins for ice cream. Rivka's motto was, "You never know a city until you find the Baskin Robbins store." [In those days Baskin Robbins was one of the few ice creams with a *hashgachah* (though it was not *chalav Yisrael*).] Rivka founded the "Ice Cream for Breakfast on Your Birthday Club." Ethel recollected how, many times, she and Rivka would have to wait until noon, when the ice cream store opened, to eat their birthday breakfast.

Challenges

At age 39, Rivka was diagnosed with cancer. She underwent surgery and chemotherapy, and survived, but from that time on she regarded every day of life as a free gift. When, two decades later, Rivka succumbed to cancer, Terry's rejoinder to her distraught friends was: "She got twenty extra years." Rivka loved life, but she never felt she got too little of it.

Eight years later, the cancer recurred. Again surgery and chemotherapy. Rivka became proactively involved in her own treatment. She kept up with every medical journal she could find, and informed her doctors of the latest cancer treatments she had read about.

Meanwhile, Rivka had spiritually outgrown San Diego. The Rakovs made *aliyah* to Israel in 1978, moving into an

Absorption Center in the Jerusalem neighborhood of Gilo. There Rivka inaugurated a weekly Torah class for English-speaking women, inviting a different speaker each week. Twenty-six years later, the weekly Gilo class is still meeting.

It was time to buy an apartment. Little wonder that Rivka gravitated to the world's holiest spot — an apartment overlooking the Kosel in Jerusalem's Old City.

Terry started a laundromat, to be followed by a deli, in the Old City's Jewish Quarter. The children grew up, married, and had children of their own. Rivka became the ultimate *"savta"* [grandma]. "She read us stories, played games, took us on trips, stayed with us when our parents needed a break, knew our friends, our likes and dislikes ... For some of us, she was also our best friend, a person with whom we could share our biggest secrets."

Even during the trying months of her final illness, Rivka displayed unlimited patience with all her grandchildren. She also talked to them candidly about her impending death, confident that even a child could be taught not to fear death.

Rivka's generosity was legendary. It extended not only to Shabbos meals and hospitality, but even to the clothes on her back. Honey Weiss, a pensioner who attended the Old City synagogue where Rivka prayed, recalls one Shabbos when Rivka, chic as ever, was wearing an elegant black velvet vest with braided trim and brightly colored stones. "Tasteful, but not gaudy," was Honey's assessment. "Oh," she exclaimed to Rivka, "that's just the sort of thing I'm looking for. Where did you — ?"

Rivka interrupted her. "Why buy one? I'll lend you mine, with pleasure! How many of these do we need in one neighborhood?"

The Rakovs loved to travel. In 1994, they flew to Africa with two other observant Jewish couples. Rivka, a seasoned camper, knew how to handle the challenge of keeping kosher in the hinterlands of Africa. They arranged for the native guides to meet them with all new pots and pans, which they toiveled in the ocean. They cooked all their meals over an open fire. Mica Fox relates one episode from their African adventure:

> *One image stands out so clearly: Rivka in Victoria Falls, dressed in a wetsuit, life vest, and crash helmet, ready to go white water rafting. She gave precise instructions to a couple of us cowards who stayed behind: "If anything should happen to me, be sure to ship my body to Jerusalem."*
>
> *The boat overturned, and the people in it were swept into the foaming water, but were retrieved. When the ordeal was over, a happy Rivka enthused, "This is really something to tell my grandchildren."*
>
> *A young woman stopped dead in her tracks and asked, "Your WHAT?"*
>
> *"My grandchildren."*
>
> *The young woman stared at Rivka in consternation and stammered, "You mean you have children who have children?"*
>
> *"Yes," replied Rivka. "I have fourteen grandchildren."*
>
> *The young woman looked incredulously at her and exclaimed, "My grandmother would never do anything like this!" Then she added, "My mother would never do it either."*

The Angel of Death

*I*n 1989, tragedy struck with the sudden death of Terry and Rivka's youngest son, 29-year-old Matthew. Rivka's grief was as private as her customary joy was public. Those of us who met her after the tragedy never knew the heartbreak concealed behind her radiant, constant smile. In this misfortune, as with the cancer that cast its menacing shadow over her life, Rivka had absolute faith in the goodness of Hashem.

At the age of 56, the Angel of Death caught up with her again; Rivka was diagnosed with ovarian cancer. It took three years until she died, and that period was perhaps the most glorious of her luminous life.

It is no exaggeration to say that Rivka retained her good cheer throughout her whole ordeal. Ruth Fogelman, who visited Rivka in the hospital after one of her abdominal surgeries, recalls Rivka bantering with her: "You know Michal. She's just had a tumor taken out the size of an orange. I did better than her; I had a tumor the size of a grapefruit! We had them in the same place. Why did she have to copy me?"

While Rivka submitted to all the conventional therapies, the treatment in which she put the most stock was prayer. She asked her friends to divide up the Book of Psalms and collectively recite the entire Book every day for her recovery. When, a few months later, she received a favorable report, she attributed it to the power of prayer.

While waiting for the reports about the state of her cancer after each series of chemotherapy, Rivka and Terry traveled to exotic places. They made a trip to China and, a year later, planned a motorcycle tour of New Zealand. When I heard about the motorcycle trip, I was flabbergasted.

How could a person fighting metastasized cancer ride a motorcycle around New Zealand? Dismissing everyone's misgivings, Rivka went — on the motorcycle — and had a fabulous time.

From the upbeat way Rivka always acted, I wondered if she understood how dismal her prognosis was. Then, one evening, I was sitting next to her at a Bar Mitzvah. She was giving me a glowing report about a gourmet glatt-kosher Thai restaurant in Jerusalem. "We're going to take all the kids and grandkids there to celebrate my 60th birthday next month."

It took me a moment to register the discrepancy. "You're not going to be 60," I corrected her. "You're going to be 59."

She chuckled at having been caught. "I know, but this restaurant is too expensive to take everyone for anything less than a major milestone. So I decided to celebrate my 60th birthday this year since I may not be around for it next year."

Perspicacious Rivka. She never lived to see 60.

Putting Others First

While protracted illness can make one self-absorbed, Rivka's hallmark during the final phase of her life was her unremitting concern for other people. A divorced woman who moved into the Jewish Quarter eight months before Rivka died recalled how solicitous Rivka was to make sure that she was never alone on Shabbos. When Rivka, whose body was declining rapidly by that time, could not host her herself, she made phone calls to friends to place the solitary woman for Shabbos meals.

Nomi, a neighbor from the Old City, relates the following story from this period: Nomi had gone to downtown Jerusalem to shop when she suddenly was overcome by a sick feeling. She made her way to the bus stop to catch the bus to the Old City, and there was Rivka, also waiting for a bus.

> *I told her that I was feeling very weak, and wasn't sure if I could make it home. Rivka immediately got us into a cab, helped me walk all the way home [a 5-minute walk from the parking*

lot of the Jewish Quarter], and tucked me into bed. Concerned by the fact that my husband was out of the country, and that I was momentarily all alone, she patiently waited for my daughter Yael to come home from school. She also called my married daughter to let her know that I was not well. Then Rivka made sure that I called a doctor, and confirmed that he would indeed be coming to see me soon.

The image is searing: Nomi, who was suffering from a virus that would last a week, being attentively cared for by Rivka, who was suffering from terminal cancer.

During that final phase of her illness, Rivka had trouble breathing. She had to go to Hadassah Hospital periodically to be drained. While I called this procedure "painful," Rivka insisted on labeling it, "uncomfortable." Once, after such a draining, Rivka had to wait around to speak to a doctor. Never wanting to waste a moment and oblivious to her own weak condition, Rivka took the hospital elevator up to the geriatric ward to see if she could help. It was lunchtime, so she set about feeding the patients. She saw an elderly Russian woman who could not feed herself. Rivka sat on the edge of her bed and spoon-fed her. In the next bed was a 90-year-old American woman who had lost all interest in eating. As she fed the Russian woman, with whom she could not communicate, Rivka talked to the American, trying to convince her to eat.

When all her coaxing failed, Rivka thought of a new tactic. "You should eat," Rivka told her, "because it will make you look prettier. It will make your cheeks pink and give a glow to your skin." Then, to accentuate the importance of looking pretty, Rivka took a lipstick from her purse, cleaned it off, and applied it to the nonagenarian's lips. Rivka then held up a mirror, so the woman could see how nice she looked. The woman ate.

Telling me this story later, Rivka was pleased that she had managed to use her time optimally by feeding two patients at once. Time was precious to her, even before it started to run out. Every day she would ask herself: "What did I do today to bring me closer to Hashem? What did I do today for others?"

Rivka's lifelong dedication to learning Torah was not an intellectual exercise. Rather, Torah for her was a path of personal transformation. She integrated everything she learned into her life, constantly working on herself until the end.

Thus, in Rebbetzin Tziporah Heller's weekly class, which Rivka faithfully attended until she became housebound, she learned that the Maharal's suggested method for overcoming anger was to recite *Tefillas HaDerech* (without using the Divine Name). A short time later, Rivka underwent yet another surgery. Afterward, she was in great pain. The nurse on duty insisted on giving her a painkiller to which Rivka knew she would have a bad reaction. Rivka told the nurse the correct painkiller to give her, which she had worked out with her doctor, but the nurse refused. The nurse insisted on following the standard orders, unless she had explicit instructions to the contrary from the doctor. Rivka begged her to call the doctor, but the nurse was too busy. Rivka, in pain and helpless, felt frustrated and angry. Then she remembered what she had learned in class, and determined to use it then and there. She recited *Tefillas HaDerech*, and it worked! She calmed down, spoke sweetly to the nurse, and convinced her to call the doctor, who ordered the nurse to give Rivka the painkiller she had requested.

I could barely look at Rivka during that period without crying. She became skeletally thin, and lost her eyesight in one eye. But whenever anyone asked her, "How are you?" she replied with a broad smile and a buoyant, *"Baruch Hashem!"* And she made herself a pink eye patch decorated with sequins.

An Ordinary Woman / 405

And even at this stage, she put others first. On her last Lag B'Omer, three months before she died, her oldest grandson Ariel had planned to build the traditional bonfire with his friend Yoel. The boys were at Rivka's house. Knowing that bonfires need adult supervision, Rivka phoned Yoel's mother and asked her, "If I can't make it up the steps, can you supervise the bonfire?"

"Of course," Ruth replied, understanding how difficult it would be for Rivka and knowing that Terry was in America.

"Uh-oh," Rivka remembered. "You're allergic to smoke. Don't worry. I'll manage."

And she did.

The Final Trip

A friend said of Rivka, "She always saw the donut, not the hole." Indeed, Rivka did more than see the donut; she ate the donut, relishing every last crumb.

One month before she died, Rivka's condition took a sudden turn for the worse. A friend hurriedly called for the neighborhood women to meet at the Kosel to recite *Tehillim*, to implore the Almighty that Rivka should live until Ariel's Bar Mitzvah, two weeks away. Knowing that Rivka would be strengthened to learn that her friends were reciting *Tehillim* for her, I telephoned to tell her. "If you look out your living room window," I suggested, "you'll be able to see us."

"I can't get out of bed without throwing up," Rivka replied weakly. She was silent for a moment, clearly casting about for a way to join our collective effort. "And I don't have the strength to say any *Tehillim* with you." She racked her brain for another moment, then triumphantly pronounced the solution: "But while you're saying *Tehillim*, I can hold the book."

Her desire to contribute was so great, undiminished by her body's devastation, that she managed to think of some way that she, too, could contribute to the group's effort. She would hold the book.

Exactly two weeks before Rivka's death, I was privileged to be allowed to see her for the last time. When I entered her bedroom, she was on her way from the bathroom to her bed. At first I was shocked to see her, so shrunken and emaciated, without the *sheitel* and makeup that had served to cover up her true condition. My horror melted as soon as Rivka greeted me with her usual broad smile.

Instead of lying down on her bed, Rivka sat down on the edge, bent over, and started rummaging through a drawer beneath the bed. She was looking for hats to give me. Her position certainly could not have been comfortable; I begged her to stop. No, she had to find three hats that matched the outfit I was wearing, lest she bequeath to me hats that didn't match my wardrobe.

We spoke about food, recipes, spices. Her zest for living had not abated, even while she was dying. Food was life. Just because she could no longer partake of it did not diminish her interest in it.

Then she told me she had chosen Terry and her three sons-in-law to give the eulogies at her funeral. "You're planning your own funeral?" I asked in consternation.

"Of course. Do you think I would give up control before I have to?" she replied, and laughed.

"Have you thought of what you will say when you see *HaKadosh Baruch Hu*?" I asked.

"I already feel so intimate with Him," was her pensive reply.

When I left, she gave me a hearty farewell hug. I was high for a week. The Baal Shem Tov said that death is like going from one room to another. For Rivka, it took more planning and preparation than that, more like going on a trip to Africa or New Zealand. She planned her journey to the Next World with the same good cheer, fearlessness, and open anticipation that she had planned her This World journeys.

A Chassidic saying asserts that there are no proofs for Hashem's existence, only witnesses. Rivka was such a witness. By the way she lived, and even more so by the way she died, she made us all witnesses.

My friend Rivka was an ordinary woman. How did she become so great?

And if she could do it, what about me and you?

For the aliyas neshamah of
Rivka bas Emmanuel.

Seeing Clearly: A Blind Woman's Vision

Being blind has not been the hardest challenge of Leah Efrat Moyal's life, but it was the first.

Born in Jerusalem in 1974 with normal vision, Leah was allergic to the formula her mother fed her. At the age of five months, weighing the same as her birth weight, she was hospitalized. One day her mother Miriam entered the neonatal unit and noticed immediately that her baby's eyes were searching rather than focusing as they usually did. Miriam called her daughter's name, but the baby did not look at her. Alarmed, Miriam ran to the doctors and cried, "My baby can't see!"

The doctors confirmed Miriam's nightmare: the baby had lost her eyesight and the damage was irreversible.

Miriam, however, was a strong woman. She was not about to let herself or her daughter be routed by a handicap. Before Leah started first grade at the local elementary school, she went for lessons to learn Braille. Equipped with her Braille typewriter, Leah attended mainstream religious schools through high school. Then she did National Service (an alternative to the army for religious girls), tutoring children from broken homes. She went on to earn her B.Ed. in music education at Michlala, a Jerusalem college for religious women. Since college, Leah has worked for Michlala's radio station.

As with many blind people, music has played a pivotal role in Leah's life. Since the age of 15, she has given concerts to women and girls, playing guitar, harmonica, and flute, and singing, often her own compositions. She has performed in "women only" concerts all over Israel, lacing her music with stories about her life and her faith in Hashem. Seven years ago, her first CD was released.

Raised in a deeply religious home, Leah has always had an intensely personal relationship with Hashem. Growing up, she recalls, "He was my best friend. He was in charge of getting my favorite singer to the top of the charts."

But Leah's life would provide ample challenges to her childhood faith.

The Baby

*M*iriam always dreamed that her blind daughter would marry a sighted man. This was the goal — the sign of having "made it" — of all of Leah's blind friends. Indeed, Leah did become engaged to a sighted man, but she soon learned that perfect vision does not make a perfect partner. She broke the engagement.

Then, at the age of 25, considered "old" in her circles, Leah married Avraham Chaim Moyal, a yeshivah student. An albino, Avraham has weak eyesight. He studies Gemara with jewelers' magnifying lenses. "Like me," Leah comments, "he's a person with tremendous strength of will. He has pushed himself far beyond the limitations of where people thought he would get."

After four years of waiting, Leah, joyfully, was expecting. She carried the baby to term. Four days after the due date, she went into labor. With blissful anticipation, Leah and Avraham went to the hospital, where, as a routine procedure, she was hooked up to the monitor. The expectant mother could hear a flurry of concerned, even panicked, voices around her bed. Then came the dreadful words: "Your baby is dead."

At first Leah did not believe them. This could not be happening, not to her, who had already undergone her share of affliction. When the terrible truth did sink in, her first response was: "I didn't know that I am such a *tzaddikah* that Hashem would give me such a test."

After that, she recited the verse from Psalms: "Hashem is good and does good. Teach me to understand Your edicts."

To her devastated family and friends, the bereaved Leah assumed the unlikely role of the paragon of faith. "People came to *me* asking why I lost my baby," she recalls with wonderment. "I had to be the teacher of *emunah* [faith]."

Yet, the hardest test was still to come.

Outgrowing Your Shoes

A few months later, Leah's mother Miriam was diagnosed with cancer. By that time, Leah was again expecting. Her condition was an uphill road running parallel to her mother's precipitous decline. Leah and Avraham's son Yoel was born in January, 2004. Two months later, despite an avalanche of fervent prayers, Miriam died at the age of 52.

Leah was shattered. She who had borne her blindness and the death of her first child with stoic faith now found herself angry with Hashem. She who had always believed in the power of prayer now found herself mouthing the words without conviction. She who had always been resilient in the face of hardship now found herself plummeting into an abyss of depression.

"*Emunah* is like shoes," Leah muses. "Sometimes you outgrow them and you have to find bigger ones."

When Leah's life outgrew her faith, she set about searching for a larger measure of faith, one that could accommodate the huge challenge of losing her mother just when she needed her most.

Her first step was to admit that she was angry at Hashem. "In my own heart and mind," she explains, "I knew that being angry at Hashem doesn't mean rejecting Him. It's like He's my father. You have a fight, but you're still together. I allowed myself to be angry at Hashem. I kept saying, 'Don't talk *about* Hashem; talk *to* Hashem.' I would say to Him, 'I don't understand why You do what You do,' but He was always there with me."

Her next step was to learn more Torah, especially teachings about the World to Come, where souls go after the death of the body. "I upgraded my faith in *Olam Haba* [the World to Come]. I came to realize that what we don't understand here, we'll understand there. I'm building my place in *Olam Haba* all the time. There is one right choice in every moment; I'm trying to discern what is right and pursue it."

Leah's definition of *emunah* is twofold: "Part one is to feel the presence of Hashem in everything that happens, to understand that nothing happens by chance. Part two is to believe that it's good. That's the harder part."

When asked, "Does Hashem love you?" Leah answers with a quiet, "Yes." How does she know He loves her? She ponders the question and replies: "I think that I know it now more than I knew it before. It took me a very long time to understand that His presence is healing, and not punishing. I was afraid of Him and did not truly love Him. Only when I started loving myself could I start loving Hashem.

"And Hashem led me to people who helped me. My best friend never saw Hashem as scary, but always as loving. She understood that just because we don't get everything we pray for doesn't mean that Hashem doesn't love us. She kept saying to me, 'Hashem is not a fairy godfather but *Keil Melech Neeman* — the faithful, powerful King.'"

Does Prayer Work?

During this cataclysmic period, Leah realized that her own special mitzvah is prayer. Although her mother's death had pierced her faith in prayer like a knife stabbing a balloon, Leah set about building a less fragile faith.

Six weeks ago, the 20-year-old son of Rabbi Motti Elon was critically injured in an automobile accident. Another occupant of the car was killed. With all of his internal organs injured, Rabbi Elon's son faced a series of lengthy surgeries to try to save his life. Leah, who knew the family well, joined in a massive prayer effort by thousands of Rabbi Elon's students and well-wishers. The result was an open miracle. The first operation concluded successfully much more quickly than the surgeons had expected, and no other surgeries were needed. Three weeks after the accident, to the shock of his doctors, the boy went home, with no permanent damage of any kind.

"Prayer works," Leah concludes. "It couldn't save my mother, because she had her own accounting with Hashem. But I saw from Rav Elon's son that prayer can work miracles. We may not get everything we want. Hashem is not a fairy godfather. But we surely get closer to Hashem and become purer people through praying."

Finally Joy

Leah has finally emerged from the pit into which she fell upon the death of her mother. Her encounter with Chassidus has played a significant role. "Through the *simchah* of Chassidus," she explains, "I realized that Hashem has always loved me."

Leah's 3-year-old son Yoeli, "the world's most adorable child," in her assessment, is also a potent contributor to her joy level. Although the first year of his life was overwhelmingly difficult, Leah, who was raised to be fiercely independent, has learned to ask for help.

One day Yoeli handed his mother a book and asked her to read it to him. "I can't, sweetie," Leah demurred.

"Please read it to me, *Ima*," Yoeli begged.

"I can't, sweetie. You know my eyes don't work."

"Then use your cane," was Yoeli's advice.

One characteristic of her more mature faith is that Leah no longer blames herself for her bouts of bitterness. "There's a difference between saying life is hard and *kvetching*. To *kvetch* is to think that someone was unjust to you. I don't consider myself the victim of injustice. *Baruch Hashem*, I'm learning to understand that being bitter over what I've suffered is okay. When I stop blaming myself for being bitter, then I stop being bitter. I'm not afraid of falling anymore. Who am I not to fall?"

Pesach Parallels

Leah was born on the eve of Pesach, and her life has embodied the eternal lessons of the Exodus from Egypt.

The Hebrew word for Egypt is *Mitzraim*, which connotes a narrow place. The inner process of redemption, available to all Jews at this time of year, is to emerge from a state of narrowness and constriction to a more expanded state. This is the process which Leah described as outgrowing your shoes and having to find larger ones.

To any observer, the young Leah was a shining example of faith and love of Hashem. But the terrible torment of losing her mother made her realize that her faith was facile and immature. It became too "narrow" for her. She had to grow into a larger, deeper, and stauncher faith. Similarly, each of us, no matter what our religious level, must grow beyond our present state into the expanded consciousness that awaits us. Seder night is the time to grasp the spiritual energy of bursting out of constriction in order to emerge into an expanded state. This is the inner Exodus from *Mitzraim*.

The Seder is replete with the contrasting symbols of suffering and redemption: the salt water, the bitter herbs, the sweet *charoses*, and the matzah, which is called both the bread of freedom and the bread of affliction. This interfacing of bitterness and freedom is intended to drive home the core lesson of Passover: that suffering leads to redemption.

Eating the "bitter herbs" is one of the four mitzvos of the Seder. Rebbetzin Tziporah Heller explains the difference between depression and bitterness. Depression paralyzes. Bitterness, on the contrary, galvanizes; when you eat something bitter, you want to spit it out.

Our national experience of Egyptian bondage was bitter. At the Seder, we are bidden to imbibe that bitterness — not to ignore it, nor gloss over it, nor paint it pink with platitudes. Hardships create yearning, and yearning breaks the illusory barrier that separates the physical from the spiritual. Only when Leah learned to accept her bitterness could she find the way to her redemption.

The quest for redemption requires much arduous inner work. Leah, who works relentlessly on herself, uses a Biblical quote to prove the point. The final words of the Book of Ruth state: "Boaz bore Oved, Oved bore Yishai, and Yishai bore David [King David, the progenitor of Mashiach, who will usher in the final redemption]."

Leah points out that the name *"Oved"* means worker. Thus, the hidden meaning of the verse is that only one who works on oneself can ultimately give birth to the redemption.

If only we could all see as clearly as this blind woman!

Unbelievable Belief: Dr. Melamed-Cohen

People all over the world turn to Dr. Rahamim Melamed-Cohen for advice, encouragement, and inspiration. A father from a religious community near Jerusalem seeks educational guidance from him in dealing with his troubled teenage son. An unmarried older girl, on the night that her most recent *shidduch* failed, finds optimism and joy in his recipe for living. A New York neurologist, scheduled to speak on medicine and ethics, asks for his input. A secular California college student diagnosed with bipolar disorder effuses: "Your spirit and love for life jumped right through the article, through my monitor, and into my own spirit." A fifth-grade girl writes to him: "You have totally changed my perspective on things." A successful gentile Texas dentist with a turbulent family situation pleads with him to help her find joy in life. A *frum* woman in Arizona undergoing marital difficulties after many years of marriage requests that Dr. Melamed-Cohen pray for her and her husband.

Letters pour into his email from Australia, South Africa, Turkey, England, Canada, Chile, Israel, Guatemala, Zimbabwe, Greece, and all over the United States.

Is Dr. Melamed-Cohen a globe-trotting motivational speaker? A radio or television personality? A best-selling author? An advice columnist turned celebrity?

No, Dr. Melamed-Cohen has galvanized this tidal-wave of inspiration from his wheelchair in his Jerusalem home where, totally paralyzed and on life-support, he communicates only by moving his eyes on his computer screen. Thirteen years after being diagnosed with Lou Gehrig's Disease (ALS), twelve years after losing his ability to walk, eight years after losing his ability to feed himself, seven and a half years after losing his ability to breathe without a respirator, Dr. Melamed-Cohen is enjoying what he calls, "the best and most important years of my life."

What is the secret of his unconquerable spirit?

Preparing for Everything Except the Worst

Rahamim Melamed-Cohen was born in Jerusalem in 1937, the scion of Jews from Syria and Persia, where his grandfather had served as Chief Rabbi of Shiraz. At the age of 22, he married Elisheva, whose parents had fled Germany before the *Shoah*. The couple has six children, 27 grandchildren, and one great-grandchild.

After getting his Ph.D. in Special Education, Dr. Melamed-Cohen held a leading position in Israel's Ministry of Education, served as Head of the Education Dept. at Michlala, a Jerusalem college for religious girls, and pioneered Special Education programs throughout Israel. The Israeli government sent him to work with Jews in India from 1963-67 and to England from 1983-85.

One day when he was 57 years old and at the apex of his career as Head of Curriculum for all Israeli government schools, Dr. Melamed-Cohen felt a weakness in his left shoulder. Soon the weakness spread down his arm to his fingers. When he made *Kiddush* on Friday night, the *Kiddush* cup shook and the wine spilled.

He and his wife Elisheva made the rounds of neurologists, until one doctor gave them the dread diagnosis: Lou Gehrig's Disease (ALS). In answer to Rahamim's searching questions, the doctor spelled out for them the entire course of the disease: first his limbs would become paralyzed, to be followed by the muscles of his neck, esophagus, and tongue. "The day will come," the physician told Rahamim, "when a fly will land on your nose and you won't be able to brush it off. You will become dependent on other people for everything." And in the final stage, his lungs would stop working. "You have three to five years to live," the doctor prognosticated.

From the beginning, Rahamim decided to stay one step ahead of the disease. Anticipating the paralysis of his legs, he installed an elevator to carry him up to his second-floor apartment. When one hand was still good enough to press the buttons on his special wheelchair, he had a control mechanism installed on the back of the wheelchair for the stage when he would not be able to drive it himself. While he could still speak clearly, he researched and located the ingenious American-made computer that is now his principal means of communication.

Yet, with all his preparations, he did not prepare for the inevitable moment that strikes all ALS sufferers: the final moment when the paralysis creeps into the lungs. One day, seven and a half years ago, Elisheva heard her husband straining to breathe. She called an ambulance. The medics arrived at the same moment that Rahamim's breathing stopped. They resuscitated him and rushed him to the hospital. There Elisheva made the decision to hook her husband up to a respirator rather than let him die.

"Everything would have been different in one minute," Elisheva recalls, "if I hadn't called the ambulance. And there was a doctor in the emergency room who said to me, 'Why did you resuscitate him?' This was very terrible to hear."

When he regained consciousness, Rahamim himself was not sure that being kept alive by a respirator was the best decision. Now, however, he asserts, "If they had let me die, I would have missed the best and most important years of my life."

A Full Schedule

It is now thirteen years since his diagnosis. Three of the doctors who attended him have since died, but Rahamim Melamed-Cohen, while completely paralyzed, is still going strong. Since the onset of his illness, he has written and published eight books. The earlier volumes, written when he could not move his hands but could still speak, were dictated to his sister; the later volumes he typed by his eye movements on his special computer. Until two years ago, when he could still speak clearly, he gave lectures on educational methodology in his living room to students from Yeshivat Shalavim. He maintains a voluminous email correspondence with a wide spectrum of people who look to him for encouragement and wisdom. He prays thrice daily and attends synagogue every Shabbos.

At 69, Dr. Melamed-Cohen's daily schedule would daunt many healthy people his age. He starts out his day by *davening Shacharis*. His friend Yitzchak comes daily to put *tefillin* on him. Then he and Yitzchak learn Torah for an hour. Then he works: writing his books, which sometimes entail considerable research; answering his email correspondence (he receives on average twenty letters a day); and doing artwork on the computer.

In addition, he administers a small yeshivah, Abir Yaakov, founded by his late father. This entails determining the curriculum, interviewing the applicants, paying the staff, and keeping daily track of the attendance and progress of each student.

He also reads books and newspapers. Twice a week he has physiotherapy. At 4 p.m., visitors start arriving — his four siblings, six children, 27 grandchildren, friends, or former colleagues. "Many people come," comments Elisheva. "This house is like a Visitors' Center."

Her husband corrects her: "No, like a World Center."

Although he had written articles and lectured extensively before his illness, this new phase of his life has opened up wellsprings of creativity. He has written eight books: one on the weekly Torah *parashah*, one on the weekly *haftarah*, two about education; one book of autobiographical anecdotes; one book of poetry; *L'Seder*, in which he provides relevant *pesukim* for every occasion for people who follow the custom of beginning their letters with a *pasuk* from the weekly *parashah*; and *Choose Life*, a collection of his musings about life and advice to the chronically ill. He is currently working on his ninth book, a second volume of poetry.

With eye movements activating his computer, Dr. Melamed-Cohen has also begun to produce works of art. One particularly engaging picture seems symbolic. Its bright colors and bold forms hide the sketched letters of Hashem's name, just as Hashem is hidden in the attention-grabbing events of our lives.

Writing poetry is another post-paralysis avocation of his. Several of his poems have been set to music and performed on the albums of various artists. A CD of ten of his poems set to music is in production.

Joy in Life

The most noticeable thing about Dr. Rahamim Melamed-Cohen, even more prominent than his reclining wheelchair and multiple tubes connected to various machines, is his relentless good cheer. Other than his eyes, the only muscles that he can still move are those by which he smiles.

According to Dr. Melamed-Cohen, humor is an important component of life. "Humor brings *simchah*," he says, speaking one word at a time in a garbled speech that his wife interprets with difficulty. "Humor is healthy for the body and the soul. I read a study that showed that humor actually expands a person's blood vessels."

The irony is searing. Here is a person suffering from a horrendous, debilitating disease, who is physically incapable of laughing, but who appreciates and dispenses humor. What part does humor play in his own life? "He tells a lot of jokes," his wife Elisheva declares. "He asks visitors to tell him jokes, and he remembers them. Also, he makes up his own jokes."

During a recent visit, one person told a joke that fell flat. Dr. Melamed-Cohen rolled his eyes, and set everyone off laughing.

Yet, Dr. Melamed-Cohen's palpable joy in life comes from something much deeper than humor. An ardently religious Jew, he has a rich inner life unimpeded by his total physical disability. "In the last year," he attests, "I feel that Hashem is drawing closer to me, and I am drawing closer to Him. But I hope that Hashem will get even closer to me."

Dr. Melamed-Cohen asserts that any living person, in any state of health, can perform mitzvos. Asked what his own three favorite mitzvos are, he responds without hesitation: helping people, maintaining the yeshivah, and *tefillah*. Notice that these correspond to the three foundations of the world according to *Chazal: Gemillas Chassadim, Torah,* and *Avodah*.

Dr. Melamed-Cohen's *emunah* and *bitachon* have grown as his physical powers have waned. Immediately after his diagnosis, he had many questions for Hashem. "Why did this happen to me?" he pondered. "What did I do wrong? All my life I tried to do good, to fulfill mitzvot, and to act properly toward my fellowman. Maybe here and there, I wasn't okay, but where is the proportion between this terrible illness and my small sins?"

But as his physical condition deteriorated, his faith grew stronger — both his faith in Hashem and his faith in himself. "There is faith in Hashem," he explains, "and within that faith in Hashem, you come to believe in your own strength. It's like a cycle. The more you believe in Hashem, the more you believe in yourself within Hashem."

His Mission

*S*ignificantly, his affliction itself seemed to spawn a remarkable spiritual growth. For one thing, he achieved a crystalline clarity about what is truly important. "I think I understand better than most people," he says, "how to appreciate the important things in life, and to ignore those things that aren't important."

On an even higher level, Dr. Melamed-Cohen has found meaning and purpose in his suffering. He perceives a mission bestowed by his crippling illness: "I feel that I have a task: to give to other people encouragement and strength."

Few of us fulfill our missions with as much zeal and dedication as Dr. Melamed-Cohen. Whether writing his books, all of which are meant to encourage others, or receiving an interviewer in his home, to whom he eagerly offers a drink of water, a gift of one of his books, and background material on his life, Dr. Melamed-Cohen is the consummate giver. While many ill people (and many healthy people as well!) are self-absorbed, Dr. Melamed-Cohen is other-directed. How did he achieve this trait? Did he work on it?

"Certainly!" he exclaims. "I tried all my life to be a giver. My motto was that of Aaron HaKohen, 'to love people and to draw them near to Torah.'"

Dr. Melamed-Cohen believes firmly that people are able to change. His own metamorphosis from a good person to a great person took place under the unlikely catalyst of his dire illness. Asked how these years of total paralysis can possibly be the best years of his life, he replies that when he was first diagnosed, he didn't believe that he had the power to overcome the gigantic challenge of ALS. But as the years passed and his physical state deteriorated, he tapped an inner strength that he didn't know he had. And in proportion to the immensity of the challenge, he discovered an immense power to meet the challenge and overcome it. That attainment, even more than his successful career or fulfilling family life, brought him an enormous satisfaction, a true sense of triumph.

Yet his battle is ongoing. Dr. Melamed-Cohen is an inveterate teacher. This made his loss of the power to speak all the more frustrating for him. People, except for his immediate family and his two hired attendants, can no longer understand what he's trying to say. "For me this was a challenge," he admits. "I had to seek an alternative."

The alternative is his EyeTech computer. A camera positioned in front of the computer screen and two sensors on the side pick up the smallest eye movements as he looks at letters on his onscreen keyboard. Looking at a letter types the letter, but the process is laborious and given to many errors as his eyes move from one letter to the next. Speaking these days is even more laborious. He pronounces one word at a time, and often has to repeat a word two or three times before his wife understands it.

On Shabbos, of course, he cannot use the computer. "It's frustrating," he admits. "If I want to give a *dvar Torah* or participate in the conversation, I can't."

Dr. Melamed-Cohen explains that he adheres to three basic coping mechanisms in his life: "The first one is *savlanut* [patience]. The second one is *savlanut*. And the third one is *savlanut*."

The Hidden Hero

The hidden hero of this story, of course, is Elisheva Melamed-Cohen, Rahamim's wife of 47 years. It was she who decided to keep him alive on life-support despite all it requires in terms of 24-hour care. While Elisheva must evince as much *savlanut* as her husband, she gets less credit for it, but she does not seek credit.

The most impressive aspect of this strong and gentle woman is her total lack of "What about me?" When asked what she *gets* from her marriage during these last years, she replies with a smile, "To see him, to see what he attains. This gives me also quality of life. To be part of what he achieves gives me great satisfaction."

Elisheva's advice for spouses/parents/children who are caretakers of disabled relatives is: "First of all, make peace with the situation. Second, try your maximum to see the good in the situation, not just the bad. No one can have everything in life. When I light Shabbat candles, I thank Hashem for the good in my life. I always say to myself, 'He's alive and he's with me and we're together.' I see the good."

Inspiring Others

Dr. Melamed's effect on other people is profound. In his book *Choose Life*, for example, he directly addresses people suffering from terminal or chronic illness. He believes that such people often give up due to three reasons:

1. *They behave according to societal expectations.*

2. *In our times, many people are spoiled.*

3. *Today's education doesn't teach people to stand up to challenges.*

While many advocates of euthanasia admit that Dr. Melamed-Cohen's life on life-support systems is definitely worth sustaining, they claim that he is an exception. Dr. Melemed-Cohen himself disagrees: "Maybe I am special, but the principles can be applied to other people as well. Not everyone has to produce so much, but everyone can fulfill his life in his own way. Rather than always talking about 'death with honor,' why not put the same effort into sustaining 'life with honor'? They can do this by encouraging patients and by bringing them volunteers to help them. Instead of prodding them to finish their lives, prod them to live their lives."

After an article I wrote about Dr. Melamed-Cohen appeared on the website of Aish HaTorah (Aish.com) last year, a woman posted a comment revealing the dramatic change of viewpoint wrought in her by Dr. Melamed-Cohen:

> *I am a hospice volunteer and I too have been a proponent of euthanasia. This holy, creative, energetic, loving man has given me a fresh perspective. His willingness to live life to the fullest despite his challenges, his generosity of spirit, his deep and abiding faith have affected me deeply. ...*
>
> *So often we hospice volunteers do in a way "prod patients to finish their lives, rather than prod them to live their lives." And it does come from the fear of being a burden. I have seen though that when a patient opens herself to receiving love through being taken care of, they give the support person the opportunity to give love selflessly. And what greater gift can a human being give another than the chance to be in that selfless state?*

In response to the same article, Dr. Melamed-Cohen received over 400 email letters from readers across the globe. (And he replied to every one of them!) The most amazing aspect of this response was the wide spectrum of people who were uplifted by Dr. Melamed-Cohen's example and words.

Some, as expected, came from people who are taking care of their handicapped or ill relatives. One mother wrote:

> *I am the mother of a 37-year-old son who was left severely handicapped at the age of 8 by encephalitis. He is 100 percent*

> *paralyzed and without any form of communication except for an occasional signal for "yes" by moving the area around his mouth. He lives with us at home and is a part of all our family activities. ...*
>
> *My husband and I have always tried to give him the best quality life that we can. However we are often troubled by not knowing what he thinks, how he feels about his situation, etc. I try to convince myself that he is glad he is alive and a part of a loving family, but you are the only one who has said that such a difficult life can be joyful and worthwhile.*
>
> *... We fight so hard to keep Yossi alive and at times I wonder if he really would rather we didn't try so hard! So thank you for expressing your beliefs and feelings — they have given us great comfort and strength.*

Most of the letters came from people who were suffering from not physical disabilities, but a whole range of psychological or emotional problems. A woman who had suffered a traumatic childhood drew parallels between Dr. Melamed-Cohen's physical paralysis and her own emotional paralysis:

> *I see striking similarities between your physical condition and my emotional one. I have dealt with great despair in my life. ... Some things said in the article have struck a very deep cord with me, and I feel encouraged. I want to thank you.*
>
> *I wonder if there is a parallel in our situations. I spend a lot of time being frustrated, angry, and defeated because of my emotional "paralysis" — maybe I have approached it wrongly. Maybe it would behoove me to stop focusing on my paralysis, and instead do my best to encourage and strengthen the joy that exists in the midst of it. Stop trying to change the paralysis, no?*
>
> *In your physical self, you cannot change anything about your condition, but there is still a very real place that is free and alive*

inside that you spend your time focusing on. I want to learn from your example in this regard. I will be praying for the wisdom to do this. To live my life the way that you do.

☙

Kal V'chomer

On the simplest level, Dr. Melamed-Cohen's miraculous effect on people operates by the principle of *"kal v'chomer."* People reason that if Dr. Melamed-Cohen, with his total paralysis, can be upbeat/active/diligent, then they, with their lesser problems, must be able to do the same.

Thus, a 58-year-old Chassid wrote to Dr. Melamed-Cohen that he had had a stroke two years before, had lost the use of one arm, and suffered chronic "discomfort" in his muscles. "Standing or sitting for *davening*," he wrote, "has long ago fallen by the wayside for me. A dear friend comes every day to help me with *tefillin*, and I usually just say the *Shema*. Now, after reading this article [about you], I have decided to try harder to *daven* properly."

The next day, the same Chassid wrote a second letter to Dr. Melamed-Cohen: "I just finished putting on *tefillin*, saying *Shema*, and *davening Shemoneh Esrei*. I would like to dedicate my new *Shemoneh Esreis* to you."

Other people, suffering from various forms of emotional or psychological distress, compare their problems to the magnitude of Dr. Melamed-Cohen's difficulties, and find their own problems shrinking in comparison. For example, one person who moved from South Africa to Australia and was always complaining about the difficulty of the move, decided, after reading about Dr. Melamed-Cohen, that he had nothing to grumble about. Another person wrote: "I feel quite ashamed that at times I have felt sorry for myself when I've had trivial challenges to face."

A 52-year-old woman wrote:

> *I have spent much of my life worrying about one problem or another and am finally ready to break free of a worry-filled life. Your story is helping me put things into perspective. Some of the problems may be serious, but I'm asking myself (and now prepared to actually change) if God gave us one trip to this world, shouldn't it be b'simchah and not complaining and obsessing and worrying? You are living proof that it is possible to do this. If you can do it, than I can too, although my handicap is much more subtle and emotional.*

Dr. Melamed-Cohen's example is the surefire antidote for all of our self-pitying complaints. "I will hold onto this story about you," wrote one reader. "And whenever I find myself complaining about this or that, I will dip into your story again."

Your Life Commands Our Lives

*Y*et, the reason Dr. Melamed-Cohen's example is life-transforming goes beyond *kal v'chomer*. His triumph over his total disability penetrates to the core of our fears and faithlessness, and reveals to us that we can not only cope with whatever Hashem sends us, but we can grow great from it.

There are certain trees whose seeds sprout only when exposed to fire. Thus, precisely when the forest is being consumed by conflagration do these seeds sprout and begin their growth into mighty trees. That we each have potentials that can be actualized only amidst the fire of difficult challenges, like these seeds, answers all of our deepest questions about suffering and the goodness of God.

As a 16-year-old girl wrote to Dr. Melamed-Cohen: "As I was reading your story, I was hit by an amazing feeling of how much anyone can do in any circumstance."

A letter from another reader, a *frum* man from California, proclaims: "Your life commands our lives. We can all be so much more, as your life so eloquently demonstrates."

Amid the forest fire, a seed sprouts and gradually grows into a towering tree. As Dr. Melamed-Cohen's father used to say in response to every situation: *"Yishtabach Shemo la'ad.* May His Name be forever praised."